CAPITAL CITIES
EUROPE

Stockholm is Sweden's capital and
the residence of the royal familiy.
In 1754, King Adolf Fredrik was the
first Swedish ruler to occupy the Royal
Palace (Kungliga Slottet), which with
its 600-odd rooms is one of the largest
residences in the world.

CAPITAL CITIES EUROPE

The Malá Strana bridge tower, on the Malá Strana district riverbank, forms one end of Prague's famous Charles Bridge. The Gothic gate tower was constructed in about 1464. In the background, the Prague Castle Hill rises, with the imposing Saint Vitus's Cathedral.

ABOUT THIS BOOK

As multifaceted as the continent itself, so are Europe's capital cities. The cradles of our Western culture once stood in Athens and Rome, and two and a half millennia later, the sublime vestiges of antiquity can still be admired in the Greek and the Italian capitals. Paris and London impress with the glory and the wealth of ancient kingdoms and colonial powers, and with the pulsating life of our own time. What do cities as different as Berlin and Madrid have in common? They are relatively young capitals – Berlin is by far the younger of the two –, attracting visitors from around the world with their vibrant nightlives. In addition, both boast – and this they again share with many other capitals – museums and art collections of international standing. Prague, one of the most history-charged metropolises in Central Europe, was once known as the "Golden City" and still shines today thanks to its great architectural riches. In Vienna and Budapest, the visitor can often still experience the sedate charm of the former Austro-Hungarian Empire, which once ruled over half of Europe. Sweden's metropolis, Stockholm, is sprawled across numerous Baltic islands, whereas Malta's capital, Valletta, rises high above the blue-shimmering Mediterranean sea, behind the mighty walls of medieval fortifications dating from the Crusades. In the Adriatic lies the Balkan peninsula with cities like Skopje and Podgorica, which only rose to the status of capitals after the disintegration of Yugoslavia. Cities like Chişinău – capital of the Republic of Moldova – or Tirana – capital of once-isolated Albania – today claim their place as European capitals in the general awareness.

These remarkably multifaceted capitals reflect the cultural and geographical diversity of the small continent of Europe, with a history that is not exactly bereft of dramatic events. This richly illustrated volume invites you on a journey to the 47 capitals of Europe, permitting you to experience their unique features as well as what they have in common.

Wolfgang Kunth

The Forum Romanum was the heart of ancient Rome. Today, the ruins of imperial monuments attest to the transience of worldly power: the triumphal Arch of Septimius Severus, the Temple of Saturn and the Temple of Vespasian in front of the baroque Church of Santi Luca e Martina.

CONTENTS

Tradition and modernity: In London, old and new are often found in close proximity. From this vantage point, St Paul's Cathedral and the skyscraper designed by Sir Norman Foster and known as the "Gherkin" to Londoners define the cityscape.

CAPITAL CITIES EUROPE

REYKJAVÍK

Iceland's capital is the most northerly in the world, beautifully located on Faxaflói Bay. Volcanic nature and modern architecture define the cityscape of the young island metropolis.

Translated, Reykjavík means "Smoke Bay", a name the Vikings allegedly gave this natural port, when, on their journeys of exploration, they first landed on the island in about 870. They founded a settlement, the oldest on Iceland, but it took another thousand years for it to become a real city. The first, hesitant boom came at the end of the 18th century, when the Danish king, the colonial ruler of the island, granted trading rights to the village and made it a bishop's see. Gradually, Reykjavík, located on the south-west coast of the Atlantic island, developed as an economic, cultural and also political center. The lengthy struggle for national independence was also conducted from here. It was not until 1944 that the Republic of Iceland could be declared, making Reykjavík the official capital. With its 120,000 inhabitants, it is by far the largest town in the country – every third Icelander lives in the capital. There is an airport and a deep-sea port, high schools, theaters, museums, shopping streets and entertainment

Church of Hallgrímur and Perlan Hot Water Storage

The cityscape is dominated by the snow-white Hallgrímskirkja, a monumental structure on a hill. It is the main work of the Icelandic star architect G. Samúelsson (1887–1950), who left his imprint on modern Reykjavík. Many decades passed between planning (1937) and final completion (1986); the majestic concert organ was not installed until 1992. It is easy to see why the unusual architecture might have been seen as controversial by some. Yet the light, spacious convinced even the skeptics. The steeple (74m/243ft) is not only Reykjavík's tallest structure, it also provides the best views. Another spectacular landmark is the Perlan, hot-water storage tanks with a giant glass dome, inaugurated in 1992. The structure combines esthetics with usefulness, because it supplies the city with hot water. In winter, even the pavements (sidewalks) are heated, so that it is not necessary to shovel snow. Geothermy is one of the most valuable natural resources of Iceland. The five giant tanks of the Perlan hold millions of liters (gallons) of hot water (85 °C/185 °F) which are extracted out of the ground. The Perlan became a tourist attraction thanks to its sixth tank – vast and dry, it houses a small Saga Museum. The ensemble is completed by a stunning observation deck, a revolving restaurant with panoramic views, an artificial geyser and the lighting effects in the dome.

The impressive glass dome of the Perlan (above). The Hallgrímskirkja is the largest church on the island; a statue of the Icelandic explorer Leif Eriksson stands in front of it (large picture).

districts. And from time to time a small earthquake! The island's capital cannot conceal its volcanic origins. People live with nature, smoke and steam billow out of the restless ground. And so the Vikings were absolutely right when they named the village located just below Mount Esja on Faxaflói Bay–Reykjavík.

It is as bright as day during the midsummer nights in Reykjavík (left). Iceland's capital is located just 270 km (168 miles) south of the Arctic Circle. In the background rises 900-m- (2,953-ft-) high Mount Esja.

Tjörnin City Pond

In the middle of the city is Tjörnin Pond, with the Town Hall built in 1992 standing on its shore. Its foyer offers a good start to an Iceland visit – on display here is a giant relief map of the island.

Árbæjarsafn Open-Air Museum

The houses of inhabitants and workers, workshops, peat huts and a horse stable: The open-air museum in the Árbær district takes visitors back to 19th-century Reykjavík.

Blue Lagoon Spa

The lava basin, filled two-thirds with seawater and one-third with fresh water, is used today as an open-air thermal pool (37–39 °C/99–102 °F).

OSLO

Oslo, the capital and royal residence of the kingdom of Norway, is the cultural and economic center of the country. It offers a high quality of life to its 500,000 inhabitants and a great diversity to its visitors.

Even at first glance does the city look impressive between the blue Oslo Fjord and the green hills of the surroundings. Sports are high priority here, with the vast Frogner Park as a popular venue. Its numerous students breathe new life into the roughly 1,000-year-old city, whose medieval layout was completely destroyed in the fire of 1624.

The Danish king, who ruled Norway at that time, had Oslo rebuilt from scratch as "Christiania", and it did not get its original name back until independence (1905). Historic monuments are few and far between, but Norway's capital has many interesting museums on offer instead. Viking ships and the legendary polar explorer "Fram" have their own mu-

seum, as does the great artist Edvard Munch and the sport of skiing. The vast National Museum exhibits art, architecture and design. Ancient Norway can be experienced at the Open-Air Museum. Oslo presents itself from its most attractive side between May and September, when the days are long and the temperatures are pleasant.

Spectacular architecture: The new Opera House of 2008 (left). Shopping is done on the Karl Johans Gate, which leads to the Royal Castle (right). The Nobel Peace Prize is awarded each year in the monumental Town Hall (1915–1950) beside the harbor, the symbol of Norwegian independence (large picture).

OSLO

Akershus Fortress

The origins of the Renaissance Akershus Fortress, located on a peninsula on the eastern side of the Oslo Fjord, date back to the time around 1300. The extensive complex, featuring a main building and auxiliary buildings as well as a park, is one of the most popular sights in the city. The crypt of the castle church is the burial place of the kings of Norway. Norway's Resistance Museum, which is housed in a protected building inside the fortress, as well as the memorial are commemorated to Norwegian patriots and the Norwegian Resistance during the German occupation in World War II.

Vigeland Park

One attraction in the Norwegian capital – for locals and visitors alike – is the Vigeland Sculpture Park, a monument Norway's most important sculptor, Gustav Vigeland (1869–1943), set for himself. The figures in this unusual open-air museum of naturalist art were mostly created between 1924 and 1943. Vigeland arranged the impressive groups of sculptures himself: 58 bronze figures stand on the

bridge that leads to the 17-m-(56-ft-) high granite monolith column, portraying human figures hewn in stone and surrounded by further monumental figures. The Vigeland Park is part of the Frogner Park, Oslo's largest park complex, comprising a sports stadium, tennis courts and an open-air swimming pool. The vast landscape park (300 ha/741 acres), featuring idyllic spots and romantic walks, groups of trees and sunbathing areas, was laid out in the 19th century around the historic Frogner Manor; it has been open to the public since 1904. The carefully restored buildings of the former agricultural property (18th century) house the Oslo City Museum.

The granite figures around the "People Column" in Vigeland Park (above). This unique sculpture park counts some one million visitors every year (large picture). It is open 24/7 and admission is free.

Viking Ship Museum

The best-preserved Viking ships in the world (9th century) and precious burial gifts can be admired in the Vikingskipshuset. Equally exciting is the documentation by archeologists who set out to search for the Viking settlements in "Vinland" (America).

The Renaissance Akershus Fortress (far left) is situated in a beautiful spot. Unique treasures can be admired at the Viking Ship Museum (left). The ships were discovered in burial places; they were intended to transport the chieftains into the realm of the dead.

Edvard Munch

Norway's most famous artist is the painter Edvard Munch (1863–1944). The Edvard Munch Museum Oslo owns the largest collection of his paintings, illustrations and prints in the world, with "Madonna" and "The Scream" (see picture) the main attractions. Another version of "The Scream" can be seen in the National Gallery.

Holmenkollen

The legendary ski jump on Oslo's local mountain, Holmenkollen, was replaced by a new, very modern complex. The Holmenkollen Ski Museum tells us what it looked like in days gone by.

COPENHAGEN

A relaxed atmosphere and people full of zest for life – that's Copenhagen. And how could it be any different when the famous Little Mermaid greets from the water, and even the royal family lead a carefree life, closely in touch with the people!

The history of Copenhagen begins in the 11th century, when it was not much more than a fishing village. Today, Copenhagen is a modern metropolis and has been the royal residence for many centuries. The Danish parliament (Folketing) resides here in one of the old royal castles, and Copenhagen is the seat of the European Environment Agency. As a major port and the hub between Central Europe and Scandinavia, Copenhagen is an important city.

Copenhagen, located in the east of Zealand Island and adjoining Amager Island, is the economic and cultural center of Denmark, and with a good half million inhabitants it is also the largest city in the country. More than 1.5 million people live in the metropolitan area of Copenhagen, which is more than a quarter of the population of the entire country. The city boasts numerous historic buildings, but some remarkable modern architecture can also be seen here in abundance. In 1996, Copenhagen was the European Capital of Culture.

Colorful houses stand in a row in the Nyhaven (New Port). Where once there was a major harbor arm, today the largest entertainment area of Copenhagen extends (left). Copenhagen's emblem seems rather melancholic in contrast: the little Mermaid by Edvard Eriksen, who longingly waits for her prince at the entrance to the port (large picture).

Amalienborg Palace, Frederick's Church

Amalienborg Palace, the Copenhagen residence of the Danish royal family and the lodgings of the Crown Prince, is probably the most outstanding Rococo building in the country. The palace was built from 1750 to plans by the Danish master-builder Nicolai Eigtved. With the Amalienborg, he did not create a single building but an ensemble of four separate city palaces, arranged around a large square. The reason was King Frederick V's wish to modernize his capital. A new district was to be created, designed in the contemporary French style, and the square with the four palaces had been chosen as its representative focal point. One of the wide boulevards that radiate from the central square is flanked on four sides by the palaces and leads directly to Frederick's Church, only a few hundred meters (yards) away. This building was also designed by Nicolai Eigtved and was originally planned as part of the royal concept of restoration, but it was not completed until considerably later.

King Frederick had not planned for the Amalienborg to become the royal palace, however. Instead, the four palaces were to be used by influential noble families, who also financed their construction. The king merely insisted that they be built according to the plans of his court

Rosenborg Castle

King Christian IV directed the fate of Denmark from 1588 until 1648. During this long period, he encouraged a brisk building activity. He was particularly fond of Rosenborg Palace, which he had built as a summer residence at the city gates. Originally, a small summerhouse, built in 1607,

stood here, which the king liked to use for his recreation. A few years later, however, Christian decided to expand the residence. Work began in 1613, when the north wing of the new palace was added, and continued apace. The palace gradually grew under the direction of master-builders Hans van Steenwinkel and Bertel Lange, but the king repeatedly changed his mind and ideas so that the result was no longer a harmonious design. It was exactly this aspect, however, that made the castle an interesting and informal structure, often referred to as the "fairy-tale castle". Today, Rosenborg Castle is a museum. Amazing treasures can be seen in the lavishly furnished rooms, ranging from enormous silver lions and precious porcelain to the Danish crown jewels.

Rosenborg Castle stands in an idyllic spot in one of the most popular parks of Copenhagen (right). The staterooms inside are furnished with precious gold and silver ornaments, giant lion sculptures and valuable tapestries (above).

architect. However, when the royal residence at Christiansborg Palace fell victim to a fire in 1794, Frederick's successor, King Christian VII, moved into the Amalienborg without further ado, thus making it the residence of the Danish royal family, which it is still today.

View from the castle square to Frederick's Church, also known as the Marble Church. The foundation stone was laid by Frederick V in person in 1749. Because of financial problems, the work was delayed, however, and later was stopped altogether. Finally in 1894, the church was completed according to a revised concept.

COPENHAGEN

Tivoli

When the Tivoli amusement park opened its doors in 1843, a veritable storm of visitors have arrived from the first day. Today, still, the park is a favorite destination among local citizens and visitors alike. Aside from the giant Ferris wheel and the many ultramodern funfair rides, there are also some very special attractions, such as the famous Pantomime Theater and the old-fashioned merry-go-rounds that are seldom found elsewhere nowadays. In contrast to some other parks of this kind, there are none of the usual glaring lights. Instead, thousands of individual lamps twinkle throughout the night.

Christiansborg Palace and Old Stock Exchange

The former royal palace exudes an air of grandeur with its 90-m- (295-ft-) tall tower and its clear, symmetrical lines just like its significance for Copenhagen and Denmark. Christiansborg Palace looks back on a turbulent, more than 800-year-old history. In the Middle Ages, the first Copenhagen castle stood here; King Christian VI had a Rococo castle built on its site in the 18th century. This, however, fell victim to the fire of 1794, which led Christian VII to re-settle in Amalienborg. From 1806 to 1828, the palace was rebuilt in the neoclassical style, but then it burned down again in 1884. The present building was constructed from 1903 and has been the seat of the Danish parliament since 1918. Some parts of the palace, comprising more than 600 rooms, are also used as a museum, where the royal carriages can be seen. In the courtyard, the horses of the royal family are still trained today. The former commodity exchange was also commissioned by Christian IV, the construction-friendly king, who influenced the Copenhagen cityscape in such a lasting way. The Renaissance structure, erected from 1619 until 1640, with its famous "dragon-tail tower", stands right next to the former royal palace, Christiansborg, on the castle islet (Slotsholmen). The Old Stock Exchange was purpose-built for the exchange in commodities from overseas. Nevertheless, the building had to comply with some of the king's extravagant demands; thus, it was not to be too tall overall, so that the views from the adjacent castle would not be blocked. In economic terms, however, the Exchange did not bear the expected fruits, and it was soon sold to a merchant. In the middle of the 19th century, the Merchants' Guild moved in, which kept up a brisk business here for a good 100 years. Today, the Old Stock Exchange is the seat of the Chamber of Commerce.

Next to the Old Stock Exchange with its distinctive tower (top right) stands Christiansborg Palace, boasting magnificent interior furnishings (right).

At Tivoli, any occasion that's worth celebrating is celebrated, whether weddings, anniversaries or business jubilees. Even Queen Margrethe was here for her 60th birthday. While the merry-go-rounds are spinning in the park (left), a statue of the fairy-tale writer Hans Christian Andersen greets visitors at the entrance (far left).

City Hall

This red-brick building, constructed from 1892 to 1905, is located at the heart of the city, on the H. C. Andersen Boulevard, just opposite Tivoli. The town hall square with the dragon fountain (picture) dating from 1904 is a busy gathering point of Copenhagen life and a popular meeting place. A statue of the fairy-tale collector and poet Hans Christian Andersen adorns the square, and there is also a column with a bronze statue of two men playing the lur. The town hall itself is in Italian Renaissance style, crowned by battlements and corner turrets, sculptures embellish the façade, including a gilded figure of the founder of the city Bishop Absalon. At 113 m (371 ft), the City Hall tower is the tallest in the country. It houses the astronomic World Clock by Jens Olsen, which consists of more than 15,000 individual components and has told the time in any place in the world since 1955.

New Carlsberg Glyptotek

When Christiansborg Palace burned down in 1884, most of the paintings kept there were also destroyed. The tragic event was the reason why the proprietor of the Carlsberg brewery, Carl Jacobsen, donated his vast private art collection to the city of Copenhagen, thus forming the starting point of the museum. Jacobsen was not only an art collector and sponsor, an energetic supporter of other projects, but he also greatly admired the Glyptothek in Munich. Using this museum as a model, the new collection was called the "Ny Carlsberg Glyptotek" – New Carlsberg Glyptotek. The present museum building was opened in 1897 and houses the largest collection of ancient art in Northern Europe. When Copenhagen became the European Capital of Culture in 1996, a large collection of French Expressionist art was added, including works by Toulouse-Lautrec, Gauguin and many others.

STOCKHOLM

Water is omnipresent in Stockholm, the capital and royal residence of the Kingdom of Sweden, which is spread across numerous islands, peninsulas and the mainland. Thanks to its location and its countless bridges, the city is also known as "Venice of the North".

Here, where Lake Malar flows into the Baltic Sea, lies the Swedish capital with its 810,000 inhabitants. A glance at the city map reveals a confusing maze of waterways, islands and skerries; in one lock, in the heart of the city, the freshwater of Lake Malar merges with the seawater from the Baltic. The historic old town (Gamla Stan) is concentrated on one island, which is also the site of the royal palace. With its leading research institutes, a university and numerous museums, Stockholm forms the cultural focal point of Sweden. The different districts convey ever-new impressions, whether you are strolling through the old town, experiencing the Stockholm nightlife in the former workers' suburb of Södermalm, shopping in the NK department store in Östermalm or visiting the great "Vasa" and the Skansen open-air museum on the Djurgården peninsula. On every visitor's must-do list is an excursion around the skerry islands and to Lake Malar, with a visit to baroque Drottningholm Palace (a UNESCO World Heritage Site).

Each year, Stockholm's City Hall, which is located on the Kungsholmen and was built between 1911 and 1923 in the style of Swedish National Romanticism, is the venue for a festive banquet for the Nobel Prize winners (left). On Riddarholmen Island, the gothic Riddarholskyrkan Church, the burial place of the kings, dominates the scenery (below).

STOCKHOLM

Royal Palace, Parliament Building

On the edge of the old town stands the Royal Palace. It was built between 1690 and 1750, at a time when Sweden's dreams of being a superpower had already been shattered. All the more surprising are the enormous dimensions of the baroque four-winged complex with its square courtyard and severely structured façade. It is easy to understand that the royal family moved their residence to the much smaller Drottningholm Palace at the gates of the city. And so the inside of the city palace can also be visited, if no act of state is imminent. However, not all of the 607 rooms are open! Worth seeing are the Royal Apartments, furnished with paintings, tapestries and furniture in the rococo style, the Hall of State with the throne, the Banquet Hall in the Empire style, the Treasury with the regalia, the Royal Armory, die Palace Chapel and the Museum of Antiquities. The Changing of the Royal Guard is always popular; it takes place daily in summer at midday on the square in front of the palace. From the palace, Helgeandsholmen Island (Islet of the Holy Spirit) is accessed via Norrbro Bridge. Here stands the Parliament Building, which was inaugurated in 1905 after eight years of construction. Neo-baroque Riksdagshuset, built using local natural stone, looks exceptionally distinguished.

Gamla Stan (Old Town)

The historic heart of Stockholm, for hundreds of years the actual city, is Gamla Stan, meaning "old town". It is spread across Stadsholmen Island, and therefore also referred to as the "town between the bridges". In the 13th century, the first fortress

guarding the route from the Baltic Sea to Lake Malar stood here. Around 1700, the royal palace was built next to Storkyrkan (13th century), Stockholm's oldest church. Visible from afar is the steeple of the "German Church", Tyska kyrkan. The heart of Gamla Stan is Stockholm's oldest square, Stortorget, which is lined by narrow town houses, some dating from the Middle Ages. The square is dominated by the Stock Exchange, the baroque Börshuset, which is the seat of the Swedish Academy and the Nobel Museum. In the picturesque alleyways, many cobbled, impressive historic façades from the Renaissance, Baroque and Classicist eras can be found. Gamla Stan is not only Stockholm's tourist flagship, it is also a sought-after residential and entertainment district. Elegant shops and exclusive restaurants are located here, although the stylish ambience is expensive. Everyone should indulge in a break at one of the many pretty cafés, however; particularly unusual is Café Gråmunken which is located in medieval vaults.

Narrow lanes are typical of the old town (above). Stockholm's oldest square is this quiet only at night. At other times of day, Stortorget buzzes with tourists (right).

Two of Stockholm's most impressive buildings stand on the adjacent islands of Stadsholmen (Gamla Stan) and Helgeandsholmen, linked by a bridge: On the left in the picture, the baroque Royal Palace can be seen (built around 1700) and on the right next to it is the neo-baroque Swedish Parliament (c. 1900).

Storkyrkan Cathedral

In commemoration of the Battle on the Brunkeberg (in the present-day district of Norrmalm), in the course of which the Swedes, assisted by the Hanseatic League, repelled the Danish Army, an artist from Lübeck created the grand sculpture "St George and the Dragon" for Stockholm's oldest church in 1489. The Church of St Nicholas, usually called Storkyrkan, stands in close proximity to the Royal Palace. For centuries, it was the coronation church and is Stockholm's Cathedral today. It was built in the 13th century and converted during the baroque period.

Tyska kirkan

The "German Church" owes its name to its beginnings as the medieval guildhall of the Hanseatic League. Only when the alliance of trading cities had largely lost its importance was the building dedicated as a church (16th century) and subsequently converted and enlarged. The steeple, at almost 100 m (328 ft) height the tallest structure in the Gamla Stan, dates from the 19th century. The carillon is very popular; it plays every day at 8 a.m., midday and 4 p.m.

STOCKHOLM

Modern City Architecture

In the 1950s and 1960s, large parts of Norrmalm were torn down in order to create a modern, car-friendly city. This urban-planning feat of completely restructuring an entire city district caused an enormous stir in Stockholm, especially abroad. But for many locals, the "faceless" architecture is still a source of annoyance today. Among the prestige projects then was Sergels torg, a square with an elliptical roundabout, underground metro station, subterranean shopping malls and the "five trumpet-blasts", as the Stockholmers call the five tall buildings.

Djurgården, Vasa Museum

Undoubtedly one of Stockholm's greatest attractions is the "Vasa", worldwide the only preserved ship dating from the 17th century, and thus a top-ranking relic of seafaring. In addition, thanks to its opulent carved-figure ornamentation, it is also a magnificent work of art. The

"Vasa" was built as a battleship from 1626 to 1628 during the Thirty Years' War. An enormous effort was made; it was to be the pride of Gustav Adolf's fleet. But, on its maiden voyage, after just one nautical mile, the "Vasa" sank. In 1961, again with a huge effort, sea archeologists salvaged the wreck and thousands of tools and pieces of equipment that had belonged to the ship as well as the remains of sailors who had drowned during the disaster. In the Vasa Museum, the fantastic shipwreck can now be admired from all sides and on seven floors. Accompanying it are exhibitions and documentations that shed light on the technical and historical background. The Vasa Museum, located on Djurgården Peninsula, is the most-visited museum in Scandinavia. The Skansen Open-Air Museum also attracts visitors: 150 historic buildings from all over Sweden bring the past 16th-century back to life.

The warship which sunk in 1628 has been restored and can now be seen in the Vasa Museum (right). Above: detail of the sculptural ornamentation.

Östermalm, Strandvägen

Östermalm, Stockholm's central city district, scores on the one hand with the Humlegården, the largest inner-city park, as well as with the discos, clubs and bars around the Stureplan on the other. The Strandvägen boulevard, Stockholm's most elegant street, is an inviting promenade.

A 37-m- (121-ft-) tall glass column adorns busy Sergelstorg Square (far left). A row of elegant houses stretches along Strandvägen, from Nybroplan to the Djurgårdsbron. In front of the Grand Hotel, cruise vessels dock for excursions to the skerry islands (left).

HELSINKI

The sea confers a special flair on Finland's capital. Located on the north coast of the Gulf of Finland, large parts of Helsinki extend across peninsulas and off-shore skerries.

Even in the actual center of the town, the densely built up inner-city area on Vironniemi Peninsula, the sea can be felt at every step. It is this maritime location to which Helsinki also owes its very existence: In the late Middle Ages, the king of Sweden, who ruled over Finland until the early 19th century, sent Swedish settlers here, who were to start up in competition with the flourishing Hanseatic city of Reval (today's Tallinn, the capital of Estonia) on the opposite shore of the Gulf of Finland. But the settlement of Helsinki remained insignificant despite the royal Swedish intervention. It was the Russian tsar who eventually conquered Finland in 1808 and made the city into a showcase of neoclassical architecture. Its real heyday did not begin until the 20th century: In 1917, Finland separated from Russia and declared itself an independent republic. The capital, Helsinki, developed as the economic and cultural center, a conurbation counting some 1.5 million inhabitants today. About every fourth Finn lives in Helsinki and its environs.

Uspenski Cathedral, the symbol of former Russian rule (1808–1917) inaugurated in 1868, is the largest Orthodox church in western Europe (left).
The many visitors enthuse especially about the opulent furnishings, such as the valuable iconostasis (right).

Senate Square and Cathedral

When Helsinki had become the capital of the Russian Grand Duchy of Finland (1812), the tsar commissioned the German architect Carl Ludwig Engel to give the hitherto insignificant place a prestigious, contemporary face. With Senate Square in the heart of the city, Engel created one of the most beautiful neoclassical squares in Europe. The successful ensemble of senate and university buildings is dominated by the Cathedral (large picture left). Built between 1830 and 1852, it is visible from afar and is today regarded as an emblem of the "White City of the North".

Esplanadi

The promenade boulevard leading to the Market Square (Kauppatori) in the southern port, popular with locals and tourists, is divided by a park into Northern and Southern Esplanadi. This culinary heart of the city, boasting a fish market, a grocery market and souvenir stalls, is a must for visitors. The ferry also leaves from here for the imposing Fortress of Suomenlinna (a UNESCO World Heritage Site), which the Swedes built in the 18th century on several of the off-shore islands.

HELSINKI

Finnish National Opera and Finlandia Hall

Opera, ballet, concerts – the Finnish National Opera, which moved into its new home in 1993, has a lot to offer. One of the most important cultural institutions in the country, the modern structure is harmoniously integrated into the graceful line of the Töölön Bay, where the Finlandia Hall also stands. This spectacular congress and concert hall, inaugurated in 1971, is completely clad in white marble. Alvar Aalto (1898–1976), the Finnish architect, town planner and designer who created it, was one of the most influential representatives of Functionalism, and active around the world.

Jean Sibelius

Jean Sibelius (1865–1957) is revered as the "father of Finnish music". The composer created his most important works at the end of the 19th and the beginning of the 20th centuries. This period was a golden era for the arts and a period of national awakening for his fatherland. In 1917, it led to the founding of the first sovereign Finnish state. Sibelius achieved legendary status through his musical interpretation of Finnish sagas and myths, such as the Kalevala. After his studies in Berlin and Vienna, he worked from 1891 as a music teacher at the Academy in Helsinki, which today carries his name and is one of the leading academies of music in Europe. One of

Rock Church

Daylight falls through the many windows in the vaulted copper roof of the subterranean Rock Church, Temppeliaukio (1969), near the park-like Hietaniemi Cemetery. The sacred space, which was hewn into the granite, is also used for concerts and has become one of Helsinki's tourist attractions.

Helsinki's many attractive parks is also named after the composer. Here, in Sibelius Park in the Töölö district, also stands the spectacular monument to the great Finnish composer.

The Sibelius monument was inaugurated in 1967. The abstract work by Eila Hiltunen, consisting of 600 steel pipes, generated vociferous criticism, but this has long since been silenced.

In Helsinki, he also designed the main building of the University of Technology (1964), another architectural icon of the 20th century. The Finlandia Hall made political history from 1973 to 1975, when it was the venue for the international Conference on Security and Co-operation in Europe (CSCE).

Around 250,000 spectators visit the performances in the modern, internationally renowned Finnish National Opera (far left) every year. Also located in the Töölö district is the Finlandia Hall (left), a creation of the Finnish star architect Alvar Aalto.

National Museum

The National Museum of Finland (1905–1910), embellished with "medieval" turrets, oriels and round arches, is characteristic of the architecture of Finnish National Romanticism, which blends elements of Historicism and Art Nouveau. It stands for the emergence of a period of national self-determination after centuries of Swedish and Russian rule. Finland confidently presents itself in its museum with a history dating back to the Stone Age. Its historic heritage is represented in six departments. Among the key themes are the early history with extensive

10,000 years of Finnish history – from the Stone Age to the present day – are brought to life at the National Museum. Even the building on Mannerheim-intie itself is a first-rate cultural monument dating from 1910.

archeological collections, everyday life in pre-industrial Finland, as well as the early 20th century including the independence and the founding of the republic. In the entrance hall, the ceiling frescoes from 1928 attract everyone's attention. The artist, Akseli Gallen-Kallela, incorporated motifs here from the Finnish national "Kalevala" epic in a work full of national pathos. Other important works by this artist can be seen at the Ateneum Art Museum (1887), a neo-Renaissance historic building on the square in front of the railway station. Part of the National Gallery is dedicated to Finnish art of the 18th to 20th centuries, especially to the exceptionally fertile golden age between 1880 and 1910.

TALLINN

Outstanding churches and noble patrician mansions, the fortified city walls and the imposing town hall, all testify to the turbulent history of the Estonian capital on the Gulf of Finland.

The historic town center of Tallinn, formerly Reval (until 1918), can be considered an outstanding example of a Northern European medieval trading port, and so UNESCO has accepted the entire old town onto its list of World Heritage Sites. The origins of the Estonian capital date back to the 12th/13th centuries, when a church and a castle first stood on top of the Cathedral Mountain. In the late Middle Ages, the settlement below developed into a leading Hanseatic city, whose upper class was composed of merchants mainly of German descent. The layout of the old town with its squares, lanes, nooks and crannies, as well as many of the historic buildings, still attest today to this period of flourishing trade. It is best to gain an overview of this superb manifestation of Hanseatic bourgeois civic life before visiting the city. You can do so in style from the observation deck in the town hall. Even farther, however, are the views from the TV tower – on a clear day up to the coast of Finland.

An impressive relic of Tsarist rule in Estonia (1710 until 1917) is the Orthodox Alexander Nevski Cathedral (far left). The lanes in the historic old town almost convey a feeling of small-town life (left). From Cathedral Mountain, superb views of fortified Tallinn and its many towers as well as the Baltic Sea can be had (large picture).

TALLINN

Kadriorg Palace

Probably the most attractive district outside the medieval old town is Kadriorg (Catherine's Valley), where you will find pretty old stone and wooden houses, the Baltic shore as well as the Kadriorg Palace and Park. The baroque complex dates back to Tsar Peter I, who ruled in the Baltic countries after the Great Northern War (1710). Until 1917, Kadriorg was very popular with the Tsar's family as a summer residence; but then the October Revolution put an end to this. Estonia became a republic and the palace a museum. The highlight of the palace is the two-floor Great Hall, one of the most glorious baroque halls in northern Europe. The vestibule, too, is preserved in its original form. Some rooms were furnished in the 1930s, in the style of Estonian National Romanticism. Neglect during the period of affiliation to the Soviet Union (1944–1990) necessitated comprehensive restoration work after the re-establishment of the Republic of Estonia. Since 2000, the palace has

Town Hall

In the middle of the old town is the Town Hall Square, a centuries-old market square and a popular meeting point for Tallinners. Surrounded by historic town houses, it is dominated by the gothic Town Hall (1404), which today still conveys an air of civic pride, but also of Hanseatic reserve. There is no ostentation here, but confident simplicity, crowned by a distinctive tower. High up in the air sits "Old Thomas" (Vana Toomas), the bearer of the weather vane and the crest of the city. The history of the building is documented in the cellar vaults. A further attraction is the historic Town Hall Pharmacy, which has operated uninterrupted since 1422 and has an impressive array of archaic remedies on display. Several traditional eateries can also be found in the square. Incidentally, fairly reliable recommendations and a guide to good restaurants is offered by the "Silverspoon", a gastronomic prize awarded each year by the city.

KUMU Art Museum

Estonian art of all periods is on show at the spectacular KUMU building, inaugurated in 2006. It forms an attractive architectural contrast with the adjacent baroque Kadriorg Palace, whose Museum of Art is dedicated to international fine art.

Tallinn's gothic Town Hall (right) dates from 1404. The town hall square has served as a central market square since the 12th century.

housed the Kadriorg Art Museum, which as well as exhibitions also organizes concerts and plays. Also part of the palace complex are small restored buildings from the 18th/19th centuries, such as the park pavilion, the guesthouse and the guard house. In the park, which was laid out at the same time as the palace, the stunning flower garden should not be missed.

Kadriorg Palace (left) was built in the Italian baroque style during the reign of Tsar Peter I, between 1718 and 1725. It has been carefully restored and now admits visitors on extensive tours.

RIGA

Riga was founded 800 years ago as a conveniently placed merchants' settlement. Today, the Latvian capital boasts numerous historic monuments and attractive landscape parks.

Riga is situated where the Daugava River flows into the Baltic Sea. After several centuries of foreign rule, it became the capital of Latvia in 1918. With its 700,000 inhabitants and a diversified industry, several universities and colleges, it is also the largest and most important city in the country. On the right bank of the Daugava rises the old town and on the left bank the new town, built in the 19th century. Both parts of the city are rich in historic buildings from different historic periods. Whereas the Renaissance and the Baroque dominate in the old town, the new town boasts an extraordinary abundance of Art Nouveau buildings.

House of the Blackheads on Town Hall Square

The impressive building on the historic Town Hall Square was erected in 1334 as a guild and assembly house. Built originally in the gothic style and converted several times later on, it received its magnificent Renaissance façade, featuring many sculptures and reliefs, in the 17th century. The building became

Historic Center

After World War II, the historic center of Riga with its picturesque lanes and squares was largely rebuilt true to the original. Today, it is a UNESCO World Heritage Site.

known as the House of the Blackheads only from the second half of the 17th century. The name harks back to the Merchants' Guild, which had been using the house for the previous 200-odd years. Members of this guild of unmarried merchants, predominantly of German origin, were known as "blackheads" in Riga and some other Baltic cities named after their black patron saint. In World War II, the building was almost completely destroyed. A good half century later, from 1995 to 1999, it was rebuilt to the original plans.

In front of the imposing backdrop of the House of the Blackheads (large picture: on the right, next to the Schwabe House) on Riga's Town Hall Square, the monumental statue of the knight Roland stands guard, the symbol of civic liberty and freedom.

View across the Daugava River of Riga's turreted old town panorama (left). The second tower on the right belongs to the Cathedral, which was donated in 1211 by the founder of Riga, Bishop Albrecht von Buxthoeven.

RIGA

New Town

A short distance north-east of the 42-m- (138-ft-) tall Freedom Monument, which with the surrounding park marks the boundary of the old town, the start of the "boulevard circle" begins. This is the name of the central area of Riga's New Town, which is delineated by three large boulevards. Here stand an impressive number of magnificent buildings, ranging from Classicism to Art Nouveau in style. South-east of the monumental statue is the Latvian National Opera. The neoclassical building, featuring columns and allegorical statues, was constructed between 1860 and 1863; the Nymph of Riga Fountain on the forecourt was added in 1887. Also unmissable in the New Town is the Palace of Culture and Science, completed in 1955, which was once named after Joseph Stalin and today houses, among other institutions, the Latvian Academy of Sciences. Also visible from afar is the more than 368-m- (1,207-ft-) high TV and Radio Tower, rising into the sky at the south-western tip of Zaķusala Island and the Daugava. Opposite is the Central Market, which was established between 1924 and 1930, and which re-uses two large Zeppelin hangars. Today, the market covers a vast area having a total of five large market halls as well as many smaller ones amount to more than 70,000 sq m (753,200 sq ft) of commercial space.

Art Nouveau

Anyone exploring Riga's New Town will discover a wealth of Art Nouveau buildings, which can easily stand comparison with the more famous Art Nouveau city centers, such as Vienna or Prague. In total, some 800 Art Nouveau buildings adorn the city. Riga's Art Nouveau is closely

connected with the name of Mikhail Eisenstein (1867–1921), father of the famous film director, Sergei Eisenstein. As the director of the civic planning authority, the architect and civil engineer created a large number of outstanding buildings from 1893. One of the most famous is the town house in Elizabetes iela 10b, which has an outstanding decorative façade featuring nine window axes and oversized heads on the gable. Decorative art almost seems to be pushing the limits of the possible here. Nearby, in Alberta iela and Strelnieku iela, as well as Smilšu iela in the Old Town, other opulently decorated façades can be admired. It was not only Mikhail Eisenstein, however, who defined the cityscape at the turn to the 20th century. Other architects too, for example Konstantins Pēkšēns, left a rich heritage, albeit with slightly more sober styling.

In Riga's New Town, one of the most remarkable collections of Art Nouveau buildings in Europe was created at the turn of the 19th to 20th centuries, featuring a wealth of shapes and sculptures (above). The staircase at Alberta iela 12 was designed by Konstantins Pēkšēns and Eižens Laube (right).

View of Riga's New Town; in the foreground the expansive terrain of the central market, on the left the Palace of Culture and Science. The TV and Radio Tower, built from 1979 to 1986 on Zaķusala Island, is the third-tallest structure in Europe. There is an observation deck at a height of almost 100 m (328 ft).

VILNIUS

The center of a large empire in the Middle Ages and since the collapse of the Soviet Union once again the capital of the independent Republic of Lithuania, Vilnius is a city with both a past and a future.

For visitors, the large (360 ha/ 890 acres), well-preserved historic center, which has been included on the UNESCO World Heritage list in its entirety, is particularly interesting. The gothic, Renaissance, baroque and classicist periods have produced valuable historic buildings dating from the 13th to 19th centuries. Particularly noticeable is the large num-

Old Town

Carefully restored town houses, winding lanes and picturesque courtyards shape the Old Town, which extends from the Castle Mountain in a southerly and westerly direction on the left bank of the Neris River. Cozy cafés, basic taverns and sophisticated restaurants invite guests to linger, and in the many small shops, a suitable souvenir can easily be found, ranging from traditional handicrafts to folkloristic kitsch. Amber, especially, is sold in all imaginable shapes. One of the oldest roads, and the most popular with tourists as well as locals, in the historic inner city is Pilies ("castle street") and its extension Didžioji ("main street"). The cosmopolitan, hospitable ambience is lively but not frantic. You can admire in peace and

quiet the magnificent historic buildings that have made the old town into a vast architectural museum. The baroque style predominates (e.g., Vilnius University and the Church of St John, St Casimir's Church), but the Gothic (St Anne's Church, Bernadine Church) and finally neoclassicism (Old Town Hall, St Stanislaus Cathedral) are also represented. Thanks to its great abundance of sights, Vilnius has become one of the most-frequented cities in Eastern Europe.

Proud town houses line the streets in the Old Town (above). A unique ensemble is formed by the dainty gothic St Anne's Church and the Bernadine Church, also gothic (right).

ber of churches worth visiting; there are Catholic, Protestant and Orthodox places of worship. Of the more than one hundred synagogues, however, that once existed in Vilnius, only one remains today. The genocide of the Jews, who before the Holocaust made up almost half the population in the city, has wiped out the rich Jewish traditions. The Polish minority,

who had also helped mark the city's life since the late Middle Ages, was expelled after World War II, when Lithuania became a Soviet Republic. Since 1991, Vilnius has once again been the capital of the free Republic of Lithuania, and it joined the EU in 2004. People are cosmopolitan and western-oriented, but also very proud of their historic heritage.

The neoclassical Basilica-Cathedral of Stanislaus (c. 1800), resembling a temple with a medieval bell tower, stands in the middle of the Old Town (far left). The Gediminas' Tower (left), the relic of a once-mighty castle, commemorates the founder of the Grand Duchy of Lithuania (since 1316).

Gate of Dawn

The eastern city gate with St Mary's Chapel, known as the "Gate of Dawn", was built in the 16th century, when Vilnius was under Polish rule and a center of the Catholic Counter-Reformation.

University

Vilnius boasts the oldest university in eastern Europe, founded in 1579. The historic university building has a picturesque library courtyard and the magnificent Pranas Smuglevicius Hall (17th century).

Museum of Genocide Victims

The museum in the former KGB building is dedicated to the countless Lithuanian victims of the Holocaust and the Soviet regime. Open to the public are the cells, guardhouse and execution chamber.

VILNIUS

Užupis Artists' Quarter

Užupis means "behind the river", referring to the Vilnia River, which separates this area from the old town. Visitors have to cross the bridge in order to immerse themselves into this charming world of artists and free-thinkers, which has sprung up in Užupis since the collapse of the So-

viet Union and Lithuania's independence (1991). The once-drab suburb, a poor people's area and red-light district that did not enjoy the best of reputations, has become much brighter. And yet, the plaster still crumbles from the historic façades, there are still idyllic backyards and winding lanes, tiny shops and inexpensive pubs. Located next to the

bridge, the artists' café Užupis Kavine is almost legendary. It is the seat of the "Parliament" of the "Republic of Užupis", which was declared in 1997 partly as a performing art and partly as an April Fool's joke. The citizens of this microstate are called upon to abide by the 41 articles of the "constitution", which can be consulted on a bronze panel in the café. It is based

on the principle of being free to do however one pleases. Thus, everyone has the right to be happy or, equally, unhappy, depending on how one feels. Animals are also considered: according to Article 12, a dog has the right to be a dog. Anyone not wishing to adopt the constitutional principles for him- or herself, should at least tolerate them in Užupis.

City Center and Europa Tower

The contrasts could not be greater than in the Šnipiskés District, on the right banks of the Neris. In the middle of a village-like neighborhood with traditional, brightly painted wooden houses, rise the skyscrapers of the sophisticated city center of Vilnius. The tallest is the Europa Tower (148 m/486 ft, 33 floors), the highest office and residential building in the Baltic States, which has an observation deck at 114 m

Trakai Castle

An attractive excursion (c. 30 km/ 19 miles) is to the ancient town of Trakai with its fairytale island castle dating from the 14th century. The redbrick complex was considered impregnable thanks to its defiant fortifications and its location, surrounded by lakes, that still define the quiet countryside.

(374 ft). The spectacular building was officially inaugurated in 2004, to mark Lithuania's entry into the European Union, a symbol of a new beginning. However, it was not greeted with unbridled enthusiasm by the populace – many historic buildings, and with them long-established inhabitants, had to make room for the business district.

In this picture, the modern skyscrapers of the Vilnius city center form a marked contrast with the Russian-Orthodox church of Our Lady of Vilnius, dedicated in 1901 (large picture).

In Užupis, a district formerly inhabited by the Jewish people of Vilnius, an artists' colony established itself after its original inhabitants were murdered in the Holocaust. The artists declared the "Republic of Užupis". The once-dilapidated houses have been creatively and colorfully renovated and today house galleries and workshops (left).

DUBLIN

Ireland enjoyed an unprecedented boom in the last decades of the 20th century, and things have been happening in the capital too. Yet Dublin has always been much more than its cliché image of Irish pubs where the Guinness flows nonstop.

With half a million inhabitants, Dublin is the largest and the most important city in the Republic of Ireland. It is also the undisputed cultural focus of the country as well as the leading location for industry and trade thanks to its port. The city is located on the mouth of the Liffey River, which flows here into the Irish Sea. The river cuts almost exactly through the middle of Dublin, dividing the prosperous residential areas and suburbs of the south from the less well-heeled areas and the most important industrial areas to the north of it. Dublin's roots go back to the ninth century. Invading Vikings erected a fortress here, which later developed into the center of the new Viking kingdom of Dublin. In 1170, it was raided by British troops, they conquered the city and, gradually the entire Irish island from here. Dublin's heyday came in the 18th century. At that time, the wide boulevards with their Georgian houses were built, which still strongly mark the appearance of the city today.

Trinity College

Trinity College, the oldest of Dublin's three universities, looks back on more than 500 years of history. It was founded in 1592 by Queen Elizabeth I, at a time when Ireland was under English rule, and the English queen was also the queen of Ireland. Although the construction of Trinity College was decreed in England, it

had to be financed by private donations and with contributions from the City of Dublin. Later, King James I, Elizabeth's successor, granted this institution of education a fixed annual sum at the crown's expense. However, such generosity was in no way based on charity alone, for Trinity College was to be a Protestant institution, and its foundation was certainly also a political statement. It took nearly 200 years before, in 1793, Catholics were first permitted to study here.

The buildings in their present form largely date back to the 18th century. Particularly impressive is the old reading room of the Library, where items from the collection of valuable old manuscripts is exhibited to the general public.

The buildings of Trinity College stand in the heart of Dublin; the main entrance is on a busy crossroads (large picture). In the Library's "Long Room" (above), measuring more than 60 m (197 ft), the famous "Book of Kells", more than 1,000 years old, is kept along with other manuscripts.

O'Connell Bridge, built across the Liffey at the end of the 18th century, is wider than it is long (left). It crosses the river as an extension of O'Connell Street, Dublin's main north-south axis.

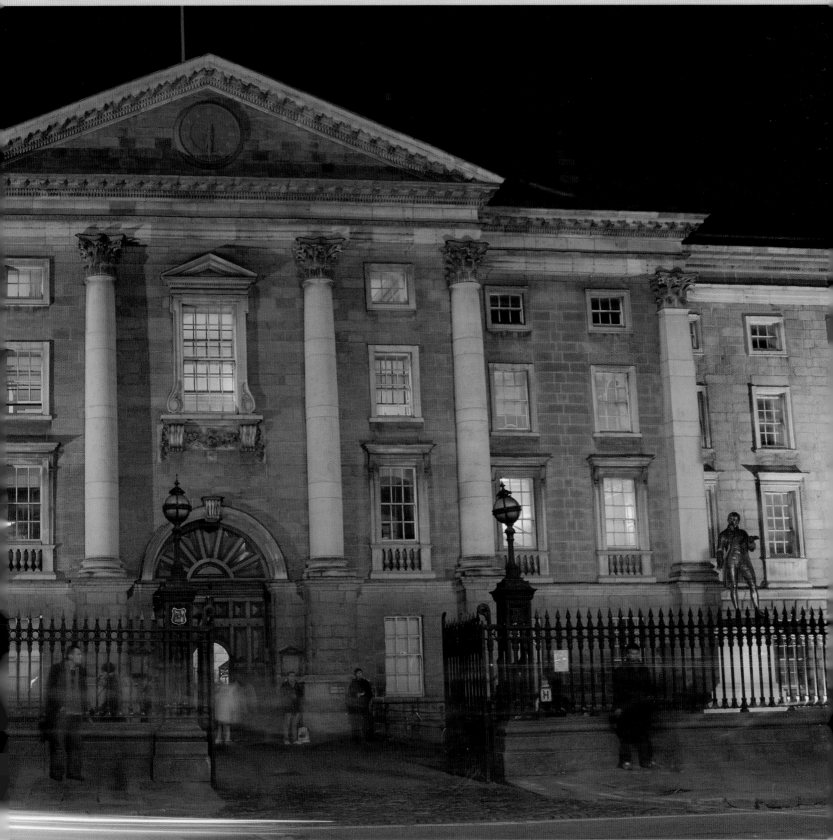

Temple Bar

Temple Bar is more than just the entertainment district of Dublin, although as such it is very popular with visitors to the city. There are countless pubs and taverns in the picturesque cobbled streets on the south bank of the Liffey. At times, though, this concentrated mass of pubs may seem like a tourist trap. After a period when Temple Bar seemed to become progressively more run down, attempts to reinvigorate and gentrify the area have been successful for a while now. In 1991, the state-run Temple Bar Properties was established to oversee the regeneration of Temple Bar as the creative heart of Dublin. Many old buildings have been restored and public spaces cleaned up; in the process, historic housing has deliberately been preserved next to the modernity of some new buildings. Today, Temple Bar is the site of numerous institutes and initiatives from almost all areas of art and culture. Nationally important establishments also have their headquarters here, for example the Irish Film Centre. Thus, it is not surprising that in summer open-air cinema screenings take place in Meeting House Square. At the weekends, a food market is based here; a book market and a fascinating designer market are also in close proximity.

Custom House

This magnificent edifice is one of the pearls of neoclassical 18th-century architecture in Dublin. The administrative building, sited right next to Butt Bridge at Custom House Quay, on the northern riverside road of the Liffey, today houses several ministries and national authorities. Originally, however, it was built as the new seat of the customs office for the nearby port. The plans for Custom House, completed in 1791, were part of a concept for the large-scale redevelopment of the cityscape and all public buildings, for which a special state commission was established in 1757 by parliamentary decree, the Wide Streets Commission. The renowned English architect James Gandon was appointed as master-builder; he designed several buildings in Dublin in the course of the same program. During the Irish War of Independence, the Custom House burned down in 1921, but it was rebuilt in 1928 true to the original.

Ha'Penny Bridge

The pedestrian bridge across the Liffey, connecting Temple Bar on the south bank with the shopping district to the north of the river is one of Dublin's landmarks. Certainly it is the best-known bridge in the city, known by several different names locally. When it was built in 1816, it was first called Wellington Bridge, after the famous duke who was born in Dublin and had, together with General Blücher, defeated Napoleon near Waterloo the year before. Now the bridge is officially called the Liffey Bridge, but locally it is mostly known as Ha'penny Bridge, short for Half-Penny Bridge. The name refers to the fact that, until 1919, a bridge toll had to be paid by anyone wishing to use this river crossing, initially half a penny, later twice as much. The cast-iron Ha'Penny Bridge was produced in a foundry in Shropshire, England, and shipped across the Irish Sea to Dublin.

In Dublin's Temple Bar District, a new, fresh joie-de-vivre set in long before the beginning of the new millennium. Aside from the countless traditional pubs that have always been here, the district now also boasts trendy nightclubs, stylish restaurants and plenty of art and culture.

Christ Church Cathedral

Officially this medieval church is called the Cathedral of the Holy Trinity, but it is most commonly known as Christ Church Cathedral. The building, today the see of the Archbishop of Dublin, stands in the heart of the oldest part of the city, where once the first fortified Viking settlement rose on the riverbank. In the same spot there was once an earlier Viking church, built by King Sigtrygg Silkbeard in the early 11th century and assigned to the first Bishop of Dublin as the bishop's see. This first church, built from wood, was torn down in 1172 and replaced by the new structure of the present cathedral. The gothic church was completed in 1240, but then repeatedly annexed and transformed. Worth seeing is the Crypt, at more than 64 m (210 ft) the longest in the British Isles, as well as the older, Romanesque portal in the transept.

St Patrick's Cathedral

Dublin's second cathedral is also the largest church in Ireland. It is dedicated to the national saint, St Patrick, who had brought Christianity to the island in the fifth century. Construction was not begun, however, until several centuries after Patrick's missionary work, namely in the year 1191. Again, another building first stood on this site – a wooden chapel that had also been built to honor the saint, marking the spot where he is alleged to have baptized the first Irish converts. Like most structures of this kind, St Patrick's Cathedral too was refashioned and enlarged several times over the centuries. At one time, the work was financed by the famous Guinness brewery dynasty. In the 18th century, Jonathan Swift, who wrote "Gulliver's Travels", was the dean at St Patrick's. Swift also has his final resting place in the church. Next to his tomb, a bust and a memorial plaque commemorate the writer and cleric.

LONDON

Courtly ceremonies and progressive modernity, alternative culture and profligate consumption – all this and much more make London what it is: one of few metropolises in Europe to undeniably truly deserve the epithet of "world city".

Big Ben and the Houses of Parliament in Westminster are among the best-known landmarks of the venerable capital of England, Great Britain and the United Kingdom. London is not only the seat of the government and the administrative center; it is also the royal capital and the epicenter of the Commonwealth, the association of states that were once British colonies and their erstwhile mother country.

The city extends on both banks of the Thames, over 70 km (43 miles) from its estuary. With more than seven million inhabitants, it is an important industrial city and one of the major finance centers in the world; more than 500 foreign banks have established their headquarters here.

This financial power is evidenced in the construction boom of recent decades, which has dramatically altered the cityscape. But London also ranks right at the top as a trendsetter in many fields of modern culture. In comparison, the monarchy may not seem in keeping with the times, but its reputation and popularity continue unabatedly.

From the entrance of the Tate Modern visitors reach the opposite bank of the Thames via the Millennium Bridge, with St Paul's Cathedral always firmly in view (left). The Houses of Parliament, Big Ben and the London Eye, the giant Ferris wheel – the Thames unites them all (large picture).

LONDON

Financial District

Long gone from the streets is the image of the elegant banker sporting a black bowler hat and an umbrella. Today, sharp bankers conduct business in the "City". Architecturally, the contrasts perfectly complement each other, for example the Victorian gem of Leadenhall Market and the adjacent avant-garde Lloyd's Building. The Bank of England (1734) and the Royal Exchange (1844) commemorate the age-old traditions of the district. Next to them, ultramodern skyscrapers, such as Tower 42 and 30 St Mary Axe, are symbolic of London's top ranking among the global finance centers.

Thames and Tower Bridge

Either side of the Thames, which crosses London from west to east, the famous historic landmarks of the city stand side by side with the daring new structures and soaring multi-story office blocks of the last few decades. Right by the river, Shakespeare's Globe opened in 1997, a faithful reproduction of the original playhouse of 1599. Opposite rise the towers of Westminster and the dome of St Paul's.

London's Pubs

Pubs are – in London as anywhere on the British Isles – a permanent feature of everyday life, convivial meeting points and places of relaxation. The peak period is in the early evening, after a stressful day at the office, when a chat with colleagues is often called for before the journey home.

Tower Bridge spans the river on the eastern limits of the city center. Inaugurated in 1894, its two towers are 65 m (213 ft) high. When the drawbridge was designed, London still boasted large dock facilities upriver all the way to London Bridge. It is therefore the only bridge in London under which taller ships may pass once the carriageway has been raised.

The upper pedestrian walkway of Tower Bridge is a feature of the permanent exhibition on the history and construction principles. On the right in the picture, the 180-m- (591-ft-) tall "Gherkin" can be seen, the office block at 30 St Mary Axe, one of the City's new landmarks.

Even on the outside, the complex of buildings that makes up the Bank of England (left), dating from 1734, demonstrates that one of the most important financial institutions is based here. Only a few blocks along, at Leadenhall Market, a filigree cast-iron and glass construction, delicacies of all kinds can be purchased (far left, in the foreground the Lloyd's Building).

The Tower of London

The vast medieval fortified complex right beside Tower Bridge was built from the year 1076. It served, among others, as a royal castle and a prison. Today, it houses the Crown Jewels.

St. Paul's Cathedral

Christopher Wren's magnificent master-piece with its 110-m- (361-ft-) tall dome was built between 1675 and 1711, after the earlier church had been destroyed by the Great Fire of London in 1666.

Guildhall

The former town hall (from 1411) is a complex of buildings comprising several characteristic late-Gothic assembly halls. Today, the Guildhall is the administrative headquarters of the City of London.

LONDON

Buckingham Palace

Since Queen Victoria's accession to the throne in 1837, Buckingham Palace with its more than 600 rooms has been the official London residence of the Royal Family. The palace, expanded several times in later years, was originally built as the private city residence for the Duke of Buckingham in 1705. After the death of Queen Victoria, the Victoria Memorial created in honor of the great monarch by Thomas Brock was set up outside the gates. However, since the palace in its appearance at that time was not deemed suitable as a backdrop for the monument, the architect Sir Aston Webb was commissioned to modify the building to achieve a better match between the two. Thus, in 1913, the neo-baroque façade was built that can be seen from the forecourt today (picture right). Visitors may admire the royal art treasures at the Queen's Gallery. In the Royal Mews, the royal stables, the gilded state carriage dating from the 18th century is on display, among others.

Trafalgar Square

The square was laid out in 1820 to 1845 and named after the naval victory over the Spanish and French fleets in 1805, during which Lord Nelson secured naval supremacy for the Empire against Napoleon. At its center the square features the spectacular column, from the top of which a statue of the admiral gazes into the distance. With its two striking curved water basins, the square is considered by many Londoners to be the heart and the real focal point of the city. It is also a popular site for public ceremonies and events.

Covent Garden

In Covent Garden, not far from Trafalgar Square, small and larger stores offer for sale anything the heart may desire. The traditional, glass-roofed market halls stand at the Covent Garden Piazza, in the heart of the shopping and entertainment district, surrounded by restaurants.

Piccadilly Circus

Several roads lead into this busy square and roundabout, including the shopping streets Piccadilly and Regent Street as well as Shaftesbury Avenue, which boasts the theaters of London's West End. The popular "Eros Fountain" of 1892, on the traffic island in the middle of the square, is in reality a monument to the Earl of Shaftesbury, and the figure at its top does not represent Eros, but Anteros, the ancient god of requited love.

Every day at 11.30 a.m., the royal infantry line up for inspection, accompanied by marching music, and this is followed by the Changing of the Guard on the forecourt of Buckingham Palace. The ceremony is a major attraction, not only thanks to the bearskin hats.

Palace of Westminster and Big Ben

The Palace of Westminster (Houses of Parliament), with its three tall towers, defines the cityscape of London on the north bank of the Thames. Westminster Hall, the oldest part of the extensive complex of buildings and the former royal hall, was erected as early as 1097. The rest was the first neo-Gothic building in Great Britain, built according to the plans of the architect Charles Barry in 1837 after the earlier structures had burned down in a fire in 1834.

At the eastern end of the main building stands the famous elegant clock tower, probably London's best-known landmark. Behind the four clock faces of the tower clock, at a height of 55 m (180 ft), Big Ben is concealed: the great bell of the clock, cast in 1858 and weighing almost 14 tons, whose name has become synonymous everywhere with the entire tower.

Westminster Abbey

The history of the British coronation church dates back to the years 1045 to 1065, when a Romanesque abbey church was built here on the orders of Edward the Confessor. The present church with its 30-m- (98-ft-) tall central nave was built from 1245, when Henry III commissioned a completely new building in the early-Gothic style. This, however, was not completed until the 18th century, when the towers were added. It was also annexed and altered over time, including the choir, which did not receive its neo-Gothic look until the 19th century.

In 1953, Queen Elizabeth II was crowned in Westminster Abbey. Yet the abbey does not serve only as a coronation church and burial place for British monarchs. Many more than 3,000 distinguished Britons have found their final resting place here, including Isaac Newton, Charles Darwin and Charles Dickens, as well as the German composer Handel.

LONGON

British Museum

The British National Museum evolved from a private collection, which the owner bequeathed to the state in 1753. Six years later, it had developed into an exhibition that was open to the general public. Today, the museum is one of the most important museums of cultural history in the world, and with more than six million items in its inventory it is also the largest museum anywhere.

One of the most famous exhibits in the main building (1848) is the Rosetta Stone, discovered in 1799. Its identical inscriptions in Demotic, classical Greek and ancient Egyptian made it possible to decipher hieroglyphics by comparing the texts.

Camden

Student district and alternative culture – these sum up Camden past and present. The city district north of the center was the home of punk in the 1970s and of the gothic movement in the 1980s. Since then, however, much has changed around here. Next to the old pubs on Cam-

Notting Hill

At one point, there were still slums in Notting Hill to the north of Hyde Park, but since the 1970s this part of town has again become a desirable residential area for the upper middle classes. It is particularly famous for its antiques market in Portobello Road and the colorful Notting Hill Carnival in August.

den High Street, classy celebrity bars and chic boutiques have opened. At the weekends, there is a huge crowd of people thronging the many popular street and indoor markets. Yet, despite all these changes since the days of punk, the old Camden has managed to preserve its very special charm to the present day.

Shops of all kinds and alternative lifestyles determine the street scene in Camden (right). The markets are concentrated in the area around the picturesque and historic Camden Lock on Regent's Canal.

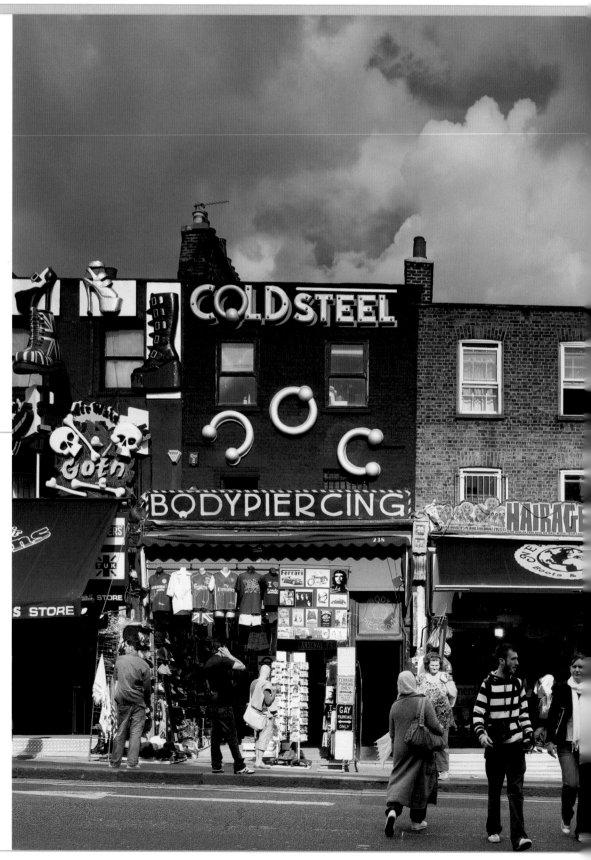

Tate Modern

When the vast collection of the Tate Gallery threatened to burst at the seams, the art museum was divided into two in 2000, creating the Tate and the Tate Modern. The latter moved into a new home in a former power station on the Thames. On more than 12,000 sq m (129,120 sq ft) of exhibition space, all major representatives of modern and contemporary art from 1900 to the present day are exhibited in the converted industrial building.

Naturally, the Tate Modern also has a museum shop as well as restaurants and cafés on offer. One of these is on the sixth floor, affording superb views of the river and city.

Canary Wharf

In the heart of the Docklands former industrial landscape in London's East End, shiny skyscrapers, visible from afar, rise into the sky today. Among them is One Canada Square, at a height of 235 m (771 ft) the tallest in the country. Canary Wharf evolved where once deep-sea vessels were unloaded in the West India Docks. Today, the Docklands Light Railway, a fully automatic city railway without a driver, transports business people and employees to their offices in the skyscrapers and to the shops of the ultramodern business district.

Harrod's

Probably the most famous department store in the world, Harrod's sales area of more than 90,000 sq m (968,400 sq ft), also makes it one of the world's largest. It evolved from a tea wholesalers', founded in 1834 by the merchant Charles Harrod. The store attaches great importance to style – anyone wearing a cropped T-shirt or skimpy sportswear will be barred from entering.

Kensington Palace

Prince Charles and Princess Diana lived in this palace after their wedding in 1981. The palace, surrounded by picturesque Kensington Gardens, however, has been a royal residence since the end of the 17th century and is used today by several members of the royal family. Queen Victoria was born here, as was Mary of Teck, Queen Elizabeth II's grandmother.

Together, Amsterdam as the capital of the Netherlands and The Hague as the royal residence and seat of government, are fascinating twin cities in the historic province of Holland.

An old town entirely constructed on wooden pikes, 80 km (50 miles) of waterways, hundreds of bridges plus a red-light district surrounding a gothic church: Amsterdam really is unique. Amsterdam's heyday was the 17th century, the Golden Century of the Netherlands, which developed during this period as a leading naval and economic power, establishing colonies and trading stations around the world. Large sums of money flowed back to the mother country, and the Amsterdam bourgeoisie invested it, not least in the beautification of their city. But they were also practical people, and the city was surrounded by a ring of canals so that goods could be transported directly to the trading houses.

Today, the canals with their rows of historic houses and bridges are synonymous with romantic Amsterdam. Like the economy, the arts also flourished during the Golden Century. The name Rembrandt, whose home is open to visitors, represents this era around the world. In The Hague, where Dutch politics has always been at home, the roots go back to

Canals

A canal cruise features on most Amsterdam tourists' list of things to do. How better to enjoy the "Venice of the North" than from the water? This convenient mode of transporting not only people but also goods was also the guiding aim of the founding fathers of Amsterdam,

when they began the systematic construction of a network of waterways in 1612. Amsterdam had the Amstel River and its canals flowing through its center since the Middle Ages, but now a semicircular belt of canals consisting of three main waterways was built around the heart of the city. Over the course of time, smaller side canals formed so that at the end of the "golden" 17th century the city boasted umpteen kilometers (miles) of navigable waterways. This necessitated the construction of bridges for pedestrians, and today Amsterdam boasts some 1,280 bridges! Numerous locks were also constructed to prevent flooding from the North Sea. Dutch water engineering was of the highest standard even then and is still impressive today. Ultimately, the quaint canals and bridges delight us today thanks to the engineering skills and the utilitarian thinking of this ancient trading city.

The tall, narrow riverside houses stand shoulder to shoulder along the Amstel (above). Prinsengracht together with Herengracht, Keizersgracht form the historic belt of canals around Amsterdam (large picture).

the Middle Ages. The seat of government and of parliament is the magnificent Binnenhof, founded in the 13th century by the counts of Holland. It is relatively recently that the queen, too, has conducted her official duties from The Hague – it was Napoleon, ultimately, who made the traditional Republic of the United Netherlands a monarchy.

Westerkerk

For the inhabitants of Amsterdam, the spire of the Westerkerk is a familiar sight. Everyone knows it, everyone loves it. This is partly because of its distinctive, ornate shape, and partly because of the carillon of 50 bells that can be heard every Tuesday between midday and 1 p.m. Anne Frank, too, who lived just around the corner, heard it from her hideout. She wrote about it in her diary.

The church itself, dedicated in 1631, is a particularly successful example of Dutch Renaissance style, whose key feature is the combination of brick and natural stone. The light interior is almost as wide as it is high (29 m/95 ft), with the central nave featuring a wooden barrel vault – it is said a stone vault would have been too heavy for the unstable ground. As the Westerkerk was built as the first large church in the Netherlands specifically for Protestant services, its interior is comparatively plain. Particularly valuable, however, is the organ, which was

Montelbaanstoren

The sight of the Montelbaanstoren conveys a good idea of the strength of the late-medieval fortifications, built by the prosperous city of Amsterdam to defend itself from hostile attack. The sturdy tower (1512) on the Oude Schans Canal houses the town watch that guarded the entrance to the port and its environs. It probably also served as a gathering point for sailors. The Montelbaans Tower is one of few surviving remains of the medieval town walls. The last fortification ring of Amsterdam dates from the late 19th century. Thanks to its ingenious technology and its extent, UNESCO has listed it as a World Heritage Site. The impressive fortification belt measures 135 km (84 miles) in length, and comprises walls and 45 forts, including the fortified island of Pampus. What is particularly unusual, however, is the flooding system: with the help of locks, the entire surroundings, most of which are below sea level, could be flooded.

Dam and Palace

Damplein is one of the most attractive squares in the old town, home to restaurants and cafés, hotels, shops and "Madame Tussaud's" wax cabinet. The Dam is dominated by the Royal Palace. Built in the middle of the 17th century as a town hall and at the time the largest secular building in Europe, it still attests today to the pride and prosperity of Amsterdam's bourgeoisie during the Golden Century. As the royal family do not live at the palace, parts of it can be visited. The nearby Nieuwe Kerk (New Church, 15th and 17th century), an impressive church in the style of the early Renaissance, is the venue of royal weddings and funerals. Anyone assuming that the name of the Dam might be something to do with the name of the city, is absolutely right. For in the 13th century, there really was a dam on the Amstel here, which protected the city from the storm tides of the North Sea, at the same time connecting the two oldest areas of the settlement.

manufactured between 1686 and 1727. Its rich sound can be appreciated during the popular church concerts.

On Sundays, the Westerkerk is only open for those attending its service, but on weekdays it is also open to sightseers.

Left: The "South Church" stands on Zuiderkerkhof Square, near Nieuwmarkt and Rembrandt House. No services have been held at the originally Protestant church since 1929. Today, the attractive Renaissance structure (1601–1611) with its richly detailed tower is used by the city information bureau.

De Waag

The impressive structure, today known just as De Waag (the scales), was however not built as the city weighhouse but as one of three main city gates in 1488. When, a good century later, the demolition of the city fortifications was begun – because within the ring of walls the flourishing, growing city simply ran out of space –, the city gate lost its function. And thus it was decided to set up the city weighhouse on the ground floor. Weighhouses served mainly to deter fraudsters: The weights cited by the merchants could not be relied on, and therefore all goods had to be weighed on the calibrated scales before a sale. On the top floor, several guilds had their assembly rooms. The surgeons even set up an anatomical theater in order to demonstrate their art to the general public. Today, visitors can visit the restaurant and café in the picturesque old building.

Rijksmuseum

Amsterdam's Rijksmuseum is not only the largest museum of art and history in the Netherlands. Its comprehensive collection, especially of Dutch masters (17th century), is renowned around the world. All the great masters are represented here: Rembrandt, Vermeer, Hals and many others. In addition, the historic department has exhibits on the history of the Golden Era. Delft porcelain, furniture, jewelry and garments convey an idea of the life of the prosperous bourgeoisie, which had a decisive influence on the period. Unlike the rest of Europe, it was not the aristocracy that set the standards in the Netherlands but the urban elite of merchants. The trade with Asia and the non-European colonies in particular brought a great deal of money to the country. This aspect of history is represented by the superb Asia Department in the Rijksmuseum and its treasures from China, Japan, India and Indonesia.

Scheveningen

From the center of The Hague it is only 6 km (4 miles) to the North Sea. The district of Scheveningen, the largest seaside resort in the Netherlands, is quickly reached by tram or bicycle. It is astonishing how it developed from a simple fishing village – the visitor is greeted by a skyline not unlike that of a major city. In fine weather, there is intense activity on the beautiful sandy beaches, and at the beach bars there is hardly a free seat to be found. Anyone preferring solitude will have to come either in winter or in the early morning hours, or alternatively, wander along the beach in a northerly direction into the dunes of Uilenbosch. The stylish mode of transport is the bicycle; an exceptionally attractive route takes cyclists to the seaside resort of Katwijk, where tourism is also in full swing. Designed for tourists also is the 381-m- (1,250-ft-) long Scheveningen Pier. Visitors walking out over the sea will find a tavern, a playroom for children, souvenir shops and an observation tower. Scheveningen is also a top location for night owls, as one pub and disco follows another along the "boulevard". The most beautiful building is the historic Kurhaus. The magnificent structure was built in the final years of the 19th century and today houses an elegant hotel and restaurant.

Binnenhof

The story of The Hague and its famous Binnenhof dates back to the 12th/13th centuries, when the counts of Holland and Zeeland acquired territories there. In 1291, Floris V, one of the most important members of the dynasty, moved the comital residence to s'Gravenhage, an earlier name of The Hague, which at times is still used today. During the reign of Floris, the enlargement of the Binnenhof also began. Ever more new buildings were added until the late 18th century, so that visitors now see a complex of representative buildings grouped around the central, rectangular courtyard and featuring a variety of different styles at the Binnenhof. The political heart of the Netherlands has been at the Binnenhof since the early days. Today, it functions as the official seat of the prime minister and parliament. The historically and architecturally most significant struc-

ture of the complex is the "Ridderzaal" (Hall of the Knights), a gothic ceremonial hall from the end of the 13th century. Each year on Prinsjesdag, the third Tuesday in September, the queen opens parliament here with her speech from the throne. The Binnenhof can be visited on a guided tour, but it is not a museum and thus it is possible that one or other of the halls will be closed because of parliament being in session.

View through the inner courtyard to the Knights' Hall with its two towers (above). Reflected in the castle pond is the north wing of the Binnenhof, which today is the official residence of the prime minister (large picture).

Left: Large hotels and apartment blocks characterize the cityscape of Scheveningen. The largest seaside resort in the Netherlands, boasting miles of sandy beaches, it is located only a stone's throw from the center of The Hague. The pier is 381 m (1,250 ft) long, with an observation tower at the end.

Peace Palace

One of The Hague's landmarks is the Peace Palace, built shortly before World War I. The American steel tycoon and philanthropist Andrew Carnegie, then the richest man in the world, donated it to the city. Symbol for the peaceful coexistence of the peoples are the contributions made by individual countries to the opulent furnishings of the monumental neo-gothic palace. Today, it houses the International Court of Justice.

Mauritshuis

Immediately next to the Binnenhof stands Holland's most beautiful neoclassical building, with one of the most exquisite art museums in the world. The centerpiece of the Royal Picture Gallery in the Mauritshuis is the collection of Dutch masters of the Golden Century. Rembrandt, Frans Hals and many other famous names are represented, including Jan Vermeer with his famous painting, "Girl with a Pearl Earring".

BRUSSELS

The Belgian capital and royal residence town, the headquarters of the EU and of many international organizations, presents itself as a true metropolis. Stunning sights make it a major tourist attraction.

The Gothic and the Baroque as well as the architectural styles of the 19th and 20th centuries define the cityscape. The historic development is also the best guide for a visit of the city. Visitors will likely begin with the easily accessible old town around the Grand-Place, one of the most attractive squares in the world. Here, Brussels is elegant and sophis-

ticated – and expensive! All around the old town, the 19th century predominates, with the magnificent buildings, boulevards and parks that bestowed prestige on the capital and royal residence of the new kingdom, founded in 1830. In 1958, the World's Fair took place here and the EEC was founded with its headquarters at Brussels, setting off a huge

wave of modernization. Brussels became a "car-friendly" city; visitors, however, are advised to park theirs. The bilingual street signs and road names alone are confusing – French and Dutch enjoy equal rights as languages in the capital of this country where a settlement between the Walloon and Flemish populations has been sought many times.

Grand-Place

The Walloons call it the Grand-Place, the Flemish Grote Markt – but all are proud of this famous square in the heart of the old town, which was a vibrant place of trade already in the Middle Ages and has preserved its attractiveness over the centuries. With its unified yet vibrant and diverse buildings, it is an ensemble of town construction of a singular quality. The dominant structure is the richly adorned Town Hall (Hôtel de Ville/Stadhuis; 15th century) with its 96-m- (315-ft-) high belfry, a superb

Art Nouveau

At the turn of the 19th to the 20th century, the architect Victor Horta created town houses and city palaces in Brussels that are fine examples of the Art Nouveau style; today they are a UNESCO World Heritage Site. The Hôtel Tassel demonstrates the bright and light style (in the picture: the lobby).

example of Brabant Late Gothic architecture. Characteristic for the Grand-Place are the tall and unusually narrow guild houses of the bakers and brewers, river navigators, grocers and all the other occupations that once defined the economic life of the city. After the destruction of the square (1695), the guild houses were rebuilt in the baroque style.

The Grand-Place – a tourist attraction, UNESCO World Cultural Heritage Site and the heart of the city – is one of Europe's most beautiful squares.

The Stock Exchange

In the 1850s and 1860s, when the young kingdom of Belgium experienced its first economic boom, it became apparent that the stock exchange needed a new, larger building in a central location. It was to be both representative and useful, to do justice to the growing impor-tance of the financial markets. In 1865, the city commissioned the architect Léon Suys with the design. As a site, the former butter market on Anspach boulevard was chosen, one of the wide, straight roads that had been laid out in the course of the modernization of the royal capital. The architectural style of the stock exchange, built over four years (1869–1873), complied entirely with the taste of the time in the flamboyant founding years: a neoclassical monumental structure with columns and opulent sculptural decoration, reminiscent of a Greek temple. King Leopold II was present for the grand opening of the magnificent stock exchange palace, and the newspapers were effusive in their enthusiasm.

Today, La Bourse/De Beurs is one of the most distinctive structures in the old town. The word "bourse/beurs" originated not far from here. The van der Beurs family is said to have lived in the Belgian city of Bruges, the trading center of Flanders in the Middle Ages, and the traders in money and securities used to meet in their taverns. The first real stock ex-

Rue des Bouchers

The Rue des Bouchers, a picturesque side street off the Grand-Place, is Brussels' legendary "mussels alley": The displays overflow with lobsters and all sorts of marine creatures; the restaurant stand cheek by jowl, and of course they serve not just "pommes frites" (chips), Belgium's national dish, but specialties from around the world. There is something for every taste, and not all the restaurants are expensive. When all the outside tables are occupied on a

Manneken Pis

The bronze fountain sculpture of the piddling boy, "Manneken Pis" (1619), is the most popular icon of Brussels. Sometimes he is dressed, e.g. in the shirt of the national football team when Belgium plays internationally.

mild evening, it is hard to squeeze past. It is also hard, here, in the "belly of Brussels", to see how magnificent all the old houses are on this historic site, the Rue des Bouchers/Beenhouwersstraat, where the butchers lived and worked back in the Middle Ages.

The "belly of Brussels", the Rue des Bouchers, is the best known of the narrow old lanes around the Grand-Place.

change in a permanent building and with fixed regulations was opened in Antwerp in 1531. The Flemish apparently always had a good nose for money – for today Flanders is once again the more prosperous region of Belgium.

Like a temple to Mammon, the Stock Exchange, inaugurated in 1873, stands on the lively Place de la Bourse, one of the central squares in the inner city of Brussels, only a short walk from the Grand-Place (left).

Cathedral

The cathedral of the Archbishopric of Mechlin-Brussels is the stage for royal weddings and state funerals and one of the finest gothic build-

View of the central nave of the cathedral, with its stunning cross-ribbed vault.

ings in Brussels. Construction of this mighty three-naved church with its tall cross-ribbed vault continued over almost 300 years (from 1226). In 1579, the interior was ransacked by reformist iconoclasts, and so its present furnishings largely date from much later. Especially noteworthy are the figures of the twelve Apostles (17th century) on the columns as

Equally famous are the stained-glass windows, dating back to the 16th century.

well as the carved baroque pulpit. The double patrocinium of the St Michael and St Gudula Cathedral dates back to the time around 1000, when a church dedicated to St Michael stood here, in which the relics of St Gudula were venerated.

BRUSSELS

Quartier Européen

When we say, "Brussels" has decided, no one thinks of the Belgian capital, but of the EU, which has its main seat here, in the European district at the western end of the Rue de la Loi/Wetstraat arterial road. The cruciform tower building of the European Commission, the Berlaymont building, is a typical 1960s monstrosity, visible from afar. More recent but no less colossal is the Justus Lipsius building (1995), seat of the Council of Europe, with a total area of more than 200,000 sq m (2,152,000 sq ft). The two administrative palaces were not particularly happy buildings – the Berlaymont was closed for years because of asbestos contamination, and at the Council of Europe, a network of listening devices was discovered in 2003, which had been installed when the building was first constructed. Brussels has been the "capital of Europe" since 1957/58, when Belgium, West Germany, France, Italy, Luxemburg and the Netherlands joined to form the European Economic Community, the precursor of the European Union founded in 1992. The origins of European union go back to the French Foreign Minister Robert Schuman, who in 1950 promoted the idea of a Franco-German coal and steel union community. The central square in the European district is named after him.

Triumphal Arch in the Jubilee Park

In 1880, on the occasion of Belgium's 50-year anniversary, the Jubelpark/Parc du Cinquantenaire was established. Here stands a 50-m- (164-ft-) tall neoclassical triumphal arch, which is reminiscent of the Arc de Triomphe in Paris as well as the Brandenburg Gate in Berlin with its quadriga. It is the focal point of an impressive group of structures housing several museums. The Royal Museums for Art and History is mainly dedicated to the Oriental, Greek and Roman Antiquity and non-European cultures. The most fascinating treasures in the Royal Museum of the Armed Forces and of Military History are the historic and modern warplanes. Classic cars can be admired at the Autoworld Museum. Beyond the complex of museums, the Jubilee Park extends for 37 ha (91 acres), where, you can go on wonderful walks away from traffic noise.

Royal Palace

In the second half of the 19th century, Belgium was one of the richest countries in the world, and it wanted to display its wealth. The self-portrayal of the young monarchy might be called pompous or even tacky – at least, the public buildings in the new capital and royal residence town had to be larger and more lavish than anything else. And of course, the king of the Belgians also needed one of the most stunning palaces in Europe.

The awakening of this national pride is understandable, for Belgium did not become a state until 1830. Instead, it was fragmented into several territories with ever-changing rulers. In 1794, revolutionary France annexed the entire area; after the fall of Napoleon, the Congress of Vienna granted it to the Netherlands in 1815.

In 1830, the Belgian Revolution led to its secession. Belgium declared its independence and was recognized by the European powers according to

In the complicated framework of EU institutions, the European Commission with its 27 Commissioners (one from each member country) is considered a "guardian of treaties" and the budget. It is based in the vast Berlaymont building (left), which was built in the European Quarter of Brussels in the 1960s.

Law Courts

When it was inaugurated in 1883, it was the largest building in the world, and today the Palace of Justice (Palais de Justice/Justitie-paleis) on Poelaert Square is still impressive thanks to its volume alone – it rises on a ground surface area of 160 by 150 m (525 by 492 ft) and is crowned by a colossal dome. Construction took 17 years; 360,000 cu m (12,713,280 cu ft) of masonry was erected around eight inner courtyards; 65,000 payloads of ten tons each were needed in order to transport the building materials; the dome's hall is nearly 100 m (328 ft) high. These impressive figures are indicative of the grandeur of the structure. In the history of architecture, the Law Courts are known as one of the most outstanding works of the 19th-century ecclecticist style, which combined the elements of various historic periods. In the magnificent interior design, the successful mélange becomes particularly apparent. The Law Courts are freely accessible on workdays.

international law. Now the country needed a king. He, in turn, was chosen by the big powers, who selected an insignificant and thus harmless prince from the house of Saxe-Coburg. Leopold I moved into the Brussels residence of his predecessor, the King of the Netherlands. After repeated conversions and enlargements, especially during the reign of Leopold II (r. 1865–1909), and eventually the neo-baroque design of the early 20th century, the royal palace emerged in its present form. It still contains, as then, the royal administration offices.

The royal family itself resides in the Royal Castle of Laeken, in the Domaine Royal to the north of Brussels. The complex also comprises the Royal Greenhouses commissioned by King Leopold II.

The state residence of the Belgian king is the Royal Castle of Laeken (far left). The Royal Greenhouses are opened to the general public for a few weeks each year in the spring (left).

LUXEMBOURG

The capital of the Grand Duchy of Luxembourg is not only a top financial center, but also a rewarding travel destination: 1,000 years of history have left impressive traces.

Even from afar, Luxembourg presents itself as a picturesque city, with its Lower Town on the Alzette River and the Upper Town, which developed around a castle in the 10th century, high up on the steep Bock Rock. One of Europe's most defiant fortresses, its remains, as well as the historic city center, are UNESCO World Heritage Sites. Located in the border triangle

Lower Town on the Alzette River

The historic Lower Town comprises the Grund, Clausen and Pfaffenthal quarters, which developed from medieval artisan settlements on the banks of the Alzette. In Pfaffenthal, two towers of the fortress dating from the baroque period are still standing. They go back to Marshall Vauban (1633–1707), King Louis XIV's famous master-builder of casemates. Also baroque in style is the Neumünster Abbey (now a cultural center) in Grund. Its Saint John's Church was mentioned for

Grand Ducal Palace

The palace serves as the official residence of the grand duke, the head of state in the constitutional monarchy of Luxembourg. The oldest part of the extensive complex of buildings is formed by the city's former late-gothic town hall (15th century).

the first time in records in 1309; the present structure dates from around 1700. In the Clausen district stands the house where Robert Schuman (1886–1963) was born. The father of the European Union became the first President of the European Parliament in 1958. Visible from afar is the 355-m- (1,165-ft-) long Red Bridge (1965), spanning the Alzette in Pfaffenthal at a height of 75 m (246 ft). It is one of several bridges that link the Upper Town with the other districts and define the entire cityscape.

between Germany, France and Belgium, Luxembourg has historically often been a bone of contention; many rulers followed one another, each time leaving their architectural mark. With its 90,000 inhabitants, the capital of the miniature state is no metropolis, but its international banks and the EU, which has its third main base here, certainly mean it is not provincial.

The Lower Town quarter of Grund (large picture) sprawls along the Alzette River. Here, mostly artisans settled in earlier days. In the lanes of the old town you can now find countless restaurants – life is good in prosperous Luxembourg (far left). In the Kirchberg district stands the Philharmonic Hall (left, with the tall buildings of the European Parliament).

Notre-Dame Cathedral

In 1870, the Jesuit church (17th century) was elevated to become the Cathedral of Our Lady. The baroque picture of the Mother of God, the patron saint of Luxembourg, is the destination of a famous pilgrimage each year at Easter.

The Late Gothic and the Renaissance define the remarkable architecture of the cathedral. The extensive enlargement work of the 20th century matches it in style.

PARIS

For France, which is centralist in its organization, Paris is the absolute center. The most important traffic routes in the country converge on the capital in a star shape; it boasts several airports and stations; and it is the seat of various international organizations. Politically, economically and culturally, everything radiates from the capital to the rest of the country.

The Seine flows through Paris in an east-west direction, dividing the city into the Rive Droite (northern right bank) and the Rive Gauche (southern left bank). On the island, Île de la Cité, stands one of Paris' landmarks, mighty Notre-Dame Cathedral.

But Paris is not only the capital of France; it is admired around the world as a hub of art and culture, and at the same time as the home of an undeniably French lifestyle of elegance and casual flair. And this town of millions can effortlessly fulfill all these expectations. With its squares and boulevards, its museums and galleries, and its temples to haute cuisine, it is simply unique.

The restaurants and street cafés in Montmartre, the artists' quarter, are the expression of a very Parisian way of life (left).
From the richly adorned Pont Alexandre III, wonderful views of the illuminated Eiffel Tower (below) can be enjoyed at dawn.

Place de la Concorde and Champs-Élysées

Probably the most famous boulevard in the world, the more than 6-km- (4-mile-) long Avenue des Champs-Élysées cuts straight through the middle of Paris. Cafés and restaurants, together with elegant hotels and noble shops, are concentrated particularly in the section near the Place Charles de Gaulle, named after the charismatic first president of the Fifth Republic. At the other end of the boulevard is the Place de la Concorde, where the over-3,000-year-old obelisk from Luxor soars into the sky. In the revolutionary year of 1793, King Louis XVI was beheaded at the guillotine here.

Pompidou Center

Even before its inauguration in 1977, the Pompidou Center stirred up some lively controversies. Architecturally, the cultural center in the Beaubourg district is indeed unconventional. The design of the building is, so to speak, turned inside out; many structural elements and technical installations that one would expect to find inside the building are on the outside: the load-bearing frame, for example, as well as the ducts and water pipes, but also the elevators and moving stairways.

Inside, the complex provides numerous artistic and cultural facilities, among them the Musée National d'Art Moderne (National Museum of Modern Art) with its collection of more than 30,000 works of art. Additionally, there is a center for architecture and industrial design as well as a theater and a public library. Thanks to the unconventional architecture of the building, there are also vast areas inside with plenty of space for exhibitions.

Notre-Dame

A church probably originally stood on this site, and before that possibly a Roman temple. Notre-Dame de Paris, a cathedral dedicated to the Blessed Virgin Mary, was built from 1163, when the construction of the choir was first begun under the aegis of the bishop of Paris. The five-aisled basilica, towering up 35 m (115 ft) high inside, was completed in the middle of the 13th century. Characteristic for the French Gothic is especially the west façade with its two 69-m- (226-ft-) high towers and the three extensively and elaborately decorated portals. The system of using flying buttresses that is typical of gothic cathedrals is largely thought to have been an invention of the master-builders of Notre-Dame. The church and the square in front of it are regarded as the center of Paris and of France. The distances between the capital and all other points in the country are measured from here.

Built between 1806 and 1836, the Arc de Triomphe on Place Charles de Gaulle immortalizes in stone Napoleon's military achievements. From the just under 50-m- (164-ft-) high observation deck, stunning views unfold over the roofs of the city.

Louvre

The rulers of France held court at this former royal palace when they stayed in Paris until 1682. Originally, a castle stood here, dating from the 12th century. In 1546, King Francis I commissioned a new residence on its site, the "Old Louvre", which was converted and expanded by almost all monarchs that followed. When the royal residence was moved to Versailles in 1682, a quiet period followed for some time, until Napoleon I again commissioned more building activity. This further enlargement, the "New Louvre", now standing in the western part of the complex, was finally completed under Napoleon III. Since 1793, the building has been a museum, and today it houses one of the most comprehensive and significant art collections in the world. Works of art, such as the Mona Lisa and the Venus de Milo, attract millions of visitors every year. The impressive glass and steel pyramid has served as the main entrance to the "Grand Louvre" since 1989.

Opéra Garnier

In 1861, Napoleon III initiated an architectural competition for the design of a new Parisian opera house. The tender was won by master-builder Charles Garnier, who proposed a neo-baroque concept for the home of the Grand Opéra. Soon after the inauguration in 1875, the Opéra Garnier became a glamorous place of encounter for Paris' high society. With its magnificent façade and the no less extravagant interior, the building is an impressive symbol for the luxurious lifestyle of the French Belle Époque.

Particularly famous are the staircase decorated in white marble and the luxurious auditorium, which with its five galleries accommodates over more than 2,000 spectators and is dominated by a chandelier weighing several tons. Gaston Leroux's novel "Phantom of the Opera" (1910), of which several film and stage versions exist, is set in the Opéra Garnier.

PARIS

Saint-Germain-des-Près

This quarter is one of the oldest on the left bank of the Seine. Here you stroll along the Boulevard St-Germain, past shops, restaurants, bookstores and cinemas, discovering much that is worth seeing in the quieter side streets. There are museums, such as the Musée de la Monnaie, a former mint in a stunning building dating from the 18th century, or the Musée d'Orsay, in a magnificent former station building, built for the Universal Exhibition in 1900. In the Church of Saint-Germain-des-Près, which gave its name to the district, the tomb of the philosopher René Descartes can be seen, and in the charming Marché de Saint-Germain, one of the last remaining covered food markets in the city, fine foods from around the world can be purchased.

The countless cafés of Saint-Germain-des-Près look back on their own history at the heart of Parisian intellectual life. In Le Procope, the oldest café in Paris, literary folk gathered as early as the 17th century. In the 20th century, the popularity of the area reached new heights, and the cafés were populated by artists, writers and philosophers. In the Café de Flore, for example, Jean-Paul Sartre and Simone de Beauvoir were regulars, and not far from here, Pablo Picasso had his "Monument to Apollinaire" erected in 1959.

Jardin du Luxembourg

Until the French Revolution of 1789, the park belonging to the former royal residence, the Palais du Luxembourg, was only open to the aristocracy. Originally, there was an Italianate baroque pleasure garden here, laid out in the first half of the 17th century. The gardens were renovated in the 19th century. The central section was transformed to be strictly symmetrical in accordance with the rules of classical French horticulture, whereas the outer areas took the English landscape garden as a model. Today, the park is a green oasis for Parisians and visitors alike.

Musée d'Orsay

The Musée d'Orsay, a former station on the left bank of the Seine, exhibits major works of art, including the "The Gates of Hell" by Auguste Rodin, as well as paintings by van Gogh, Manet and many other famous artists.

Pont Neuf

Supported by twelve stone arches, the 275-m- (902-ft-) long Pont Neuf spans the Seine either side of the Île de la Cité. Although it is called the "new" (neuf) bridge, it is in fact the oldest of the currently more than 30 bridges across Seine in Paris. Begun in 1578 by Henry III, it was ceremonialy opened in 1607 by Henry IV. The Pont Neuf experienced the perhaps most extraordinary event in its history in 1985, when the "wrap artist" Christo made the bridge disappear under 42,000 sq m (451,920 sq ft) of woven fabric.

The famous Café Les Deux Magots was once a gathering place for intellectuals. Among its regulars then was Ernest Hemingway. Two sculptures of Chinese merchants (magots), who gave the café its name hang inside.

Panthéon

The inside of this memorial site, originally built in 1790 as a church, is adorned with the statues and monuments of famous personalities, who found their final resting place here.

Les Invalides

Almost 20 years after his death, the body of Napoleon Bonaparte was transferred to Paris and laid to rest at Les Invalides.

Eiffel Tower

The Eiffel Tower is the Paris landmark par excellence. Built for the Universal Exhibition in 1889, the 300-m- (984-ft-) high tower by Gustave Eiffel was for years the tallest structure in the world.

PARIS

La Défense

Parts of this systematically laid out new district on the western limits of the city were created as early as the late 1950s. At the beginning of the 1960s, the complex was then integrated into a large-scale modernization program for all of Paris, and in the 1980s, the then-president Mitterrand launched his so-called "Grands Projets". The center of La Défense is formed by a giant elevated pedestrian zone, surrounded by tower blocks of glass and steel. Below this car-free area are the access roads and parking spaces. As well as immense office spaces, the hypermodern buildings also house apartments, shops, a shopping mall, restaurants, cafés and hotels. Spectacular large sculptures by well-known contemporary artists adorn the spaces between the buildings. The symbol of La Défense, visible from afar, is the 110-m- (361-ft-) high triumphal arch, La Grande Arche. With its idiosyncratic cube shape, it is regarded by some as the new emblem of Paris. The angular marble structure was inaugurated in 1989, on the occasion of the 200-year jubilee of the French Revolution. Other buildings worth seeing are the Tour Fiat, one of Europe's tallest skyscrapers, and the Palais Defénse, also known as CNIT (Centre des Nouvelles Industries et Technologies), with its distinctive circular roof.

The "Moulin Rouge" in Montmartre is the epitome of cabaret and scantily clad entertainment.

Sacré-Cœur Montmartre

As early as the beginning of the 19th century, artists and writers were attracted to this district of Paris, situated on a hill in the north of the city. Among the many artists of international standing who lived and worked here, making Montmartre the artists' quarter per se, were figures like Picasso, Modigliani and van Gogh, to name but a few. The lively heart of the district is the Place du Tertre with charming restaurants and all-too-eager street artists and painters, offering their work for sale. The picturesque square, on the peak of Montmartre, is dominated by the white Sacré-Coeur Basilica. The campanile of the church, dedicated in 1919, houses a bell weighing 18.5 tons, one of the heaviest in the world. Above the main portal, an impressive statue of Christ stands enthroned, and the reliefs on the bronze doors depict scenes from the Life of Jesus.

The white Sacré-Coeur Basilica towers impressively above the renowned artists' district of Montmartre (right). Seen from afar, the unusual conical dome and the 83-m- (272-ft-) high campanile are particularly memorable.

La Grande Arche in the La Défense district is lined up to form an axis together with the Arc de Triomphe and the Louvre Pyramid. Inside, the gate-shaped structure houses mainly offices on its 35 floors (left).

Père-Lachaise Cemetery

In 1803, Napoleon Bonaparte had the former site of the Père Lachaise Cemetery bought up and a new, park-like cemetery established there. This became so sought-after as a final resting place for Parisian society that it had to be enlarged several times. Now you can visit the graves and tombs of famous personalities here, including Frédéric Chopin, Oscar Wilde, Heinrich Heine, Edith Piaf and Jim Morrison.

Bois de Boulogne

This park on the western margins of Paris once formed part of the French monarch's private hunting grounds. In the 19th century, the untouched forest of the area was transformed, creating the present-day Bois de Boulogne. Hyde Park in London served as a model. Many smaller individual facilities now define the look of the vast park. Aside from woods and artificial lakes, it also features a racecourse as well as the Parc de Bagatelle, with its small palace and beautiful rose garden.

MONACO

The city-state on the Côte d'Azur is a popular (second) residence for the rich and the beautiful thanks to its spectacular location and advantageous tax laws. It has been ruled for centuries by the princes of the Grimaldi dynasty.

A rock and a narrow strip of coastline below: The territory of the Principality of Monaco extends across an area of less than 2 sq km (494 acres). The fact that it is densely built up with high-rise blocks has made it possible for 30,000 people to live here, as well as providing space for an army of tourists and even a venue for a Formula One race. Until the middle of the 19th century, Monaco was a sleepy hamlet. But then the casino and new railway links created the first boom in tourism. Even then, Monaco was elegant; but it only became internationally famous when Prince Rainier married the Hollywood star Grace Kelly. Since then, the Grimaldis have also reigned supreme in the headlines of the tabloid papers. As there is no income or inheritance tax, the principality is a haven for tax refugees. The Opera House and the Oceanographic Museum with its first-rate research department are world famous.

From the sea, an imposing backdrop of high-rise houses presents itself that is Monaco, the "Mediterranean Manhattan" (right).

Rock of Monaco

In 1297, the Grimaldis, a noble family from Genoa, conquered the steep castle rock above the coast, yet their rule did not remain unchallenged. The strategically important fortress was just too interesting for more powerful rivals. Only after the fall of Napoleon in 1815 did Monaco become an independent and autonomous principality ruled by the Grimaldis. Their palace sits enthroned on the Rock of Monaco, and this is also where the picturesque old town is located. As early as the 13th century, the naval power from Genoa set up a fortress on the rock. Its remains – three towers crowned by battlements – can still be seen from the palace forecourt on the right. In the 17th to 19th centuries,

the fortress was enlarged to make a prestigious seat for the rulers. Worth noting is the east wing, lavishly designed in Renaissance style and featuring beautiful wall paintings in the double loggia. Aside from the stunning views, other sights worth visiting in the old town are the cathedral and the magnificent park that continues down to the Oceanographic Museum on the seashore. During a stroll through the old town, it becomes apparent that Monaco has always suffered from a lack of space: the lanes are narrow and crowded, even more when tourist parties throng the lanes in the high season. The restaurants, cafés and souvenir shops rely on day visitors for a living.

There is room even in the smallest place: On the Rock of Monaco, the Prince's Palace (above) and the old-town houses (large picture) stand closely side by side.

Prince's Palace

The Princely Palace in Monaco features on every tourist's must-see list. Even the interior can be visited – albeit only when the Prince's family are not "at home".

Notre-Dame-Immaculée Cathedral

Built between 1875 and 1884, the neo-Romanesque cathedral of the archbishopric of Monaco is the venue for princely weddings. The Altar of St Nicholas (c. 1500) is worth seeing.

Casino

The flamboyant Casino, opened 1858 in the Monte Carlo district, was immediately a tremendous success. For decades, the microstate practically financed itself from the casino's takings.

BERLIN

The German capital, a pulsating global city and a cultural metropolis of international standing, as well as a focal point of history, yet also young, trendy and cosmopolitan: The once-divided city on the Spree River greets its visitors with a world of contrasts.

With some 3.5 million inhabitants and covering an area of nearly 900 sq km (347 sq miles), Berlin is in every respect Germany's greatest city. The Brandenburg Gate in the heart of Berlin was not freely accessible for nearly 30 years and is today a symbol of conquest over the division of the city into two hostile blocks, Germany and the world. The historic Mitte (meaning center) district with the Unter den Linden boulevard, the Gendarmenmarkt and the Museum Island in the Spree is located in the (former political) east of the city, as are the trendy districts of Prenzlauer Berg and Friedrichshain, the latter now joined by the former West Berlin district of Kreuzberg to form a single administrative unit. The districts of Charlottenburg-Wilmersdorf with baroque Charlottenburg Palace, the Kaiser Wilhelm Memorial Church and the Kurfürstendamm, and Spandau with the Citadel, as well as the Reichstag and the Chancellery are located in former West Berlin. The old imperial and new federal city is one of the liveliest and most diverse metropolises in Europe.

The Wall divided the city for 28 years. Near the Oberbaum Bridge, the "East Side Gallery" (left), designed by artists from around the world, is one of few remaining sections of the border wall. Probably the most famous symbol of the city's division was the Brandenburg Gate, which today shines in new splendor, as seen from Pariser Platz (below).

BERLIN

Museum Island

Thousands of visitors flock every day to Berlin's Museum Island, which, as an outstanding cultural ensemble, is a UNESCO World Heritage Site. Five grand museums present treasures of international standing, including Nefertiti, Berlin's "most beautiful woman". The unique museum landscape was built between 1830 and 1930. After serious destruction in World War II and the neglect of the GDR years, a master plan was agreed in 1999, which is still not fully implemented. However, you can still explore the island: At the southern tip stands the Altes Museum (Old Museum) with its collection of antiquities. The impressive columned façade facing the park marks this neoclassical structure as the principal work of the great Prussian architect Karl Friedrich Schinkel. His student, Friedrich August Stüler, built the Neues Museum (New Museum), which since its reconstruction in 2009 to plans by David Chipperfield has housed the Egyptian Museum. Art of the 19th century is exhibited at the Alte Nationalgalerie (Old National Gallery), another building by Stüler. The main attraction is the vast Pergamon Museum, the newest building on the island. At the northern end of Museum Island lies the Bode Museum, a domed neo-baroque structure housing sculptures and Byzantine art.

Historic Mitte

Strolling along Unter den Linden, Berlin's "most beautiful avenue", between the Brandenburg Gate and the Schlossbrücke, you are on history-charged ground. Under the Great Elector (17th c), the 1.5-km- (1-mile-) long and 60-m- (197-ft-) wide road was a popular bridleway. Under Frederick the Great (r. 1740–1786), it became a grand boulevard flanked by superb historic buildings such as

In about 1900, Wilhelm II commissioned the Berliner Dom (Berlin Cathedral), a magnificent neoclassical building. Worth seeing are the Imperial Stairs and the Hohenzollern Crypt.

Schinkel's classicist Neue Wache (New Guardhouse, 1816–1818), which today is Germany's memorial to the victims of war and tyranny. The oldest complex is the baroque Zeughaus (Arsenal, 1695–1730), today the Deutsches Historisches Museum (German Historical Museum). Here you will also find Berlin's most beautiful square, the Gendarmenmarkt. Flanking the classicist Schauspielhaus (Playhouse, today a Concert Hall) by Schinkel, built from 1818 to 1821 are the Französischer Dom (French Cathedral) and the Deutscher Dom (German Cathedral), both built in the early 1700s and given their elegant tower superstructures in 1785.

Often described as the most beautiful square north of the Alps, Gendarmenmarkt is a unified work of town planning art. The name refers to the regiment of gendarmes who were stationed here in the 18th century.

No one can escape the fascination radiating from the Pergamon Altar (2nd century BC), which gave its name to the Pergamon Museum on Museum Island. There are further ancient monumental structures to be admired here, for example the Babylonian Ishtar Gate.

Unter den Linden

In the center of the avenue Unter den Linden (Under the Linden Trees) stands "Old Fritz": The equestrian statue of the Prussian King Frederick II is part of the Forum Fridericianum, laid out in the middle of the 18th century.

Alexanderplatz

The best views of Berlin and its environs can be enjoyed from the observation deck and revolving restaurant in the 365-m- (1,198-ft-) high "Alex" Fernsehturm (TV Tower) on Alexanderplatz.

Hackesche Höfe

When they were built in the early 20th century, the Hackesche Höfe in the Scheunenviertel district formed the largest residential and working complex in Europe. Today, they are very trendy.

BERLIN

Holocaust Memorial

In the heart of Berlin and only a few paces south of the Brandenburg Gate, on an area of about 19,000 sq m (204,440 sq ft), stands a field of stelae – Germany's main Holocaust Memorial. The Memorial to the Murdered Jews of Europe, designed by the internationally renowned American architect Peter Eisenman, consists of about 2,700 concrete slabs arranged on a grid-like plan. Because of their varying heights and the irregularly sloping ground, it creates an impression of waves that can be perceived from every position afresh. This truly exceptional memorial site, which defies all conventions, is freely accessible from all sides, to everyone, with special routes marked for the disabled and 24/7. The field of stelae is complemented by the Ort der Information (Place of Information), located underground in the south-eastern corner by Eisenman. In an exhibition space of about 800 sq m (8,608 sq ft), information is made available to visitors about the victims. In contrast with the abstract memorial, remembrance here becomes tangible and personal through the names of the murdered Jews and examples of life and family stories. Information on the memorial places that have been established in the former Nazi death camps reveals the extent of the genocide.

Reichstag Building

Millions of visitors, thousands every day! The Reichstag building is a veritable tourist magnet. This is thanks not least to the superb accessible glass dome, from where fantastic views can be had over the city as well as down into the assembly hall, the meeting place of the federal parliament. The British star architect Sir Norman Foster designed the dome in the course of the conversion (1994–1999) that became necessary when the federal government moved from Bonn to Berlin. The Reichstag building was built during the German Empire (1884–1894) and badly destroyed in World War II. It had to be rebuilt and redesigned as a parliamentary building fitting to the times. The 800-ton, 23.5-m- (77-ft-) high glass and steel dome was, in a way, the icing on the cake; it is also symbolic of the resumption of the pan-German parliamentary tradition after reunification. The glass dome is accessible every day and to everyone from 8 a.m. to midnight.

Hauptbahnhof

In May 2006, the new Hauptbahnhof (Central Station) was glitzily inaugurated, and ever since Berlin has again become a "rail hub", as before the division. Reunification had made a reconceptualization of the rail traffic imperative, and so the German capital was given the largest and the most modern crossing station in Europe. It sets new standards not only with its spectacular architecture, but also with the idea of the tower station. The long-distance, regional and city rail traffic runs on two levels – six platform lines are on the upper level, with eight lines running perpendicular to them on the lower level. In addition, there are three floors with about 80 shops, open until 10 p.m., even at the weekend. A visual highlight of the station, designed by the Hamburg architect Meinhard von Gerkan, are the two arched structures containing commercial properties that span the top track.

The strict radicalism by which the memorial for the murdered Jews in Europe in the heart of the German capital refuses to comply with conventional monuments is symbolic of a way of remembrance that is commensurate with the worst mass murder in history (left).

Potsdamer Platz

It is hard to imagine now, but after the Fall of the Wall the Potsdamer Platz was only a barren wasteland. The square, at one time the busiest in Europe, had been almost completely destroyed by World War II bombs and, because it straddled East and West, the East German government did not rebuild it. Divided by the Wall in 1961, it became a barren no man's land. After 1989, when Potsdamer Platz was once more located in the heart of the re-unified city, global corporations, such as Daimler and Sony, occupied this prime slice of the Berlin property market. Renowned architects were employed to design a new district for the city. The avant-garde architecture, the shopping malls and hotels, the casino and the "Panorama-Punkt", the restaurants and cinemas, and last but not least, the Berlin Film Museum, made Potsdamer Platz an sophisticated part of the city and a tourist attraction.

Bundeskanzleramt

Covering an area of 12,000 sq m (129,120 sq ft), the monumental postmodern structure in the bend of the Spree housing the Bundeskanzleramt (Federal Chancellery) since 2001 is one of the most impressive government buildings in the world. Allegedly, it is eight times the size of the White House in Washington. The demands were great, when in 1990 it was decided to move the federal government from Bonn to Berlin, and a new government district was planned where East and West meet, near the Reichstag building. Reunified Germany set great store by representation. For security reasons, tourists can admire the Federal Chancellery only from afar. What can be seen is the symmetrical façade with the vaulted entrance area and the two flanking office wings. In front of the building stands the vast, nearly-90-ton iron sculpture "Berlin" by the Basque sculptor Eduardo Chillida, a symbol of both division and reunification.

BERLIN

Prenzlauer Berg, Kreuzberg

The old city districts Prenzlauer Berg, Friedrichshain and Kreuzberg provide the native Berliner with his "kiez" or neighborhood, and the newly arrived Berliner with a hip scene. Many historic buildings and a mix of lifestyles define the former residential areas of workers and the lower middle classes. Anyone wishing to paint the town red, pull an all-nighter in the cozy pubs or trendy clubs or enjoy the original and hip art scene, is in the right place here. One of the most popular meeting points in Prenzlauer Berg is the area around Kollwitz-platz, named after the sculptress Käthe Kollwitz (1867–1945), who lived here. And there is Friedrichshain public park, laid out in the 19th century as a green area amid dense housing. Kreuzberg boasts two major museums: the Deutsches Technik-museum (German Museum of Technology) and the Jüdisches Museum (Jewish Museum), in the spectacular building by architect Daniel Libeskind.

Kurfürstendamm, Charlottenburg Palace, Zoo

Breitscheidplatz with the ruin of the steeple of the Kaiser-Wilhelm-Gedächtniskirche (Kaiser Wilhelm Memorial Church), Tauentzienstrasse with the KaDeWe (a top department store) and above all of course the Kurfürstendamm (short, Ku'damm), the legendary shopping and prome-

nade avenue – together they form the pulsating, cosmopolitan heart of former West Berlin. Close by is the Zoo, Germany's oldest zoological garden (1844), with the greatest number of species worldwide. It is best entered via the amazing Elephant Gate.

Among the city's top sights is the baroque Charlottenburg Palace with its gardens (1695–1746). Here, the ruling Hohenzollerns' appetite for architecture, flamboyancy and esthetics becomes evident. A must is a visit to the historic rooms, which have been restored to their original splendor after wartime destruction.

Charlottenburg Palace (top), Zoological Gardens (above, the Elephant Gate at the main entrance) as well as the ruin of the Kaiser Wilhelm Memorial Church (right) are among the main sights in former West Berlin.

Since the Fall of the Wall, many houses from the founding period (1871–1873) have been redeveloped in the Prenzlauer Berg district, one of Germany's largest ensembles of pre-World War II buildings (far left). In the neighborhood around trendy Kollwitz-platz is the KulturBrauerei (left), a cultural center on the site of the former Schultheiss Brewery.

BERN

When the traditionally federalist Swiss founded their state in 1848, they did not want to create a proper capital from which everything would be centrally governed. Bern thus became the Bundesstadt or "Federal City", as the Swiss call their de facto capital.

Bern's Old Town lies picturesquely on a plateau situated in a bend of the Aare River. This is where, according to legend, Duke Berchthold V of Zähringen founded the city in 1191. The military expansion allowed the free imperial city to radically expand its territory from 1218; it became the largest city-state north of the Alps in the 16th century. Today, the metro- politan area measures around 15 km (9 miles) in length and an average of approximately 4 km (2.5 miles) in breadth. Of all Switzerland's cities today, the Federal City is only the fourth largest. Even in terms of in- ternational importance as an eco- nomic center, it has been clearly over- taken by the financial metropolises of Zurich and Geneva and industrial- ized Basel. However, Bern is by no means "provincial"; it is the political center of Switzerland and a popular tourist destination with a wide range of cultural attractions. Bern is, in fact, a very international city, giv- en that some 20 percent of its popu- lation is of foreign ancestry. The best-preserved features in the me- dieval nucleus of this city, which has

Zytgloggeturm clock tower

Every hour on the hour, tourists gath- er in front of Bern's main landmark, the mighty medieval Zytgloggeturm (clock tower) with its famous glock- enspiel. However, you need to be there early to avoid missing the prel- ude, because the rooster crows and the jester rings the bells four minutes before the hour strikes and the armed bears begin their proces- sion. The bearded god Chronos, the personification of time, holding a scepter and hourglass, gives the command for the gold knight

The Piper Fountain

Eleven gorgeous statue fountains from the Renaissance adorn the Old Town, including the Piper Fountain (mid-16th century) on Spitalgasse. The expressive sculp- ture of the bagpiper was modeled on a drawing by Dürer.

perched high above in the spire to strike the hour. The Zytgloggeturm was originally the western city gate. Built around 1220, it also served as a defense tower for the city fortress ex- isting at the time. The first astronom- ical clock was incorporated around 1400; the glockenspiel and the mech- anized clock in the tower structure were added in 1530. In those days, a city clock which officially set the time for everyone was very expensive.

The Zytgloggeturm is one of the city's landmarks, and, with its glockenspiel, also a tourist attraction.

just under 130,000 inhabitants, are found in the stately guild houses and middle-class villas, the late-Gothic cathedral, the baroque Church of the Holy Spirit (Heiliggeistkirche), the imposing gate towers, the magnificent fountain, and last but not least the romantic arcades which blend harmoniously into the townscape. UNESCO named Bern's Old Town a World Heritage Site as early as 1983. The antique splendor stretches over a relatively small area, essentially following three historic longitudinal axes which can still be seen today. The most important of these was the central Kramgasse ("Grocers' Alley"/ Gerechtigkeits-gasse ("Justice Alley"), in the middle of which the city stream once flowed.

Not only does a bear adorn Bern's coat of arms; living versions are also kept in an enclosure situated at the end of the Nydeggbrücke Bridge. This was a cramped bear pit until 2009, when it was expanded to form a 6,000-sq-m (64,560-sq ft-) nature reserve on the banks of the Aare, now known as the BärenPark ("Bear Park").

BERN

Cathedral and archways

The architecture of the Old Town is characterized by the picturesque arcades, which the Bern locals prosaically call "pipes". Opening out onto the street, they supplement the façades of the historic townhouses. Even though it is no longer obvious nowadays, the arcades are actually subsequent additions which came into fashion in the 15th century. The houses were built on top of them, thereby adding more living space, although the alleyways became narrower as a result. Right from the start, craftspeople and grocers would offer their wares in the corridors of these arcades, and even today, the Bern "pipes", which extend

Old Town

The Inner City, as Bern locals call their Old Town, ensnared in the loops of the Aare, is ideal for visitors: The regular, planned layout with three parallel main laneways makes it virtually impossible to get lost. The central railway station, located in the west, is the starting point of the main artery – comprising Spitalgasse, Marktgasse, Kramgasse and Gerechtigkeitsgasse – which cuts

Bern Cathedral

The 100-m- (328-ft-) tall spire of Bern's Münster (cathedral), which was not completed until the 19th century, soars up above the rooftops of the Old Town. Construction on Switzerland's largest and architecturally most famous late-gothic structure began in 1421 and lasted 150 years.

through the historic center, named a UNESCO World Heritage Site in 1983. You need time to really feel the full impact of this unique ensemble. The reformed Nydeggkirche church (c. 1345) forms the eastern end of the Inner City.

The view over Bern's rooftops (large picture). Soaring up on the left in the foreground is the late-Gothic Nydegkirche church, which was erected on the site of a demolished fortress.

over a total of 6 km (4 miles), are conducive to "weatherproof" shopping expeditions. Construction on the late-Gothic cathedral also began in the 15th century, and its main porch (1490–1500), richly decorated with figurines, is one of the city's most famous attractions. Inside, the stained-glass windows of the chancel particularly delight visitors.

The arcaded Marktgasse (far left) culminates in the Käfigturm (Prison Tower), which was completed as a defense tower for the city fortifications in 1256. It was not given its name until 1405, when it was used as a prison. Left: the elegant townhouses of the Inner City are festively decorated with flags.

Untertorbrücke

For a long time, the Untertorbrücke was the only bridge over the Aare for miles. Today, it is Bern's oldest surviving bridge, built in the east of the Old Town from 1460 to 1490.

Fountains at Bundesplatz

The people of Bern love their beautiful fountains – both the ancient and modern. The twenty-six fountains in the water feature at Bundes-platz represent the twenty-six Swiss cantons.

Holländerturm

Like the Käfigturm, the 'Dutch Tower' is one of the defense towers in the ring of fortifications erected from 1250 onward, which was used to protect the free imperial city of Bern from enemy attacks.

VADUZ

Vaduz is not a capital city per se, because it lacks the city charter for this. However, with its some 5,000 inhabitants, it is the capital town of the fourth smallest European, and smallest German-speaking, state. Vaduz was first officially mentioned in the 12th century; its name is presumably derived from Latin. Liechtenstein forms a customs union with neighboring Switzerland, and previously also had close ties with Austria, because the dynasty, which is among the oldest aristocratic families in Europe, has its roots in Lower Austria. 900-year-old Vaduz has belonged to the dynasty since the 18th century, and the Liechtensteiners have resided in the castle high above the town since 1938. They are actively involved in politics. Unlike other constitutional monarchies such as England and Sweden, where the monarchs are mainly figureheads, power in Liechtenstein is shared equally between the people and the prince. The national day on August 15 is even called Prince's Day.

Liechtenstein's "Städtle"

Those wanting to get the best view of Vaduz and its spectacular surrounds should climb up to the castle, the symbol of the "Städtle", as the locals call their town. A fortress was perched atop the rocky terrace as early as the 14th century, and was taken over by the Liechtensteiners in 1712, who transformed it into a castle. It is worth walking up there just for the magnificent view alone. The castle itself cannot be visited. It is the main residence of the royal family, who shun publicity. The prince and his sons only make the headlines if it is a matter concerning Liechtenstein as a financial center and its illegal earnings. Fifteen banks, including the historic Liechtensteinische Landesbank, are based in Vaduz, as are some fifty international insurance companies, and hundreds of trust companies and shell corporations. The Städtle is buzzing, despite the fact that it is actually little more than a village.

It also has a few cultural attractions. Apart from ancient traditions, which enjoy great importance in the alpine principality, contemporary art is also a main focus. The new art gallery is famous nationwide. An art space has been created in the "Engländerbau" as a meeting place for young artists; the unusual name relates to the British lottery manager who commissioned its construction in the 1930s. The Liechtenstein national museum has exhibits pertaining to the country's natural and cultural history, while former ski racer Noldi Beck has amassed a unique collection of historic winter-sports objects for his ski museum. Vaduz's plus points must also include its surrounding area; it is just a few minutes' walk before you find yourself out amongst nature, with vast forests and babbling brooks.

View of Vaduz and its spectacular alpine surroundings. The royal castle is perched high above the town.

Vaduz's most striking buildings include St Florin's Cathedral, which rises up next to the government building, erected in 1905. The triple-naved neo-gothic cathedral was constructed in 1873 as the parish church of the small town of 5,000 (left). When the pope established the archbishopric of Vaduz in 1997, it was raised to the status of a cathedral. The royal crypt is located next door.

Art Gallery

The solid structure made from black basalt and dyed-black cement, with a façade sanded by hand and containing naturally colored pebbles, is worth seeing in itself. Inside, the State Museum for Modern and Contemporary Art, opened in the year 2000, is bright and easy to get around. The collection, specializing in contemporary sculptures, objects and installation art, is presented in completely white surroundings.

Liechtenstein Landtag

Traditional shapes and materials with a modern interpretation: the parliamentary building, inaugurated in 2008, is the arena for the twenty-five members of Liechtenstein's Parliament.

VIENNA

It's not just the magnificent buildings from the Habsburg monarchy which reflect the historic grandeur of the empire; the alleyways of Vienna's Old Town and coffeehouse parlors still also bear unmistakable traces of the dual Austro-Hungarian monarchy.

The former imperial city of Vienna is the capital, and also one of the nine federal states, of the Republic of Austria. With a population of over 1.6 million, it is also the country's largest city. Modern Vienna stretches over both sides of the frequently tamed and straightened Danube – the "New Danube". The Old Town, however, which bears evidence of settlements from as early as ancient times, lies south-west of the present-day river, by the smaller Danube Canal, which was actually the river bed in the Middle Ages. Vienna was one of Europe's largest political and social centers even before the time of the Austria-Hungary Dual Monarchy. Although the city lost importance after World War II, Austria's constitutionally guaranteed neutrality has today made Vienna the headquarters of numerous international organizations, such as the United Nations, the Organization of Petroleum Exporting Countries (OPEC) and the International Atomic Energy Agency.

Large picture: St Peter's Church with its imposing dome (left) and St Stephen's Cathedral with its southern spire (right) tower impressively over the rooftops of Vienna's Old Town. Left: Viennese coffeehouse culture is as lively as ever. A group of artists which later became the "Vienna Secession" would meet at "Café Sperl" as early as 1900.

VIENNA

St Stephen's Cathedral

In the 12th and 13th century, a Romanesque church stood on the site in Vienna's pedestrian zone where the mighty St Stephen's Cathedral, with its 136-m- (446-ft-) high spire, today soars skywards. The church made way for a new Gothic building in the 14th century. The first section, the chancel, was consecrated in 1340 and later became the present-day cathedral. However, parts of the predecessor structure were also incorporated: the "Riesentor" ("Giant's Gate"), the main porch, and the two "Heidentürme" ("Heathen Towers") on either side. The ducal crypt is the final resting place of personalities such as Emperor Frederick III.

Hofburg and Heldenplatz

For centuries, Vienna's imperial palace (the Hofburg) was the center of one of Europe's mightiest monarchies. It was here that the Habsburg dynasty lived and reigned, initially as lords of Austria, then as emperors of the Holy Roman Empire of the German Nation from 1452 to 1806, and finally, between the latter's dissolution and proclamation of the republic in 1918, as emperors of Austria and Austria-Hungary.

Capuchin crypt

Members of the Habsburg and Habsburg-Lothringen dynasties (e.g. Maria Theresa) are buried in the Capuchin or Imperial Crypt beneath the Capuchin church. The crypt was created in the 17th century by the Capuchin Order, which still looks after it today.

The oldest section of the vast complex was built in the late 13th century. Thereafter, almost every ruler expanded the residence, until it eventually reached its present-day dimensions – with 2,600 rooms, spread over eighteen wings surrounding nineteen interior courtyards. Today, the Hofburg is the official residence of the president. Several art collections and museums, including a "Sisi" museum dedicated to Empress Elizabeth of Austria, are open to the public.

The Neue Burg, with the equestrian statue of Prince Eugene of Savoy (right), forms the south-eastern end of the Hofburg. It was originally designed to be part of the gigantic imperial forum which was never built. Today, it is home to various museums and the Austrian National Library.

Jewish Vienna

Vienna's Jewish quarter was established around the Judenplatz or "Jews' Square" (pictured left with the Lessing monument and Holocaust memorial by Rachel Whiteread) as early as the Middle Ages. Since this time, Jewish residents such as Sigmund Freud have helped to define-

itively characterize the metropolis. The Jewish Museum in Eskeles Palace documents the history of Jewish Vienna in a catchy way: from the prospering municipalities in the Middle Ages, to the great pogrom of the 15th century and the persecution and murder of tens of thousands of Austrian Jews by the National Socialists, to contemporary Jewish life.

Imperial apartments

The imperial apartments are part of the museum complex at the Hofburg. Emperor Franz Joseph I and Elizabeth, known as "Sisi" (a portrait is on the right of the picture), lived in the 19 rooms, which have been preserved in original style.

Imperial Riding School

Vienna's Imperial Riding School, founded in 1572, is home to the "High School" of classical dressage. The members of the imperial family also learned how to ride here.

National Library

The baroque ceremonial room at the Hofburg, built in the early 18th century, is the most impressive room in the Austrian National Library. It contains 200,000 precious tomes from the period between 1501 and 1850.

VIENNA

Museum quarter

This modern museum complex situated not far from the Hofburg and opposite the Museums of Art History and Natural History was built on the vast site of the former Court stables, the royal stud of the Austrian emperor. It was erected during the first half of the 18th century at the command of Charles VI. At the time, it was located outside the city center, but still within easy reach of the Hofburg. In 1922, after the monarchy had ended, and pack animals and horse-drawn carriages rapidly lost importance, the buildings were used by Vienna's Exhibition and Conference Center (the Wiener Messe), founded in 1921, which prompted major modifications. After relocation of the Messe in 1995, and a three-year, greatly discussed reconstruction, the present-day museum quarter finally opened its doors in 2001. Architecturally, the cultural center is well laid out, comprising variously designed modern museum buildings in and around the interior courtyards of the original baroque ensemble. The most striking structure is undoubtedly the cuboid Museum of Modern Art (MUMOK), with its almost windowless façade made completely of grey stone slabs. Flanking it are the Vienna Kunsthalle (art gallery), the Leopold Museum and a children's museum.

Burgtheater

Vienna's Burgtheater (former imperial court theater) is undisputedly one of the leading German-language stages. Even during Vienna's imperial days, it enjoyed a fine reputation which stretched well beyond the city and national borders. Anyone who performed here as an actor or director at this time was considered part of their field's elite. The theater was founded by Empress Maria Theresa in 1741, and in 1776, Emperor Joseph III raised its status to that of a national theater. The performances were originally held in an imperial ballroom which was converted into a theater. In 1888, the venue finally moved to its present-day home on Ringstrasse. The interior of the neo-baroque structure designed by Gottfried Semper and Karl von Hasenauer reflects the building's importance and the popular style at the time. Paintings by Gustav Klimt adorn the walls of the stairwells, of which the "Kaiserstiege" ("Emperor's Staircase") was previously only reserved for the emperor.

Museum of Art History

Opened in 1918, the Museum of Art History ("Kunsthistorisches Museum", KHM) is one of the most famous of its kind anywhere in the world. It was designed to display imperial collections from the Habsburg times, including the antiquities collection, the Egyptian-Oriental collection and the art gallery with prominent works of European art history. The KHM also includes branch establishments such as the Ephesus Museum in the Neue Burg and the Wagenburg (carriage museum) at Schönbrunn Palace. The imposing main building on Vienna's Ringstrasse – designed by Gottfried Semper and Karl von Hasenauer based on the Italian Renaissance style – faces the almost identical Museum of Natural History opposite. The symmetry of the two buildings is emphasized by the similarly symmetrical Maria-Theresia-Platz in between.

Museumsplatz (Museum Square), with the baroque façade of the museum quarter and main entrance to the large interior courtyard (left). It is home to more of the red (and also blue) outdoor furniture known as "Enzis", named after a museum quarter staff member.

Karlsplatz and St Charles' Church

Karlsplatz is one of Vienna's central traffic hubs. Various statues, including a monument to Johannes Brahms, adorn the large square, which is partly also a park (Ressel-park). The main eye-catchers are the old entrance hall to the former metropolitan railway and the unmistakable St Charles' Church (1716–1737), a masterpiece by architect Johann Bernhard Fischer von Erlach, interestingly contrasted with Henry Moore's sculptures in front.

Naschmarkt

Picturesque stalls, rustic restaurants and airy bistros – this "fruit and vegetable market" offers virtually anything your heart desires. On Saturdays, a giant flea market with an authentic Balkan atmosphere is held on the adjacent square.

Secession

What people in Vienna simply call "the Secession" was originally the exhibition hall of a group of artists founded in 1897 by Gustav Klimt and others, who deviated from academic art and developed their own variety of Art Nouveau – the "Secessionist style" or "Vienna Secession". The building, erected near Karlsplatz in 1898, and which has a compact gold dome above the entrance, today displays a wide range of contemporary art.

VIENNA

Belvedere Palace

When the baroque Belvedere Palace, with its terraced garden measuring over 1.5 km (0.9 miles) in length, was built in the 3rd municipal district of Vienna, the designated land was still located outside the city. The main buildings, the Upper and Lower Belvedere, face each another at the outer ends of the elongated garden. The sheer size of the ensemble means there is a considerable distance between the two. The complex was designed by Johann Lucas von Hildebrandt, one of the most prominent master-builders of the baroque, who created the masterpiece of his extremely successful career in the form of Vienna's Belvedere. He was commissioned by Prince Eugene of Savoy, the field marshal who, in 1697, secured the crucial victory at Zenta during the Great Turkish War. Prince Eugene was not only considered the most skilful military strategist of his time, but also made a name for himself as a patron of arts and science. The Lower Belvedere was built first, from 1714 to 1716, as a residence for Prince Eugene. A pavilion was planned for the other end of the terraced garden; however, it was later decided that a second palace, The Upper Belvedere (1717–1723), would be built instead. Unlike its counterpart, it was primarily designed for representational purposes. Today, the Belvedere houses a famous art collection.

Prater

The Vienna Prater is actually a vast park which stretches between the Danube and the Danube Canal in the city's 2nd municipal district. The amusement park with its famous 64-m-(210-ft-) high Ferris wheel, which is usually synonymous with the name, was originally called "Wurstelprater", and was renamed "Volksprater" for the World Exhibition in 1873.

Hundertwasser House

This amazing urban residential complex in Vienna's 3rd municipal district, Landstrasse, is named after the artist who designed it: Friedrich Stowasser, alias Friedensreich Hundertwasser, who attained great importance as a painter and graphic artist heavily influenced by the Secessionist style. Hundertwasser primarily became known by a broader audience for his usually ecologically-inspired public campaigns and the striking designs of thirty-seven diverse residential and purpose-built constructions. This house was created from 1983 to 1986, in collaboration with the architect Josef Krawina. It is a fine example of Hundertwasser's concept of programmatic ecology in terms of nature-oriented living. There are hardly any angular corners, floors are purposely uneven, the façade looks irregular, and the terraces are overgrown with trees and bushes. There is a gallery café and shop on the ground floor.

From 1899 to 1914, The Upper Belvedere was used as the residential palace for the imperial family (left). This was where the treaty considered to be the birth certificate of modern Austria was signed in 1955.

Schönbrunn Palace

The former summer residence of the Austrian imperial family is located in a vast park in Vienna's western district. Both Schönbrunn Palace and the palace grounds have been a UNESCO World Heritage Site since 1966. Work began on the palace in 1696, but it was not until well into the second half of the 18th century that the buildings attained their present-day early-classicist appearance. From 1780, in the twenty years before her death, Maria Theresa gradually had the interior reconstructed in rococo style.

The palace grounds are laid out in the classic French manner, and are home to Franz Joseph I's palm house, a maze, and the world's oldest zoo, founded in 1752. The park, which was opened to the public in the late 18th century, stretches from the palace grounds, up the Schönbrunn Hill to the classicist colonnades of the Gloriette, built in 1775.

Grinzing

The Grinzing hills, in Vienna's rugged 19th municipal district at the edge of the Vienna Woods, are home to the famous Wiener Heuriger taverns. Until 1891, when it was incorporated among the bigger municipalities, Grinzing was an independent wine-growing town. However, even at this time, the village had long been a popular daytrip destination for the residents of the nearby metropolis, who came to the Heurige in their droves, as they still do today. The term "Heuriger" denotes both the wine obtained from the latest harvest, and also a tavern where this is served. The Grinzing wine-growers, or "Weinhauers", as they are called here, obtained a license to sell alcoholic beverages when Emperor Joseph II enacted the relevant decree. Roman legionaries stationed here probably pressed the first Grinzing wine as early as the 3rd century.

PRAGUE

The "Golden City" has enjoyed the reputation of being one of the world's most beautiful cities since as early as the Middle Ages. And, given its many magnificent buildings, hardly anyone will dispute this.

The capital and seat of government of the Czech Republic is located in a basin of the Vltava River and on the adjacent hills. For centuries, Prague has been considered one of the strongholds of European spiritual and cultural life. Charles University, founded by Emperor Charles IV in 1348, is one of the oldest in Europe, and was the first in the Holy Roman Empire of the German Nation. Today, Prague is home to numerous universities and academies, as well as many prominent museums, including the National Gallery, with collections at several different locations, and the National Museum, housed in its imposing building at central Wenceslas Square. There are over twenty theaters with permanent performance schedules. However, as a modern metropolis, Prague is also the center of business and trade in the Czech Republic. The symbols of the city – Hradčany castle hill above the left bank of the Vltava River, which dominates the city with Prague Castle and St Vitus Cathedral, as well as the 14th-century Charles Bridge – are world famous.

Romantic autumn atmosphere on the famous Charles Bridge (left). The elevation of Letná Park provides superb panoramic views over the Vltava River and bridges of the inner city (below).

PRAGUE

Jewish Quarter

Prague's Jewish population has been living in the Josefov district since the 13th century. The rest of the population maintained a fickle relationship with the quarter, depending on the general situation at the time. However, even during good times, the Josefov district was a ghetto where Jews had to settle if they wanted to live in Prague. This regulation was not abolished until 1848. Six synagogues have been preserved as old evidence of Jewish life, as have the Jewish Town Hall and Jewish Cemetery (pictured right), where all of Prague's Jews were buried until 1787. The former ceremonial hall is today part of the Jewish Museum.

Charles Bridge

This is where Prague's first stone bridge, the 12th-century Judith Bridge, originally spanned the Vltava River. After it caved in during a flood in 1342, a replacement was needed, as a permanent connection over the river was vital for the city. However, construction on the new bridge did not start until 1357, when the foundation stone was laid by Emperor Charles IV; it was completed after some fifty years. The structure has borne the name of Charles Bridge since 1870. For a long time, it was said that eggs were added to the mortar between the stone blocks to reinforce the approximately 500-m-(1,641-ft-) long bridge, and this was later also confirmed by modern methods. The baroque sculptures on the railings on both sides depict saints and were added in the 17th century. The Old Town Bridge Tower, which leads from the Charles Bridge to the Old Town, is a fine example of Gothic tower construction.

Wenceslas Square, National Museum, Art Nouveau

Wenceslas Square in the center of the New Town is an astonishing 750 m (2,461 ft) long and 60 m (197 ft) wide setting, making it one of Europe's largest municipal squares. However, in actual fact, it is not a square, but a magnificent boulevard of wide traffic lanes and a vast central median strip. Wenceslas Square was created out of the former Horse Market, which had been the focal point since the founding of the New Town in the 14th century, and which was rebuilt and renamed in 1848. It then became Wenceslas Square, with the word "Square". Today, Wenceslas Square is the city's most important shopping street, lined with large malls and many smaller stores. An entertainment district has now emerged at the lower end of the boulevard, with hot-dog stands and fast-food restaurants, discotheques, bars, as well as cinemas and street cafés, which are still

Astronomical Clock

On the southern façade of the Old Town Hall, Prague's famous Astronomical Clock reaches up as far as the base of the tower. On the hour, the two small doors beneath the protruding roof open, and the figures of the twelve apostles appear. The clock not only displays the time on its large 24-hour face, but also the phases of the moon, planet constellations, and the position of the sun, among other things. It was built in the 15th century, whereby the mechanism itself, as well as the clock face, was created in 1410. The Gothic statues were only added in later years.

The Astronomical Clock on the Old Town Hall is one of the oldest of its kind. The calendar, displaying the current date and sign of the zodiac, was added at the end of the 15th century. The hourly chiming and procession of the apostle figures never fails to enchant the many passers-by.

Old Town Square

The square in the heart of Prague's Old Town is home to many historic buildings in Renaissance and baroque style, whose foundations date well back to the Middle Ages. Solid stone buildings have stood here since at least the 12th century. The square was presumably home to merchants at the time, but it almost certainly also served as a marketplace, and was already an important and very central part of the city even then. Today's Old Town Square is no different. It is busy and lively at almost any time. Standing in the center of the square is the Art Nouveau monument to the reformer Jan Hus, who was burned at the stake as a heretic in 1415. All around the Square are some of the city's most prominent structures: apart from the Old Town Hall, there are also the baroque Kinský Palace, the Gothic "House of the Stone Bell" residential building (14th century), set back from the square, the Gothic Teyn Church, and many more.

full of people even late in the evening. Despite these developments, however, Wenceslas Square has largely managed to preserve its traditional character. Numerous buildings display beautiful baroque façades. There are also Art Nouveau buildings, such as the historic "Europa" hotel dating back to 1900, which, with its elaborate and richly decorated designs, once again gleams in the luxurious splendor of the Wilhelminian era. Perched at the upper end of Wenceslas Square is the mighty National Museum building, the country's most prominent natural science museum, erected between 1885 and 1890. The impressive neo-Renaissance structure, with its façade over 100 m (328 ft) long, dominates the surrounding area, and is one of the most important buildings of its time in all of the Czech Republic. Below the museum stands the equestrian statue of St Wenceslas, the national patron and saint of the Czech Republic. The statue was created by Josef Myslbek in 1912.

PRAGUE

St Vitus Cathedral

The monumental Gothic cathedral was built from 1344 to mark Prague's promotion from a diocese to an archbishopric. The first master-builder was Matthias of Arras, who was followed by many others. In 1929, after almost 600 years, Czech architect, Kamil Hilbert, announced that the building was complete. The triple-naved basilica, whose interior reaches a height of 33 m (108 ft), captivates visitors with precious frescoes and magnificent stained-glass windows (pictured right). Five saints are buried here, as well as numerous emperors and kings. The Crown of St Wenceslas is housed in the cathedral, as is a famous relic: the head of St Vitus.

Malá Strana Quarter, Hradčany

Prague's Malá Strana is the district beneath the castle and Hradčany castle hill. A walk through the quarter, with its countless magnificent palaces, is like traveling back through time. After King Ottokar II recruited German settlers as new inhabitants of Malá Strana and gave the quarter its own town charter in the 13th century, for a long time, the district was virtually independent. Many of the palaces were built during this time, and were not given their baroque and Renaissance façades until later. The center of the Malá Strana quarter is the Lesser Town Square (Malostranské náměstí). This is home to buildings such as the St Nicholas Church, a showpiece of baroque church architecture, the neo-classical Liechtenstein Palace, and the Malá Strana Town Hall, which was an important place of negotiation during the religious conflicts of the 16th century. The rococo building "At the Stone Table" is home to the famous "Malá Strana Coffee House" (Malostranské Kavárna), which was previously frequented by writers such as Franz Werfel, Franz Kafka and Max Brod. Towering above Malá Strana is the awe-inspiring Hradčany, where the up to 99-m- (325-ft-) tall spires of St Vitus Cathedral soar strikingly towards the heavens. The Hradčany castle district also includes numerous palaces, some of which today house ministries and exhibition rooms of the National Gallery. The castle itself was built as a royal residence in the 9th century, and was frequently rebuilt and expanded by the kings and emperors who resided here. It covers an area of 800 by 180 m (2,625 by 591 ft), and is considered the largest inhabited castle complex in the world. Today, it is the residence of the Czech president. The vast complex also includes the baroque royal palace – the scene of the famous Defenestration of Prague –, several churches and St Vitus Cathedral.

Right: View of the Vltava and Hradčany, with the castle and St Vitus Cathedral, and the old Malá Strana district. Above: Stained-glass windows and reticulated vaulting in St Vitus Cathedral.

Petřín

When viewed more closely, the wooded hill not far from the city center emerges as a vast park with lots of interesting tourist attractions, including a funicular railway built in 1891, which takes visitors up to the top. St Laurentius Church, which was later rebuilt in baroque style, has stood on the Petřín since at least 1135, or perhaps even 991. Among other things, there still remains an observatory and a mirror maze built in 1891, whose interior looks like that of a cathedral. The wooden St Michael's Church was originally located in the Ukraine, and was moved to the Petřín in 1929.

The 60-m- (197-ft-) high observation tower on Petřín Hill provides a spectacular panoramic view over the city. As with the mirror maze and funicular railway, the tower was also built for the Prague anniversary exhibition in 1891, just two years after its famous role model, Paris' Eiffel Tower.

Golden Lane

The Golden Lane, with its picturesque little houses dating back to the 17th century, is located right on the castle wall. According to tradition, this is where alchemists were said to have tried to make gold by order of Rudolf II.

Strahov Monastery

Strahov Monastery (Strahovský klašter) in the Hradčany district was founded in the 12th century, and has a prized library with over 50,000 books.

Hradčany

The entrance gate to Prague Castle leads from Hradčany Square to the Court of Honor, which was added to the castle complex in the 18th century. There is a changing of the guard every hour, but a larger one with gala uniforms takes place every day at midday.

BRATISLAVA

For many years, Bratislava appeared to stand in the shadow of larger metropolises such as Vienna, Budapest and Prague. But it was still home to important earthly and spiritual rulers, and has its own place in history.

When Czechoslovakia (ČSSR) was divided after the Cold War, Bratislava became the capital of the new state of Slovakia in 1993. The city lies on the left bank of the Danube, in a region at the foot of the Lesser Carpathian Mountains which, for centuries, was inhabited by people of several different nationalities, primarily Slovaks, Hungarians and Germans. In the Middle Ages, German town charter ruled; later on, Bratislava belonged to Habsburg Hungary, and in the 20th century, it became part of the federation with the Czech Republic. Bratislava is Slovakia's seat of government and cultural center, a university town, an important inland port, and a trading city with diverse industry.

The Old Town is full of historic buildings from various eras since the Middle Ages. Most striking are the numerous baroque palaces and the large number of fountains throughout the Old Town. However, the townscape is dominated by Bratislava Castle on the hillside and its aesthetic antithesis, the "New Bridge" over the Danube.

Bratislava Castle

Perched high above the Danube is the eye-catching landmark of the city – vast Bratislava Castle, built on a square ground plan. A castle complex has stood on the cliff since at least the 10th century. Construction was smooth and rapid, and it was the birthplace of St Elizabeth in 1207, after whom a church in Bratislava is also named. Over time, the fortress was constantly rebuilt until it was essentially given its pres-

A statue of St Elizabeth of Hungary stands on the castle grounds.

ent-day appearance in the 18th century. In 1811, a fire destroyed the entire complex, and the ruins looked down over the city for almost one and a half centuries. It was not until 1953 that reconstruction began, and the Slovakian national symbol was rebuilt true to the original. Today, the castle complex is home to sections of the National Museum, and is sometimes also used by the National Assembly – the Slovakian Parliament – for ceremonies. The Slovakian constitution was officially signed here in 1992.

Vast Bratislava Castle (right) sits high above the Danube, with the New Bridge and St Martin's Cathedral.

Grassalkovich Palace is the official residence of the president of Slovakia (left). The magnificent baroque building was built in 1760 by order of Maria Theresia's financial administrator, Count Grassalkovich, who organized balls and concerts, and occasionally also had Joseph Haydn's works performed here.

BRATISLAVA

St Martin's Cathedral, New Danube Bridge

Two worlds collide on the northern banks of the Danube, near Bratislava's Old Town: the Gothic cathedral and an urban highway, which crosses the river along a futuristic bridge. 14th-century St Martin's Cathedral is one of the city's most prominent buildings. Once northern Hungary had fallen to the Habsburgs in the 16th century, Bratislava became the capital of the "Hungarian half of the empire" in 1536. Thereafter, the cathedral was the coronation church of Hungary's Habsburg monarchs until 1830. Maria Theresa was also enthroned here. The interior of the triple-naved church con-

Town Hall at the Main Square

The Main Square (Hlavné námestie) is not only the lively central square of Bratislava's Old Town, where events are regularly held, but also the site of important buildings and city palaces. One such building is the palace of the Esterházy, a Hungarian magnate family of noble lineage; today, it is home to the French embassy. Before the Esterházy acquired the two-story palace, built in 1762, it belonged to the Baron of Kutschersfeld – the custodian of the royal estates – and is thus also known as Kutschersfeld Palace.

Somewhat to one side of the center of the square stands a large, striking Renaissance fountain, the Maximilian or Roland Fountain. The impressive water feature was built in 1572, by order of Emperor Maximilian II, after a massive fire swept through the city. The ambiguity surrounding the name is caused by the figure on the richly adorned central column: it could either represent the donor, Emperor Maximilian, or the legendary knight, Roland, the protector of cities.

At the other end of the square is the Old Town Hall (Stará radnica), which is distinguished by its sloping red tiled roof, with the multi-colored, triangular dormer windows and tall clock tower. The Gothic structure is a complex comprising three buildings, extended and rebuilt in later architectural styles. The oldest section was built as a residential home for "Mayor Jacob" in the 14th century. From the 15th to the 19th century, the buildings served as Bratislava's town hall; today, it is home to the City Museum. It was not until the 20th century that the neo-Gothic eastern section, and the connection to the neighboring Primatial Palace, the former cardinals' residence, was built. The main doorway, on the other hand, is late-Gothic, with an overlying oriel window flanked on either side by two statues and turrets. Finally, the interior courtyard lined with arcades is also worth seeing.

The Main Square, with the Maximilian Fountain (Roland Fountain) and Old Town Hall, is also picturesque at night (right).

tains four chapels and numerous works of art, including a bust of Franz Liszt. The cathedral's spire is the tallest in the city, and, at 85 m (279 ft), even surpasses the two pylons of the Danube bridge, opened on the opposite side of the river in 1972. Perched at a dizzying height on this unique supporting structure of the over-430-m- (1,411-ft-) long, asymmetrically suspended New Bridge is a restaurant whose exterior is reminiscent of a flying saucer, and which is fittingly called "UFO". While St Martin's Cathedral is one of Slovakia's national cultural monuments, the restaurant belongs to the exclusive World Federation of Great Towers (WFGT).

Just next to St Martin's Cathedral are the ramps up to the New Bridge across the Danube (far left). The 18th-century baroque Trinitarian Church (left) stands in Comitatus Square (Župné námestie). The church has an unusual concave façade (left) and interesting frescoes in the interior dome.

Primatial Palace

Construction of the classicist palace, in which the Peace of Pressburg was signed with Napoleonic France in 1805, was commissioned by Archbishop Jozef Batthyány in 1781. Today, it houses the city's art gallery.

New Bridge

Parts of the Old Town had to make way for the New Bridge (Novy Mosty) to be built over the Danube. The "UFO" restaurant in the left pylon is accessed via an elevator. Visitors are rewarded with a fantastic view over the city.

National Theater

The Old National Theater at Hviezdo-slavovo Square was built in neo-Renaissance style in 1886. The New National Theater has also stood there since 2007.

WARSAW

Largely destroyed in World War II, Warsaw once again gleams in its former splendor thanks to exemplary restoration work. Its Old Town has been listed as a UNESCO World Cultural Heritage Site since 1980.

With some 1.7 million inhabitants, the Polish capital of Warsaw extends over both sides of the Vistula. The city is Poland's seat of government, as well as its cultural and economic hub. On the west bank of the Vistula lie the central squares of the Old Town, founded at the turn of the 14th century, while the eastern side of the river is home to the New Town, which is 100 years younger. The dominant building of the modern city is the Palace of Culture, erected between 1952 and 1955. Once built as a sign of Soviet-Polish friendship, today the skyscraper is an office block and commercial building, considered by many Warsaw locals to be the symbol of their city. In Old Warsaw, the main attraction is the Royal Route (Trakt Królewski), a long boulevard with numerous representative buildings and baroque palaces. The most important monuments include the castle square with Zygmunt's Column, and the Old Town marketplace, which was created as early as the 13th century.

Modern skyscrapers and the Palace of Culture, erected in wedding-cake style in the 1950s, as well as the reconstructed historic buildings of the Old Town and New Town, form an impressive skyline when viewed from the opposite side of the Vistula (left). The marketplace (large picture) is the lively center of the Old Town.

WARSAW

Syrenka, the Warsaw Mermaid

She can be seen in several places around the city; her image has adorned the Warsaw coat of arms since the 14th century; and she appears at the top of old documents: Syrenka, the Warsaw Mermaid. Her face has been circulating for many centuries, patiently watching over the city. If tradition is to be believed, two mermaids were once swimming through the Baltic Sea when their paths separated. While one continued westward, arrived in Denmark and today still sits on the famous rock in the port of Copenhagen, the other swam to Poland's shores and then migrated up the Vistula. When she emerged from the waters in Warsaw to take a break, she decided to stay there, because of the city's beauty. But a merchant wanted to capitalize on the unusual visitor, and put her on show as a funfair attraction. So he trapped the mermaid and kept her imprisoned in a hut. But the city's residents heard her wails and set her free. To express her gratitude, the mermaid promised always to protect the people and their beautiful city. Today, a statue of the Warsaw Siren (Warszawska Syrenka) watches over the Powiśle district on the banks of the Vistula, next to the bridgehead of the modern Holy Cross Bridge (Most Świętokrzyski). However, what is probably the best-

Presidential Palace

The Presidential Palace (Pałac Prezydencki) was built in 1643 based on the plans of the royal master-builder, Constantino Tencalla, and was the private domicile of the noble Koniecpolski family. The stately building is thus often also known as Koniecpolski Palace, after these first owners. However, it is also called the Radziwill Palace, after the family who later acquired the palace. Once the Russian governors had taken over Poland's government and established their residence here in 1818, the building was given the still widely used name of Namiestnikowski Palace. During this time, the palace was redesigned in classicist style. After 1918, it was the seat of the Council of Ministers, and the Warsaw Pact was signed here in 1955. The building has been the Polish president's residence since 1994. The equestrian statue in front of the palace depicts Prince Józef Poniatowski, who was killed in the Battle of the Nations in 1913.

Teatr Wielki

The Teatr Wielki (Great Theater) is home to the Polish State Opera and the National Theater. The classicist building was constructed between 1825 and 1833 as a prominent masterpiece by Italian Antonio Corazzi, who designed many of Warsaw's main buildings. The theater underwent difficult tough times on several occasions. Before its inauguration, it was severely damaged in the uprising of November 1830. In 1939, it burned down when the German troops invaded, and the Nazis executed many people amongst the ruins during the Warsaw Uprising of 1944. A commemorative plaque at the entrance is a reminder of these tragic events. The theater was finally reopened in 1965, but a fire destroyed the west wing in 1985, and this was not rebuilt until 1997. The impressive stage is 50 m (164 ft) wide and 54 m (177 ft) deep. Apart from the two state theaters, the building is also home to the Warsaw Theater Museum.

known representation of the famous symbol of Warsaw can be found in the middle of the Old Town's central marketplace. The bronze statue crafted by sculptor Konstanty Hegel was erected there in 1855, on the very spot where the medieval town hall had stood until 1817.

The statue of the Warsaw Mermaid on the Old Town marketplace (left) is armed with a sword and shield, for she is supposed to protect the city in times of danger and need.

Royal Castle with Zygmunt's Column

The Royal Castle (Zamek Królewski) lies in the southern part of the Old Town, in the center of Warsaw, and was erected in its present-day form in the late 16th century. The builder was Sigismund III, who had moved the royal residence from Krakow to Warsaw in 1596, and had had a fitting palace built in the new capital. Sigismund's successors reconstructed the residence many times, and the most dramatic of these reconstructions came under the last king of Poland, Stanisław II August. Until his abdication in 1795, the castle was the residence of the Polish monarchs; today, it is a museum. The magnificent ballroom, the throne room, adorned with gold, and other exhibits provide an insight into the life of the Polish monarchs in the 18th century. Towering over the forecourt is the baroque Zygmunt's Column, topped with a statue of Sigismund III, who made Warsaw the capital of Poland.

Old Town Marketplace

The main square of the Old Town was laid out in an almost square shape in the 13th century. The old town hall had stood in the center of the square since the early 15th century, but was demolished in 1817; the Syrenka mermaid today stands in its place. Many of the surrounding buildings were destroyed during World War II, but were rebuilt in the early 1950s. Today, the square offers a wonderful ensemble of historic architecture, with exquisitely decorated baroque and Renaissance façades, and numerous shops, street cafés and restaurants. Two 18th-century fountains also adorn the square. The many interesting buildings include the Warsaw City Museum and the Jesuit church, erected in Polish Mannerist style between 1609 and 1626. The four sides of the square each have different names, after prominent figures who once lived there.

Krasiński Palace

Krasiński Palace (Pałac Krasińskich) on Krasiński Square in the New Town is one of the city's largest and most impressive. The baroque gem was built for Jan Krasiński, the Voivode (similar to an English prince or duke) of Płock, north-west of Warsaw, from 1677 to 1683. The Dutch-Polish master-builder, Tylman van Gameren, who served Maria Kazimiera, the wife of King John III Sobieski, and designed many of Warsaw's most magnificent baroque buildings, had been commissioned to construct the palace. The structure's interior and exterior were both elaborately decorated. A large historicized gable relief and numerous statues, all crafted by the great Hamburg sculptor, Andreas Schlüter, adorn the façade. The interior is graced with frescoes by the Polish king's Italian court painter, Michelangelo Palloni. In 1764, the then Polish "Noble Republic" bought the palace and used it as its financial administration headquarters, which is why the building is also known as the Palace of the Republic (Pałac Rzeczypospolitej). Today, the palace, which was rebuilt after World War II, houses the State Library's manuscript and incunabulum collection. Standing in the forecourt is a cast-iron fountain designed by architect Chrystian Piotr Aigner in 1824.

Sapieha Palace

The mansion is another prominent baroque palace in the New Town district. It was built between 1731 and 1746 for Jan Fryderyk Sapieha who, as the Lithuanian chancellor in the Polish-Lithuanian Commonwealth, was one of the most powerful men in the country. The palace was designed by the architect and engineers' corps officer, Jan Zygmunt

Capuchin Church

King John III Sobieski donated the church in 1683 in return for his victory over the Turks in Vienna. An urn in the royal chapel contains the entrails of Augustus the Strong, who also ruled Poland as Augustus II.

Deybel. After the collapse of the Polish-Lithuanian Commonwealth in 1795, the palace's military tradition was upheld, and it was converted into barracks from 1818 to 1820. The building was destroyed during World War II, but rebuilt from 1950, with the baroque façade being reconstructed true to the original design. Only the male busts are missing. Instead, visitors today see images of the head architect's daughters. The interior, on the other hand, has been redesigned to suit the palace's new purpose; it is now a school.

The Krasiński Palace is the largest of the many baroque palaces in the New Town district, and also one of the most beautiful in the entire capital (left).

The late-baroque Sapieha Palace in the north of the New Town was built for the chancellor of Lithuania, Jan Fryderyk Sapieha, from 1731 to 1746 (large picture).

MINSK

The largest city and capital of the Republic of White Russia/Belarus is 1,000 years old. But the past has left very few traces behind, for Minsk was almost completely destroyed during World War II.

When it was rebuilt, Minsk was completely restructured and redesigned so that the present-day center is distinguished by wide, straight residential streets and vast squares, some of which have imposing public buildings in the grand socialist style. Most of the almost 1.8 million inhabitants live in satellite cities around the inner city, giving Minsk the typical appearance of a Soviet metropolis; the independence gained by the Republic of White Russia, which is called Belarus in official documents, at the end of 1991 did not alter this greatly either. Russia and the CIS countries continue to be its most important trading partners; its attempts at a rapprochement with the EU for economic reasons have so far failed due to the undemocratic conditions in the country. Tourism plays a secondary role in Minsk, but there are around thirty hotels and numerous restaurants of varying price ranges. A subway and bus lines serve as public transportation. Taxi fares should be negotiated before getting into the vehicle.

Old Town

Winding alleyways, small cafés and a few interesting monuments can be found in Minsk's Old Town, the former uptown, as well as in the suburb of Traetskaye, located down by the river. A few sections escaped the wartime destruction, and others were rebuilt after the war based on historic plans, allowing people to get at least an impression of what the old Minsk was like.

The classicist Old Town Hall from the 19th century is a very recent reconstruction (2005). The two largest churches in Minsk – the Orthodox Holy Spirit Cathedral and the Catholic St Mary's Cathedral – date back to baroque times, as do the buildings of the Bernardine convent, erected in 1628 and the Jesuit monastery, built in 1710. Several Catholic orders had settled in the city from the mid-16th century onwards, and their buildings determined the townscape. At the time, Minsk was not only developing into an important Eastern European trading city, but also a religious center, which was particularly distinguished by its religious tolerance until well into the 20th century. Its people lived peacefully together – Russian Orthodox and Roman Catholic Christians, as well as the large Jewish community. At the end of the 19th century, every second inhabitant was of the Jewish faith; in 1941, during the German attack on the Soviet Union, it was every third inhabitant. Present-day religious life is concentrated on the Orthodox Holy Spirit Cathedral. Processions are once again held here on special festivals. Several church services are held daily, and last up to three hours, depending on the traditional rite. As there is constant coming and going, even amongst the faithful, you can easily go and mingle, but should show the due respect.

Past and present: A Soviet monument towers over a fashion boutique in the center of the capital of Belarus.

Grand Soviet architecture from the period of reconstruction after World War II characterizes the appearance of Independence Avenue, which cuts diagonally through the city. This representational street is also home to the traditional GUM department store.

MINSK

National Library

The vast foyer of the city's most spectacular new building is located on Francisk Scorina Avenue. With its large, diamond-shaped glass structure, somewhat reminiscent of Rem Koolhaas' famous Seattle Library, the Minsk National Library certainly attracts everyone's atten-

Important squares

The Battle of Białystok-Minsk in June 1941 practically razed the old city to the ground. By the time it was liberated from German occupation in 1944, around 95 percent of the old building fabric had been destroyed. Its reconstruction, for which thousands of German prisoners of war were also used, saw the capital of the Byelorussian Soviet Socialist Republic adopt a completely new layout, with vast squares often surrounded by representational buildings. These urban public spaces characterize the face of Minsk. Anyone arriving by train is met at the large Railway Station Square by two tower-like, high-rise buildings, which act as a city gate. Behind the station lies Independence Square, with modern governmental buildings, delightfully contrasted by the historic Red Church, a brick building dedicated to Saints Simeon and Helena. It continues along Independence Avenue, the main residential street in the inner city. This Soviet-style avenue encourages taking a stroll and shopping at the GUM department store. It leads to October Square, which commemorates the Russian Revolution of October 1917, and is home to more governmental and administrative buildings. Finally, one reaches Victory Square, the city's central and particularly representational square, which owes its name to the victory of the Red Army during World War II. After the war, Minsk was one of twelve Soviet cities to be given the honorary title of a Hero City in acknowledgement of its wartime suffering and resistance to the German occupation. Soaring up in the center of the square is the Victory Column, with the eternal flame in memory of the countless war victims. Anyone wanting to experience the everyday life of the locals should visit the square in front of the stadium of the Dinamo Minsk Football Club, where a market is regularly held. The traveling hawkers primarily sell clothing and household items. Another square worth seeing in the Old Town is Freedom Square, near the baroque Holy Spirit Cathedral.

tion. In its short lifetime, it has quickly become the city's main landmark, as well as an icon of national identity. Due to the destruction of the National Library during World War II and the various stop-gap measures that the citizens were forced to deal with in the interim, it was decided in 1989 that the original building from 1922 be re-

placed by a new edifice. As the center of research and science, with twelve state and five private universities, several academies and research institutes, as well as numerous other educational establishments, the Belarusian capital simply needed a large, central library. However, it was not just about the practical benefits, but also the

trend-setting impact such an educational institution would have on the people's sense of identity. In 1989, an international architectural competition was held, from which Viktor Kramarenko and Mikhail Vinogradov emerged victorious. But the laying of the foundation stone was delayed until 2002. The new National Library has been open to

students and academics since 2007. The various rooms contain a total of 2,000 reading areas, including numerous computer workstations. The shelf area spans 2,700 sq m (29,052 sq ft), and the stock covers 14 million books, periodicals, maps, notes and new media.

The new symbol of Minsk: the National Library, opened in 2007, with a 72-m- (236-ft-) high observation deck (left).
In the period after World War II, a whole series of Stalinist wedding-cake-style buildings sprang up in Minsk, including this ensemble at Railway Station Square (below).

Commemorative churches

The little church "In Honor of the Icon of the Mother of God, the Joy of All the Bereaved" is dedicated to the numerous victims of the Chernobyl reactor disaster (1986), which occured near the Ukrainian-Belarusian border. Hundreds of thousands were evacuated and resettled at the time, but around 5 million people still live today in the contaminated region in Belarus and the Ukraine.

The Great Patriotic War Museum

The grandiose Soviet-style buildings dominating the inner city also include the Museum of the History of the Great Patriotic War. World War II began in Minsk with the Battle of Białystok-Minsk between the German Wehrmacht and the Red Army in late June 1941. When the Soviet units finally surrendered, there were hardly any buildings left standing. The German occupation had meant a death sentence for tens of thousands of Jews, and the remaining population was also significantly depleted by hunger and terror by the time of the liberation in 1944.

MOSCOW

Europe's largest city is also the capital of the largest country on earth. Moscow presents itself as a metropolis of superlatives and contrasts: bound to tradition and looking to the future.

With some 10 million inhabitants across an area of more than 1,000 sq km (386 sq miles), Moscow stretches over both sides of the Moskva River as an urban sprawl, with another almost 5 million people in the catchment area. Although old "Mother Moscow" (Matuska Moskva) has long been part of history, the city has still remained a Russian place of longing and desire. "Yes! To Moscow! To Moscow as quickly as possible!", cry the characters in Anton Chekhov's play, "The Three Sisters". Legal and illegal immigrants from all over follow the calling – the city is growing! And upward too, as is evident from the modern skyline of the "new" post-Soviet Moscow. Meanwhile, people are also focusing their attention on ancient Russian traditions once more. Historic monuments, which were often neglected during the Communist era, are being carefully restored. And the 600 churches of the "Orthodox Rome" have again become lively places of faith and worship. The rich and glamorous stroll down cosmopolitan boulevards such as Tverskaya Street;

even the range of products at the GUM department store is up with the times. Museums and galleries are home to international art treasures, and imposing monuments attest to the city's turbulent history. The center of political power, which, for years, has been based in the Kremlin, the former city fortress, and Red Square, is overwhelming in terms of its size.

Red Square is home to what is probably the most beautiful of all of Moscow's 600 churches: St Basil's Cathedral, with its nine different onion domes, built around 1560 by Ivan the Terrible (large picture). No less impressive are the golden domes of the Church of the Deposition of the Robe in the Kremlin (left).

MOSCOW

Red Square

A Moscow tour itinerary would not be complete without a visit to Red Square. Its name, which originally meant "Beautiful Square", is known all around the world. For Russians, it is virtually a national legend, a symbol of Russia's history, power and splendor. Its sheer size is impressive enough: Red Square is one of the world's largest squares and, surrounded by magnificent buildings from several centuries, it is now also one of the most beautiful. UNESCO included it, along with the Kremlin, on its World Heritage list in 1990. The square was created in 1493. Before that, merchants and craftsmen had done

Kremlin

Moscow's history began around the year 1150 with the Kremlin, the prince's castle, which became the center of power of a constantly growing empire once the Grand Duchy of Moscow was founded (around 1350). Even today, the Russian president's official residence is the Kremlin (Senate, 18th century), which is why the vast area on the left bank of the Moskva can only be partly visited by tourists after passing through a security check. However, you should not miss out on seeing this unique "open-air museum",

with its magnificent palaces and churches. The Kremlin was given its present-day appearance under Grand Duke Ivan I (r. 1462–1505). This period saw the erection of the most important churches, the mighty wall with its twenty redbrick towers, as well as the Palace of Facets, which was incorporated into the new classicist Grand Palace in the 19th century. Sealed off as a seat of government during the Soviet era, the Kremlin was re-opened to the public during the "thaw" period of Gorbachev's perestroika. It has been a UNESCO World Heritage Site since 1990.

The grand Alexander Hall in the Great Kremlin Palace (above). The Cathedral of the Annunciation (1484–1489) in the Kremlin was the private church of the tsars. It is home to one of Russia's most precious iconostases (large picture).

their deals within the Kremlin walls, but were then forced to leave the grand ducal fortified town and set up their shacks outside. Red Square was thus initially only a marketplace in front of the eastern Kremlin walls. Its enhancement began with St Basil's Cathedral, which Ivan the Terrible had built at the southern end in 1555: The

stunningly beautiful church, with its nine domes, is one of Moscow's most famous monuments. Also world famous is the giant GUM department store, erected at the eastern end of the square in 1893. Soaring up on the western side is Lenin's Mausoleum (1924), which was the most-frequented attraction of the metropolis during Soviet

times. The collapse of the Soviet Union saw an intense need to reconnect with ancient Russian history, and so two 17th-century structures, which Stalin had had demolished, were faithfully rebuilt in the original style; today, the Kazan Cathedral and Resurrection Gate once again adorn Red Square.

Moscow's most historically significant and representational square – and, spanning 70 by 330 m (230 by 1,083 ft), also one of the largest squares in the world – is a popular venue for military parades, such as those commemorating the Great Patriotic War, as World War II is known in Russia (left).

GUM department store

The vast mecca to consumerism, with its glass-covered walkways, was built during the late 19th century in the historicist style in vogue at the time. GUM is not a typical department store, but rather a large shopping mall with some 200 stores.

Lenin's Mausoleum

The Soviet "Cult of Personality" yielded strange results: Millions went on pilgrimages to the mausoleum at Red Square, where the embalmed corpse of the leader of the Russian Revolution, Lenin (1870–1924), is still displayed today.

Resurrection Gate

Stalin had the former city gate (1680) at Red Square demolished. The Resurrection Gate was rebuilt when attention shifted back to the splendor of ancient Russia in the 1990s, after the collapse of the Soviet Union.

MOSCOW

Gorky Park of Culture and Leisure

It is the most popular of Moscow's many parks. The vast 1.2-sq-km- (0.5-sq-mile-) area on the right bank of the Moskva is not only conducive to walking, picnicking, boating or, in winter, ice-skating, but is also an amusement park with a Fer-ris wheel. In addition, there is an area for open-air concerts, as well as a cinema in an unusual location: the "Buran" space shuttle that has been set up here. The person after whom the park is named, Maxim Gorky (1868–1936), was highly regarded during Soviet times as a "proletarian writer".

Arbat

Moscow's historic center is home to the Arbat, one of the city's loveliest streets, with residential and commercial buildings dating back to the 19th and early 20th centuries. Many writers and artists lived here. Today, the Arbat is the preferred residential district, and the focal point of a hip neighborhood. It stretches for around 1 km (0.6 miles) from Arbatskaya Square to Smolenskaya Square, which both also have metro stations with the same names. The Arbat has been a pedestrian zone since the 1980s, which was a completely new concept in Russia at the time. It is a popular place for strolling, particularly in summer. Empire-style façades alternate with Art Nouveau façades, with traces of neo-Gothic and functionalist elements in between. The avant-garde apartment block constructed by prominent architect, Konstantin Melnikov (1890–1974), in a side street of the Arbat around 1930 is another heritage-listed building.

Pushkin Museum of Fine Arts

Moscow's Pushkin Museum contains Russia's second largest collection of art after St Petersburg's Hermitage. It displays works from Antiquity as well as European art (13th–20th century), and is housed in a museum complex comprising a total of six buildings. The main building on Volkhonka Street, adorned with Greek columns, was ceremonially opened in the presence of the tsar in 1912. Its imposing halls, designed in various historic styles, make it a main tourist attraction. The collections of Italian Renaissance and Flemish and Dutch paintings from the 16th–17th centuries, as well as the French Impressionist paintings, are world famous. Moscow's finest museum was named after the city's greatest son, the national poet Alexander Pushkin (1799 to 1837), who is considered to be the founder of modern Russian literature.

Stalinist high-rises

Stalin's despotism (1924–1953) also left its mark on architecture. The seven "wedding-cake-style" high-rise buildings, which the dictator had constructed on Moscow's more exposed squares, are striking examples of gigantomania. They continue to dominate the city skyline even today.

Gorky Park, opened in 1927, on the right bank of the Moskva River, is a popular amusement park. The Kotelnicheskaya Embankment is home to one of the "Seven Sisters" – the nickname for the seven immense high-rise buildings, which Stalin had constructed in Moscow after the war (from left).

Metro stations

It is a question of whether you want to really connect with the 2.5 billion passengers who travel on Moscow's metro every year. In the world's deepest subway system, the crush of people is not just limited to peak hours. However, there is no question that a visit to one of the underground "Palaces for the People" must be included on everyone's tour itinerary because some of Moscow's 177 metro stations were lavishly designed as prestigious Socialist accomplishments under Stalinist rule. The showpiece is the "baroque" Komsomolskaya metro station (pictured right), opened in 1952, underneath the square of the same name. In contrast with this is the futuristic, 1930s-style Mayakovskaya Station (1938), dedicated to Soviet Russian aviation. The Bauhaus-style Frunzenskaya Station on Line 1, built in 1935 as the first of what are now twelve underground lines, is also worth seeing.

Bolshoi Theater

The Bolshoi Theater, where Peter Tchaikovsky's great ballet, "Swan Lake", was first performed in 1877, is synonymous around the world with traditional Russian ballet. But the Bolshoi is also an opera stage, and anyone lucky enough to attend a show will never forget it. Its opulent furnishings and exquisite architecture in Russian classicist style make the theater, which was opened in 1835, one of the finest in the world. However, the building is currently closed for large-scale restoration, but is expected to re-open by 2012. Until then, visitors can only see the grandiose façade with columns and Apollo's chariot on the portico. The Bolshoi Theater blends harmoniously into Theater Square, which is also a stone's throw from one of Moscow's most exclusive hotels: the renovated "Metropol", opened in 1899, and designed in superb Art Nouveau style.

MOSCOW

Tsaritsino Castle

A popular daytrip in Moscow's southern districts is to Tsaritsino Castle, with its lovely park. The "Place of the Tsarina" is the literal translation of "Tsaritsino", referring to its builder, Catherine II, the Great. The German princess, who became Russia's tsarina (r. 1762–1796), had bought the land, which, at that time, was located just outside Moscow, in 1775 to have a pleasure palace built for herself in a rural paradise. When, after ten years of construction, she visited Tsaritsino on one of her inspection trips, she did not like the castle at all, and had it demolished without further ado. The palace complex was now to be built in a pseudo-Gothic style, but construction ceased in 1793. Tsaritsino Castle thus remained as very picturesque and romantic ruins – until 2004, when the city of Moscow had the construction completed. The plan to erect Moscow's largest art gallery in the representative castle complex has not yet been implemented.

Moscow City, Ostankino TV Tower

After the collapse of the Soviet Union, Russia quickly became a leading economic power, and the Moscow International Business Center on the left bank of the Moskva River symbolizes this new wealth. Moscow City is an ultra-modern commercial district with spectacular architecture, although it is currently still a giant construction site. Building complexes with up to sixty stories and measuring 500 m (1,641 ft) in height are planned. Moscow clearly wants to play in the premier league of economic metropolises!

The Bagration Bridge, a two-level, covered pedestrian bridge with a 200-m (323-yd-) stretch of restaurants and shops, leads from the 34-story Tower 2000 office block over the Moskva River. The Ostankino TV Tower (1967), which, at a height of 540 m (1,772 ft), is one of the tallest constructions in the world, was a prestige project of the Soviet era. An elevator takes visitors up to the 37-m- (121-ft-) high observation deck.

The Ostankino TV Tower (above) is one of the world's tallest structures. Skyscrapers such as the Naberezhnaya Tower and the Capital City (still under construction) are now also growing in number in Moscow City (right).

Imposing Tsaritsino Castle was not completed until 2007, before which it had just been picturesque ruins with a park – Catherine the Great had the construction work stopped in 1793. A small museum has been established here since 1980, but bigger things are in the pipeline: Tsaritsino is set to become "Moscow's Hermitage".

KIEV

The capital of Ukraine is one of the oldest and most historically significant cities in Eastern Europe. Kiev experienced its first heyday as early as 1,000 years ago, when it became the "Mother of all Russian cities".

From the 10th to the 12th century, Kiev was splendidly developed as the noble residence of the Kievan Rus, from whose empire Ukraine and Russia later emerged. The magnificent St Sophia Cathedral, with its thirteen domes, and the unique Cave Monastery (both UNESCO World Heritage Sites) continue to attest to this "golden era". Like the

other important attractions, they are located in the historic center, on the western bank of the Dnieper River. Today, Kiev has a population of almost three million, and is the political, economic and cultural center of Ukraine, Europe's second largest nation after Russia. The tourist infrastructure, however, is still yet to be properly developed.

Dnieper cruise ships moored in Kiev's port (far left). Heroic monuments throughout the city reveal the country's history – such as the sculptures on the fountain at Independence Square (left) or the equestrian statue of the Cossack leader, Bogdan Khmelnitsky, in front of the gold-domed St Sophia Cathedral (large picture).

KIEV

National Museum of the History of the Great Patriotic War

After World War II – known as the Great Patriotic War in the Soviet Union –, Kiev was given the honorary title of Hero City. This title was awarded to cities which had fought particularly gallantly against the Germans, and had suffered an especially high number of victims. The museum and "Mother Motherland" statue were built in memory of this in 1981. However, no mention was made of the fact that numerous Ukrainians had fought alongside the Germans against the Red Army. The extermination of Kiev's large Jewish communities, which still had 175,000 members at the time of the German invasion in 1941, was similarly not worthy of being remembered in the anti-Semitic climate of the Soviet Union. It was not until after Ukraine gained independence in 1991 that a memorial was erected to honor the murdered Jews. It is located in the Babi Yar ravine (today an urban district), which was the scene of a brutal Jewish massacre.

Independence Square

The Maidan, Kiev's largest and finest square in the heart of the city, has borne the official name of "Independence Square" since 1991 – the founding of the Ukrainian state marking the end of almost 500 years of Russian rule under the tsars and the Soviet regime. There is always something happening on the Maidan and adjacent 19th-century Shevchenko Boulevard, including the ritzy shopping center beneath the Maidan. Although it only sells Western products which hardly

Golden Gate

In around 1020, the Kievan Rus ordered the construction of a mighty city gate as part of the city's fortifications. Visitors can admire the reconstructed Golden Gate, for the original suffered severe damage and destruction on the Mongol siege of 1240, during which the Kievan Rus Empire collapsed.

anyone in Kiev can afford, people still come to browse and dream of wealth – something even the "Orange Revolution", which started off with high hopes on the Maidan in 2004, has not been able to bring.

The Maidan, officially known as "Independence Square", is the heart of the city. A folk-festival atmosphere prevails during the summertime open-air concerts and Independence Day festivities (24 August).

Podil district

Residential and commercial buildings with historic façades, small restaurants and churches with gold domes, the enormous Dnieper port, the lively Kontraktova Square and the main street which is car-free on Sundays: The commercial and port suburb of Podil, which developed by the river as early as the Kievan Rus era, is home to many attractions and has become the city's hip, trendy quarter. Before the Holocaust, most of Kiev's Jews, who comprised one quarter of the city's population, lived here. The well-renovated Podil Synagogue (1895), which was inaugurated under the Soviet regime (1929–1990), serves as a reminder of this.

The monumental "Mother Motherland" statue, erected in 1981, is part of the memorial attached to the Museum of the History of the Great Patriotic War (far left). Left: Street scene from the historic commercial and port quarter of Podil, which is today a very hip district.

Mariinsky Palace

Mariinsky Palace, built in baroque style by Russian Tsarina Elizabeth I around 1750, is today used for receptions held by the Ukrainian government. Its location in the middle of a park high above the Dnieper is particularly charming.

Cave Monastery

The Cave Monastery, founded by hermits on the banks of the Dnieper in 1051 (a UNESCO World Heritage Site), has three underground churches (12th century), cave tombs and caverns. The magnificent above-ground structures are baroque.

St Michael's Monastery

The restored St Michael's Monastery is a brilliant example of Ukrainian baroque (18th century). Under Stalin, the medieval monastery was destroyed and its art treasures stolen.

LISBON

The "White City on the Atlantic", is what the locals call their capital, although, in fact, Lisbon is a few miles inland from the sea, on the north bank of the River Tagus. It was from here that the Portuguese explorers set off on their journeys to conquer an empire for Portugal.

Lisbon was built on the slopes of a craggy hill chain, varying considerably – more than 200 m (656 ft) – in altitude, which has led to the division of the city into the Upper Town and the Lower Town. Portugal's largest city, Lisbon is on the one hand a modern, dynamic metropolis, but on the other hand its attitude toward life is also marked by a certain melancholic world wariness, the typically Portuguese "saudade", is so vividly reflected in the ardent songs of fado that developed here. In the course of its history, Lisbon has had to overcome several catastrophes, such as the earthquake of 1344 and the devastating "Great Lisbon Earthquake" of 1755, as well as a serious firestorm in the old town in 1988. All three events caused immeasurable damage and brought about extensive reconstruction measures, which have left their mark on the organically grown cityscape. Lisbon is the seat of government and the industrial and financial heart of the country. In 1998, it was the venue for the "Expo", the Lisbon World Exposition.

The more than 17-km- (11-mile-) long Vasco da Gama Bridge across the Tagus was built on the occasion of the World's Fair in 1998 (left). The Torre de Belém, Lisbon's landmark and since 1983 a World Heritage Site, was built as a lighthouse in the Tagus estuary in 1521 (large picture).

Eléctrico

Tramline No. 28, which runs straight across Lisbon in an east-west direction, is served by historic carriages known as eléctricos. They offer a pleasantly nostalgic way of taking a sightseeing tour of the city.

Elevador de Santa Justa

Since 1901, this elevator (lift) has linked the Lower Town with the elegant Chiado shopping district in the Upper Town. There are superb views from the top of the 45-m- (148-ft-) tall tower.

Bairro Alto

In the streets of the Bairro Alto (Upper Town), especially in the Rua da Rosa and the Rua do Norte, elegant restaurants and chic clubs stand cheek by jowl with smoky pubs and fado bars. Anyone wishing to go shopping is in the right place here, too, for in between the taverns there are numerous boutiques and shops of all kinds. Lisbon's entertainment district attracts visitors and locals in large numbers, especially at night. During the day, however, all is calm and peaceful, and life continues in its unspectacular manner in the narrow shady lanes. For a long time, the Bairro Alto was the focal point of Lisbon's newspaper landscape, with the editorial offices of virtually all major print media being based here. The papers attracted intellectuals who found work nearby or simply enjoyed life. Today, the newspapers have left and installed their editorial teams in districts that offer more room for the modern production technology, but the district has preserved its vitality. Worth seeing is the Igreja de São Roque Jesuit church dating from 1566. The building has a simple, slanted roof, but inside it boasts ceiling paintings that make the viewer believe the church must have a dome. From the Lower Town, it is particularly convenient to reach the higher locations of the Upper Town via the "Elevador da Glória", which has operated here

Castelo de São Jorge

The origins of this vast system of fortifications, located on a hill above the old town (Alfama), date back to the time of Moorish rule in the Iberian Peninsula. When it was conquered by Alfonso I, the first king of Portugal, in 1147, the fortress served as the royal castle until 1511, when Manuel I moved the royal residence to a more modern palace. After that, the castle was mainly used as a prison. During the great earthquake of 1775, the structures were not spared but were largely destroyed. The outer rampart walls, however, were later rebuilt. Today, the ruins of the Castelo de São Jorge is a compelling combination of an historical sight and idyllic park. While tourists climb the towers and enjoy the overwhelming views across Lisbon and the Tagus, ducks wander about in the palace gardens, and the locals play boules or backgammon on the open spaces between the castle buildings.

Alfama

It was at the end of the 18th century, when the poorest of the poor lived in the old town district of Alfama, crime flourished and sailors came and went, that the plaintive Portuguese songs of fado first appeared. The picture of the small streets and the narrow lanes, immersed into the shade of the houses seems perfect as the backdrop for this cultural specialty of Portugal. And as could be expected, there is no shortage of fado bars. The Alfama suffered relatively little during the fateful earthquake of 1755, so that much of it still exudes an enchanted Moorish-medieval atmosphere today. The district is dominated by the late-renaissance São Vicente de Fora Church, built from 1590, which holds the tombs of many Portuguese rulers. At the end of the Campo de Santa Clara, not far from the Pantheon, the large Feira da Ladra (Thieves' Market) fleamarket takes place twice a week.

since 1885. Over a distance of just 265 m (869 ft), the funicular railway scales the difference in altitude of 48 m (157 ft). The upper entrance to the famous "Elevador de Santa Justa" is also located in the Bairro Alto, granting visitors at the same time beautiful views over Lisbon.

During the day, the Bairro Alto (left) is a place of peace and contemplation. But in the evening, the scene in the normally romantic streets is transformed, and high life rule reigns supreme in the bars and cafés of the entertainment district.

National Pantheon

After the destruction of the Igreja de Santa Engrácia (Church of Santa Engrácia) in 1681, work to rebuild a new church began in the following year. However, construction progressed more than sluggishly, and not at all for lengthy periods at times. In the end, work on the structure took centuries and was not completed until 1966. On the orders of the dictator Antonio Salazar, the impressive building was not used as a church, however, but as a pantheon or national place of commemoration. Inside, marble-adorned niches surround the central square room of the crossing; they contain the tombs and memorials for the great personalities of Portuguese history, including Vasco da Gama and Henry the Navigator. Aside from explorers and presidents, major artists are also remembered here. The poet João de Deus (1830–1896), among others, found his final resting place in the Pantheon, as did Amália Rodrigues, the "Queen of Fado", who died in 1999.

Sé de Lisboa Cathedral

After the re-conquest of Lisbon from the Moors in 1147, the construction of this distinctive cathedral, probably a conversion of a mosque, was begun the following year. As a consequence of the earthquake of 1344, substantial parts of the church had to be restored, but this was now done in the more fashionable style of the Gothic. Thus, the oldest church of Lisbon today boasts elements of both great medieval church architecture styles. Although further style elements were added during the reconstruction after the earthquake of 1755, these were removed again in the 20th century. The Catedral Sé is the central church of the city and at the same time the patriarchate church of Lisbon. Inside it lies the sarcophagus of King Alfonso IV (1291–1357) as well as a baptismal font dating from the 12th century, which was allegedly used to baptize Saint Anthony, Lisbon's patron saint. His relics can be seen in the adjacent church museum.

LISBON

Rossio – Center of the Baixa

The elongated square on the limits of the Lower Town (Cidade Baixa), which extends down to the banks of the Tagus, was officially named Praça Dom Pedro IV in 1874, but it continues to be known as Rossio, meaning "uninhabited field". The Rossio has long been the heart of Lisbon, an important traffic hub and popular meeting place for the local citizens. Kings built their palaces on the Rossio; during the 15th century the Inquisition had its headquarters here; and later the nobility gathered in the palaces around the square. In more recent times, revolutions also started out from the Rossio. The square received its present look largely in the 18th century, during the reconstruction work after the great earthquake of 1755, which had laid waste almost all the buildings on the Rossio as well as the surrounding districts. During this time, the newly developed Baixa district also received its rectangular grid of roads. Many important buildings line the Rossio, for example the neoclassical National Theater, opened in 1847, on the north side of the square and impressive Rossio Station. Also dating from the 19th century are the two bronze fountains as well as the statue of King Pedro IV in the middle of the Rossio, together with the column on which it stands.

Praça do Comércio

Anyone coming from the Rossio via the pedestrianized Rua Augusta will see the Arco da Rua Augusta from afar, the largest arch at the end of the road, at the point where it leads into the Praça do Comércio. Before the great earthquake, this was the stately forecourt of the royal palace.

Near the Elevador de Santa Justa stand the ruins of the Gothic church of the Convento do Carmo, built around 1400.

After the quake, it was decided not to reconstruct the palace but to completely redesign the layout of the square. And so, the shape of the square was created only after 1775, and the same holds true for the buildings that frame it on three sides, boasting spectacular façades with long arcades. Today, most of them house ministries. The Praça do Comércio is open toward the south, overlooking the wide riverside road and the Tagus. A marble staircase lined by columns leads down to the river.

The Arco da Rua Augusta triumphal arch and an equestrian statue of José I dominate the Praça do Comércio (right).

The Rossio is lined with numerous fascinating historic buildings. Also on the busy town center square, and known to all Lisbon citizens, however, is the Café Suiça, which sells chocolates and marzipan creations from its own confectionary. The Café Nicola, also on the Rossio, even serves its own brand of coffee.

Hieronymite Monastery of Belém

The Hieronymite Monastery in the suburb of Belém is a superb example of the Manueline style, which is characterized by rich ornamentation. King Manuel I had it built from 1502 to honor Vasco da Gama. The great navigator, whose discovery of the sea route to India made the financing of the monastery possible, rests in a sarcophagus in a side aisle of the monastery church, together with several of Portugal's monarchs (above).

Santa Maria Monastery Church, a hall church between late Gothic and early Renaissance in style, does not seem massive despite being 92 m (302 ft) long and 25 m (82 ft) wide, thanks to the slim pillars, which are richly embellished with Renaissance ornaments (above).

MADRID

Spain's capital, founded over 1,000 years ago as a Moorish castle and the center of an empire 500 years ago, is today a modern, vibrant metropolis and a city that never sleeps.

For night owls, Madrid is the perfect city. Tapas bars and trendy discos, sophisticated nightclubs and flamenco tablaos – there is something here for everyone. At the weekends, the nights become day, and the traffic at 4 a.m. is as busy as it is during the rush hours in other cities. Anyone looking for peace and quiet should come during the hot month of August, when the Madrileños escape to the seaside. The winters can be harsh; after all, the city is located on the Castilian plateau at an altitude of 668 m (2,192 ft). Madrid is the center of the country not only in geographic terms, but also politically, as the seat of government and royal residence. Although not necessarily loved by the rest of the country, there is a huge population influx to the capital so that a giant conurbation has developed. Madrid itself has 3.3 million inhabitants, making it the largest city in Spain by far, and Europe's fifth-largest metropolis. The Museo del Prado with its excellent royal collection of paintings is one of the largest and most important art museums in the world.

Pulsating with life 24/7: the Plaza del Dos de Mayo (left) in the fashionable Malasaña district. The busy Plaza de Cibeles with its stunning baroque fountain is also the place where Real Madrid fans celebrate their team's victories (large picture).

MADRID

Plaza de España, Cervantes Memorial

Spain's metropolis is renowned for its spacious squares. An impressive example is the Plaza de España with its two distinctive 1950s tower buildings. Equally unmissable is the monument for Spain's national poet, Miguel de Cervantes (1547–1616),

erected in 1930. From his lofty height he looks down on the two world-famous heroes of his novel, Don Quixote and Sancho Panza. The Gran Vía, which ends at the Plaza de España, is fringed by theaters and cinemas, cafés, restaurants and many shops – it is one of Madrid's most elegant promenades.

La Almudena Cathedral

Madrid is not a city of beautiful old churches. Until 1885, Spain's capital was not even a bishop's see. After that date, the building of the cathedral was begun. It was to take a long time: the monumental neo-Gothic religious building with a neoclassical façade was not completed and dedicated by the Pope until 1993. In 2004, on the occasion of the wedding of Prince Felipe and Princess Letizia, the artist Kiko Argüello was commissioned to paint the interior. However, his gaudy frescoes did not find favor with conservative Madrileños. The name La Almudena refers to a sculpture of the Virgin Mary (Virgen de la Almudena); according to legend, it was hidden during the Moorish invasion in the eighth century and rediscovered in 1085, during the Christian reconquest of Madrid, as if by a miracle. In honor of La Almudena, who is also Madrid's patron saint, there is a solemn procession each year on November 9.

Puerta del Sol

Madrid's pulsating heart is Plaza Puerta del Sol, named for a medieval city gate that no longer exists. It is the central transportation hub, from which the most important roads of the country radiate. A plaque on the south side of the square marks this "zero kilometer". This is a favorite spot to meet for an evening out. Unlike the Plaza Mayor, the Puerta del Sol was not built as planned but rather it was the result of the rapid and uncontrolled expansion of the new capital after 1561. The buildings that define the Puerta del Sol today were largely constructed in the 18th/19th centuries during the reign of the Bourbon dynasty who followed the Habsburgs onto the Spanish throne. The Statue of Charles III (r. 1759 to 1787), who promoted the makeover and modernization of the capital, rises in the middle of the square that is so typical for Madrid with its big-city bustle.

Monasterio de las Descalzas reales

In the heart of the old town, not far from the Plaza Mayor, stands the well-preserved 16th-century Convent of the Royal Barefoot Nuns, one of only few historic buildings in Madrid that were built in the Plateresque style of the Spanish Renaissance. The Infanta Juana de Austria, the sister of King Philip II and the daughter of Emperor Charles V, founded the convent. It was destined for aristocratic ladies, who furnished it with precious objects. Today, it also functions as an arts repository, where courtly splendor and Catholic piety have forged a unique bond.

The Plaza de España is adorned by the imposing Cervantes Memorial with Don Quixote and Sancho Panza (far left). The Covent of the Royal Barefoot Nuns in the heart of Madrid was founded in the 16th century by the daughter of the first Habsburg ruler on the Spanish throne (left).

Palacio Real

The Palacio Real excels among the historic secular buildings in Madrid. The gigantic classicist palace complex, covering a total surface area of 135,000 sq m (1,452,600 sq ft), was built from 1734 to 1755 on the orders of Philip V, and has been the official residence of the Spanish monarchs since 1764. The royal family has now moved their residence away from the noisy center of Madrid to Zarzuela Palace, and so the staterooms of the Palacio Real are open to the public. The palace stands on the spot where the history of Madrid began: In 856, the Moors built an alcázar or fortress here, around which the city developed. During the Reconquista, it was then seized by the Christians in 1085. Madrid played a political role as early as the Middle Ages, as the place of assembly for the Castilian parliament. But it did not become the shining capital and residence city until the 16th century, under King Philip II.

Plaza Mayor

In 1561, Philip II transferred his court to Madrid, which up to then, although located in the geographical center of the country, was rather provincial. This also meant that the Plaza Mayor (Great Square), the former market place, became the city's main square, boasting impressive dimensions (120 by 94 m/394 ft by 308 ft) and surrounded by closed rows of houses. It became the model for the design of public squares throughout the entire Spanish empire. After a big fire in 1790, the square was restored in the neoclassical style; older town houses are preserved only in the south-western corner. Into the 19th century, the Plaza Mayor was the venue for royal receptions, public festivals and bullfights, but also for executions and the infamous auto-da-fés of the Inquisition. Today, Madrid's most prestigious historic square is a popular meeting place, and it offers an orientation aid to tourists in the confusing city center.

MADRID

Buen Retiro Park

Not the largest but without doubt the most attractive park in central Madrid is the Parque del Buen Retiro, which you can enter in style via the Puerta del Alcalá triumphal arch (1778) on the Plaza de la Indepencia. The centerpiece of the 130-ha (321-acre) Retiro Park is formed by the almost rectangular artificial lake (estanque) with boat hire. A short walk takes visitors to the Palacio Velázquez, an exhibition and cultural center, and from there to the Palacio de Cristal, the park's jewel. The entire park is crisscrossed by a dense network of walking tracks. Time after time, these pass imaginative fountains. In the Fuente de los Galápagos, tortoises spit water, whereas devils fulfill this task in the Fuente del Ángel caído, the "Fountain of the Fallen Angel". In the southern half of the park, visitors should not miss the beautiful rose garden (Rosaledo del Retiro). Although there are also quiet spots in this green oasis in the heart of the big city, there is plenty of life in the central parts, at least at the weekends, with numerous sun worshipers and sports-loving people, lovers and families. You will be entertained by street musicians and can have your fortunes told by clairvoyants. Puppeteers and magicians also showcase their talents; they are part of the Retiro Park's tradition.

Museum Triangle on the Paseo del Prado

Madrid's most important sights are its art museums. The three most famous ones are located on the Paseo del Prado, between Plaza de Cibeles and the Botanical Gardens. The Museo del Prado, founded in the 16th century by the first Habsburg rulers, Charles V and Philip II, enjoys a worldwide reputation with its royal collection of paintings, containing works by Bosch, Dürer, Titian, El Gre-

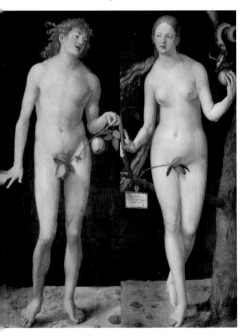

co, Velázquez, Murillo, Rubens, Goya and many other great masters. One of the most famous international private collections can be viewed at the Palacio Villahermosa, where the Thyssen Bornemisza Museum showcases art from the 14th to the 20th centuries. The Reina Sofía Museum is dedicated to modernism and contemporary art. The focus in this collection is on Spanish painting of the 20th century, excellently represented by Picasso, Miró and Dalí.

Among the treasures of the Prado is Albrecht Dürer's painting "Adam and Eve" (above). With its first-class collection of paintings, the Museo del Prado, opened in 1819, is a veritable temple to fine art (right).

Left: The main sight in the Retiro Park is the Palacio de Cristal of 1887, which is used today for art exhibitions. The stunning glass structure, which blends so harmoniously into the park landscape, was modeled on the once worldfamous Crystal Palace in London.

MADRID

Las Ventas Bullring

With 25,000 seats, Las Ventas is Spain's largest bullfighting arena (Plaza de Toros) and, after the one in Mexico City, it is also the second-largest in the world. The "cathedral", as Las Ventas is known by its fans, is located in the Avenida de los Toreros, in the Guindalera district. It was inaugurated in 1931, although in the eyes of traditionalists it has since been "desecrated", for the monumental arena is no longer reserved only for the corrida – it now also hosts pop concerts and motocross races. There are economic reasons for that since the interest in bullfights among the Spanish population has considerably diminished, especially among young people. For its advocates, it still represents an essential aspect of the Spanish cultural identity, and criticism by animal rights activists is rejected by pointing out that the fighting bulls – unlike the bulls that are bred purely for slaughter – lead a life befitting to their species before they are killed in the arena. Yet for many, the bloody spectacle is no longer fitting for the present day. Bullfighting is undergoing a crisis; the 250-year-old tradition seems to be in decline. But then, another star is born, a toreador who is celebrated like a god and who, with his courage and panache, transports the crowds into a frenzy of enthusiasm that is otherwise only known from soccer games in Spain.

Plaza de Castilla – Spain's modern architecture

The economic boom enjoyed by Spain since it joined the European Union in 1986, is apparent not least in the avant-garde architecture of the business districts that developed beyond the inner city of Madrid. One of the most recent prestige projects are the skyscrapers of the Cuatro Torres Business Area on the former training grounds of Real Madrid. The best-known high-rise buildings, how-

Cuatro Torres

All previous records for tall buildings in Spain were broken by the four skyscrapers of the Cuatro Torres Business Area: the Torre Caja Madrid, designed by star architect Sir Norman Foster and completed in 2008, is 250 m (820 ft) high, and its neighbor, the Torre Espacio, only slightly smaller (223 m/732 ft).

ever, are probably the twin towers of the Puerta de Europa, also known as Torres KIO. At an angle of 15 degrees, they have been conspicuous landmarks near the vast round Plaza de Castilla in the northern Chamartín district since 1996.

A cathedral to aviation: Terminal T4 at Madrid Barajas Airport, completed in 2006, was designed by star architect Richard Rogers.

In that case, every last seat in Las Ventas is sold out, and even the king will not want to miss the event. The newspapers outdo each other with their rave reviews. And the fiesta at five o'clock in the afternoon that was already believed dead awakens to a new life.

The front of Spain's largest bullfighting arena, the Plaza Monumental de Toros de las Ventas in the Salamanca district of Madrid, was opened in 1931. The vast arena holds 25,000 spectators, and when a celebrated matador appears, it is transformed into a seething cauldron.

Estación de Atocha

The historic station hall (1888 to 1892), a spectacular glass and cast-iron construction, became Spain's most stunning waiting hall when the Atocha Station in the heart of Madrid was newly built in 1992. On March 11, 2004, it was the location of an Islamist terror attack, in which 191 people died and thousands were injured.

Estadio Bernabéu

The vast football stadium of Real ("royal") Madrid was built as early as the 1940s – for 125,000 spectators. Today, for security reasons, it takes "only" 90,000. During guided tours on days when there is no game, the changing rooms of the stars can also be visited.

ANDORRA LA VELLA

Among Europe's microstates, Andorra is the largest in surface area. Its capital city, Andorra la Vella, is centrally located, set in the wildly romantic mountain world of the Pyrenees between France and Spain.

Visitors come to this, Europe's highest capital city (1,000 m/3,281 ft), mainly to ski or shop. During the last few decades, the Grandvalira high mountain valley with its spectacular mountain landscape has been upgraded as a winter sports center, attracting mainly vacationers from Spain. Since Catalan and Spanish are spoken in Andorra, they feel perfectly at home

Principality in the Pyrenees

The national pride of the small Pyrenean state rests on the alleged foundation of Andorra by Charlemagne in the ninth century. But, in fact, the oldest documentary proof of the existence of the principality dates from the year 1278. It was not independent, for feudal rule was shared by the so-called co-princes, which for centuries were the bishops of Urgell and the counts of Foix, later the presidents of France. In 1993 Andorra finally became a sovereign state with

Caldea Thermal Spa

Hot sulfur springs, a "water palace" with avant-garde architecture and an attractive wellness range and mountain air on offer: the Caldea spa, a few kilometers outside the capital.

a democratic constitution, and with Andorra la Vella as the official capital. Even so, together the co-princes still play an important role as combined heads of state. This constellation is unique in Europe, and a highly rated tradition in the microstate in the Pyrenees.

View of Andorra la Vella: In recent decades, the capital of the principality developed at a rapid pace. The sleepy mountain hamlet has become a busy small town.

here. As a tax haven, the town in the Pyrenees is the seat of countless letterbox companies. The many shops along its main street offer attractive prices. It is hard to imagine now that, until well into the 20th century, Andorra la Vella was isolated from the rest of the world. However, it can still only be reached by car or bus.

Andorra la Vella lives mainly off tourism. Thanks to its low-tax and duty-free status, the prices here are lower than those in neighboring France or Spain. Many day-trippers from both countries therefore use the opportunity to purchase luxury articles at reduced prices from one of the numerous shops in the capital (left).

Old Town

Granite, the rock of the eastern Pyrenees, supplies the traditional building material of Andorra. Thus, the houses and churches in the lanes of the old town are predominantly characterized by modest natural stone buildings.

Sant Esteve Church

The venerable church on the Plaça Princep Benllock goes back to the Romanesque period; it has been enlarged and rebuilt several times. The distinctive bell tower was not built until about 1940, in the style of Catalan Modernismo.

Casa de la Vall

The "House of the Valley", built in 1580, is the court building and the seat of parliament. The rooms with their original furnishings, partially adorned with frescoes, are open to visitors.

ROME

Italy's capital is known as the "eternal city". Its incomparable wealth of art treasures and architectural monuments attests to its great history. Yet Rome does not dwell in the past – it is as vibrant and alive as ever.

With 2.7 million inhabitants the "Eternal City", the capital of the Imperium Romanum once known as "caput mundi – head of the world", is today the largest city and the capital of the Republic of Italy, and is also considered its cultural center. Rome is located about 20 km (12 miles) inland from the Tyrrhenian Sea, on the Tiber River. Its actual urban area, comprising 22 inner and 35 outer districts as well as six "suburbi" or suburbs, covers some 90 sq km (35 sq miles).

Legendary are the Seven Hills of Rome – the Aventine, Capitoline, Caelian, Palatine, Viminal, Quirinal and Esquiline Hills (in rising order of height) –, on and around which the city developed over more than two and a half millennia since its official foundation by Romulus on April 21, 753 BC. The famous monuments of antiquity are mostly found on the left bank of the Tiber. On the right bank lie the Vatican City, which does not belong to Rome, and the old quarter of Trastevere, which has since become very desirable. Opposite this is the Tiber Island, which was strategically important in Antiquity.

The Arch of Constantine was originally built to celebrate Emperor Constantine I's victory at the Milvian Bridge in the year 312 (left). The Coliseum, built in the year 80, held more than 50,000 spectators, making it the largest amphitheater of the Roman Empire (below).

ROME

Capitoline and Palatine Hills

Mythology tells of the hills on which Rome was built as having used the sacred figure seven. It is obvious that the first inhabitants would have preferred the higher reaches to the marshy lowlands of the Tiber: up there the air was simply fresher and healthier! The Capitoline and the Palatine Hills are the classic "foundation hills". They delineate the first center of the city in the hollow between them. Archeological finds on the Palatine Hill date back to a time around 1000 BC. Thus, this was the nucleus of the future great power of antiquity. Dating from the early days of the Empire (1st century AD) are the remains of elegant palaces as well as the Arch of Titus on the Forum Romanum. On the neighboring Capitoline Hill, the main temple dedicated to the god Jupiter had been built as early as the sixth century BC. Around 1540, the Capitoline Square, which can be reached via impressive cordonata stairs, was completely redesigned according to plans by Michelangelo. It is a place of perfect harmony. The central eye-catcher is the equestrian statue of Emperor Marcus Aurelius, although this is only a copy. The original (2nd century AD) can be admired in the Capitoline Museums, which are housed in the magnificent buildings flanking the Palazzo dei Conservatori (1568) and the Palazzo Nuovo (1655).

Largo Argentina

The Largo di Torre Argentina, in short Largo Argentina, is a congested square in the old city quarter of Pigna. Who would suspect a major excavation site from the period of the Roman Republic here, in these unspectacular surroundings? Yet a few meters (yards) below road level, the preserved columns indicate the way to the Area Sacra, a sacred district of the Republican era, which lasted from the expulsion of the last kings (509 BC) to the beginning of the imperial period under Augustus (27 BC). Four temples have been unearthed on the Largo Argentina. The oldest was built at the end of the fourth century/beginning of the third century AD, the newest around 100 AD. It is no longer possible to ascertain to which deities they were dedicated. The excavation site can easily be seen from all sides, but there is no access to it. The site is left to the countless cats that romp around the ruins, unperturbed by cars and passers-by.

Theater of Marcellus

In the immediate vicinity of the Temple of Apollo Sosianus (fifth and first centuries BC), between Capitoline Hill and the Tiber, stands the Theater of Marcellus (17 BC), which Augustus dedicated to his deceased favorite nephew. The amphitheater, which was originally a good 30-m- (98-ft-) high, is considered the model for the later Coliseum in terms of its construction methods. Around 15,000 spectators could be accommodated in this, the largest theater of Rome of its day. The two lower rows of arcades in the semicircular structure are very well-preserved, which is due not least to the later use of the building – in the Middle Ages, the theater was converted as a fortress for the aristocracy. The supporting walls, which were erected during the Renaissance, can be seen at the back. It is not hard to tell the ancient structural components from the later ones. The mixture even provides the complex with a particular charm. The ancient ruins are still inhabited even today.

The Capitoline Museums on Capitoline Hill – which incidentally are the oldest public museums in the world – hold a comprehensive collection of antiquities, among them the equestrian statue of the philosopher-emperor Marcus Aurelius. A copy of the original greets visitors on the square in front of the Palazzo Nuovo (left).

Forum Romanum

A highlight of every visit to Rome is a walk across the Forum Romanum, for centuries the heart of the ancient city and its political, religious and economic nucleus. Situated in the hollow between the Palatine and Capitoline Hills, it became the model for all the forums in the towns of the Roman Empire. Yet the splendor of the original remained unsurpassed. The archeological park conveys at least an impression of the abundance of marble temples, public buildings and market halls, as well as of the statues and memorials that once stood close together in this small space. Visitors should not worry about the tourist throngs but instead consider that even in Roman days there would have been plenty of lively bustling here. On a warm summer evening the mood is romantic. From the main entrance on the Via dei Fori Imperiali, you can easily reach Imperial Forums. Especially worth seeing here is Trajan's Column (AD 107) on Trajan's Forum as well as Trajan's Market.

Pantheon

Who built the largest dome in the ancient world? The Romans, of course, those ingenious master-builders and design engineers. The unique domed structure on the elegant Piazza Rotonda is known as the Pantheon, the temple dedicated to "all gods". The Pantheon was built in its present shape at the beginning of the second century AD, during the reign of Emperor Hadrian. It is considered the best-preserved building from Antiquity, which may also be due to the fact that, from the seventh century, it was used as a Christian church. Through the entrance porch with its triangular pediment, visitors reach the perfect rotunda: the entire circular ground plan is spanned by a mighty dome (with an interior diameter 43.3 m/142 ft). The only source of light inside this room is the oculus, a round opening at the zenith of the cupola, whose waffle-slab ceiling directs the gaze upward. It is the most conspicuous decorative element in the solemn room.

ROME

Castel Sant'Angelo

Few edifices can look back on a history as turbulent as the Angels' Castle (Castel Sant'Angelo). It was built outside Rome, as a mausoleum for Emperor Hadrian (r. AD 117–138). At the end of the third century, when Rome began to fortify itself against the onslaught of Germanic tribes, the imperial mausoleum was integrated into the Aurelian Walls. The Castel Sant'Angelo preserved its defensive character into the modern era, and it also became the treasury and prison of the popes. Today, it is a museum. A visit is worthwhile, not only to see the papal apartments, but also because of the fabulous all-round views that can be enjoyed from here.

Piazza Navona

The most beautiful square in the city, perhaps even anywhere in the world, is the Piazza Navona; most Romans are agreed on that. You can sit in street cafés with an elegant baroque backdrop: "To see and be seen", is the motto here, in the summer months till way after midnight. The elongated oval ground plan of the square, laid out in the 17th cen-

Fontana di Trevi

The Trevi Fountain, dating from the 18th century, has become legendary and even immortalized in a film. And, quite rightly, no visitor to Rome will miss this spectacle of water and stone: on a mussel chariot pulled by mythical creatures stands Neptune, the ruler of the seas, in front of a backdrop panel that was modeled on a triumphal arch from antiquity.

tury, dates back to the stadium commissioned by Emperor Domitian in 86 AD. Churches, palaces of the aristocracy and plain town houses in finely matched colors line the 275-m- (902-ft-) long Piazza. The focal point in the center is the famous Four Rivers Fountain.

The Four Rivers Fountain (Fontana dei Quattro Fiumi) on the Piazza Navona was the masterpiece of the baroque sculptor and architect Bernini. He created this animated composition in 1651, on the orders of the Pope.

Villa Borghese

Rome's largest and most beautiful public park is the Villa Borghese, a green oasis of calm and of the arts – the idyllic park is home to one of the most famous art collections in the world, the Museo e Galleria Borghese in the elegant Casino Borghese (1609).

Raphael, Titian, Caravaggio, Correggio, Rubens ... works by the greatest masters are among the treasures of the Galleria Borghese. Anyone wishing to admire them will have to reserve a ticket in advance – the number of visitors is strictly limited!

Piazza del Popolo

Before the advent of the railway, the Piazza del Popolo with its Egyptian obelisk and twin churches (15th century) was the city's reception hall for travelers from the north. The city gate stood here even in Antiquity.

Campo de' Fiori

In the heart of the old town, in the bend of the Tiber, visitors will find one of the most atmospheric and popular squares of the entire city. In the morning, the Campo de' Fiori is a flower and food market; in the evening, people gather here or meet up with friends.

Spanish Steps

Without doubt the best known of the many Roman stairs are the Scalinata di Trinità dei Monti or Spanish Steps, which have climbed majestically up the hill from the Piazza di Spagna since 1726. A must for every Rome tourist!

ROME

Via Appia

"All roads lead to Rome." With a few exceptions, the old saying really was true in Antiquity, for the Romans were passionate road builders. They needed good communication in order to administer their vast empire. The most famous of the Roman roads leading from the capital into all parts of the Empire is the Via Appia. Like the other arterial roads, the Romans used it also as a "cemetery"; after all, burials within the confines of the city were strictly forbidden. For a walk along the Via Appia Antica (in contrast to the Via Appia Nuova), it is best to set aside a Sunday or public holiday, for on these days the normally congested road is closed, at least to private cars. A good starting point is the Porta San Sebastiano from the year 277, behind which stands the first milestone. Soon you will come across the ruins of ancient tombs, such as the tomb of Cecilia Metella with its distinctive towerlike superstructure. The largest subterranean burial place in Rome is located at the second milestone: the Catacombs of Saint Callixtus (visits only on guided tours) extend in a labyrinthine fashion across several levels. 150,000 graves have been archeologically documented, and pagan as well as Christian frescoes have also been unearthed.

Tiber Island, Trastevere

The folksy atmosphere of the former artisans' district of Trastevere (meaning "beyond the Tiber") now also attracts the rich and the beautiful, and of course the tourists. They still exist, the Italian mammas, who gather in the backyards for a gossip and who still speak the old dialect. Yet overall

this "Rome of the little people" has become a trendy nightlife district; a popular meeting point is, for example, the Piazza Belli. Numerous bars and restaurants for every budget can be found on the idyllic Tiber Island,

which in Antiquity was the city's most important transshipment place for goods as well as a sanctuary of Aesculapius and an infirmary. As early as the second century BC, a stone bridge connected the city and the island; its remains can still be seen jutting out of the river.

The former "little people's district" of Trastevere (top). Plain on the outside, exquisite on the inside: the medieval church Santa Maria in Trastevere (above). The Tiber Island in the Tiber Bend, linked with the old town of Rome and with Trastevere by bridges (large picture).

The Via Appia Antica, the ancient
Roman state road, runs through the
charming countryside of the Cam-
pagna. It was initially built as far as
Capua in 312 BC and then extended
to the Roman "oriental port" of
Brindisi in 191 BC.

VATICAN CITY

To the right of the Tiber River, surrounded by the city of Rome, is the Città del Vaticano, the Vatican City State. It is the world's smallest nation, but what a gem! And it is not just pious pilgrims who are awestruck by the center of Catholicism.

Rome's importance in Europe's history and culture is closely linked to the Papacy, because the Bishop of Rome – the pope and leader of occidental Christians according to a tradition dating back to the Late Antiquity – also became the main figure of secular power during the Middle Ages. That is now history. The pope's dominion is now just a miniature walled state covering an area of 44 sq km (17 sq miles). It comprises Vatican Hill and St Peter's Square, as well as extraterritorial possessions in the Roman metropolitan area. The head of state is the pope of the time, currently Benedict XVI. The diminutive size of the national territory is juxtaposed with the Vatican City's greatness as a haven of the arts. St Peter's Square and St Peter's Basilica are architectural cornerstones. Art treasures from every era can be viewed in the Vatican museums. The Renaissance popes in particular excelled as patrons and collectors, and it was they who commissioned artists such as Michelangelo, Raphael and Bernini to create works of immortal beauty.

Vast St Peter's Square, bordered by Bernini's colonnades, forms a grand entrance to St Peter's Basilica (large picture and left). This is where hundreds of thousands of faithful gather to hear the Pope's address, and constitute the "beating heart of the Catholic Church".

VATICAN CITY

Sistine Chapel

The Cappella Sistina, built as the main chapel for Pope Sixtus IV (1475–1481), which is today the papal chapel and meeting place for the conclave during the papal election, is one of the world's most famous places of worship. The first thing visitors do is look up at the ceiling fresco. Michelangelo spent four years creating this (1508–1512), standing on a 20-m- (66-ft-) high scaffold every day, "hunched over like a Syrian arch" – a titanic feat, the artistic result of which is quite simply overwhelming! The scenes in the trompe-l'œil paintings depict Genesis, which reaches its climax with the "Creation of Adam", i.e. man. At age seventy in 1534, Michelangelo crafted another extremely impressive piece of work with Judgment Day on the front wall of the Sistine Chapel. Given the power and beauty of these works, you may be forgiven for underestimating the frescoes on the side walls. But they too were created by first-class masters such as Botticelli, Perugino and Ghirlandaio. The Sistine Chapel can be visited as part of the Vatican Museum. Only those who get to the ticket desk early in the morning and stride through the museum's rooms in double-quick time will be able to have this masterpiece to themselves without the crush of tourists.

St Peter's Basilica

The first church from Late Antiquity, built over the tomb of Peter the Apostle, fell into disrepair in the mid-15th century. A new structure was to be erected, and thus began the complex construction history of San Pietro in Vaticano, which lasted until well into the 17th century. Plans were rejected, master-builders came and went, and then money also ran out. In its present form, St Peter's Basilica is mostly the work of Bramante, who designed the cross-shaped floor plan in 1506, and Michelangelo, who took over con-

struction management in 1547 and built the inimitably elegant dome. The triple-naved interior, with transept and choir apse, is impressive in terms of its enormous size, as well as the many magnificent funerary monuments to the popes of the 16th to the 19th centuries. The sacristy houses St Peter's treasury, while the Lower Church (Sacre Grotte Vaticane) is home to numerous papal tombs, as well as what is thought to be the tomb of Peter the Apostle — which has been an important pilgrimage site since ancient times.

The bronze statue of St Peter (13th century) in St Peter's Basilica is highly revered (above). The papal altar, beneath Bernini's richly decorated baldachin (1624 to 1633), is situated directly under the cupola of St Peter's (large picture).

The Sistine Chapel (left) is completely covered in frescoes. The sidewalls depict scenes from the life of Christ and Moses. Michelangelo's altar fresco (in the background) illustrates Judgment Day; he also painted the ceiling fresco portraying themes from the genesis and the Fall of Man.

The Pietà

Sculpture at its very best! And yet, Michelangelo was just 25 years old when he created the famous Pietà in St Peter's Basilica.

Raphael's stanzas

The former private apartments of the pope, known as stanzas and loggias, which Raphael adorned with a series of magnificent frescoes from 1508 to 1520, are one of the highlights of the Vatican Museum.

Laocoön and his sons

This ancient masterpiece (first century AD) was discovered in Rome in 1506. Today, it can be admired in the antiquities collection at the Vatican Museum.

Santa Maria Maggiore

The Vatican City's extraterritorial possessions situated in Roman territory include four so-called patriarchal basilicas ("papal churches"), one of which is Santa Maria Maggiore in the Esquilino district. It dates back to the fifth century and, despite many subsequent reconstructions,

has still preserved the basic design of an early-Christian basilica in its triple-aisled nave. The ancient columns, as well as the mosaics on the nave walls and the mosaic on the triumphal arch, attest to the building's very long history. The mosaic of the Coronation of Mary in the apses, as well as the marble floor decorated with marquetry ("Cosmati-

style floor"), are medieval (13th century). The counterpart of this marble floor is found in the gold-plated coffered ceiling which Columbus brought back from America. Lots of gold and ornate decorations characterize the furnishings and side chapels, which were added when the original church was redesigned in baroque style. The magnificent façade on the apse side

is also baroque, while the elegant main façade is classicist. Anyone who happens to be in Rome on August 5 should not miss the "Miracle of the Snow" festival, when it rains white petals to commemorate the miraculous snowfall which occurred in August of the year 325, and which, according to legend, prompted the pope to build this basilica.

San Giovanni in Laterano

St John Lateran is revered as the "mother of all churches". It is the church of the Bishop of Rome, and therefore the actual papal church, making it even more sacred than St Peter's Basilica. The popes did not move from the Lateran to the better-fortified Vatican until 1377. The Lateran was a vast area which Emperor Constantine the Great gifted to Rome's early Christian community at the start of the fourth century. This was the site of Rome's first Christian church built in the ancient basilica design (three-aisled nave). The present-day structure, erected around 910, was given its precious Cosmati-style floor, the gold-plated coffered

ceiling and the striking apse mosaic in the Late Middle Ages. In the 17th century, under the direction of baroque master builder Borromini, it was transformed into a majestic yet bright sanctuary reflecting the contemporary tastes of the time. The grandiose façade is also baroque, but the mighty bronze door of the main entrance dates back to ancient times. The splendid medieval cloister of San Giovanni is also worth a visit, as are the papal apartments in the adjacent Lateran Palace (1586).

The faithful climb the "holy staircase" in the Lateran church of Salvatore della Scala Santa, said to originate from Pontius Pilate's palace, on their knees in memory of the sufferings of Christ (above). The complex of the Basilica of St John Lateran and the papal palace also includes the octagonal baptistery from Late Antiquity (large picture).

Around the year 1600, Pope Sixtus V and the Borghese family had their own chapels added onto the church of Santa Maria Maggiore (left), whose twin domes gave the basilica from the Late Antiquity a completely new look. Reputable artists helped design the interior of the grand side chapels.

San Paolo fuori le Mura

Standing outside the ancient city walls ("fuori le mura") since the fourth century is the Basilica of St Paul, one of four Roman patriarchal basilicas, and, it is said, once the most magnificent Christian church. But a fire destroyed the venerable basilica in 1823; only a few pieces of furniture were saved (and can today be seen in the sacristy and museum). San Paolo was rebuilt on the old base walls of the giant five-naved basilica, but this time in the historicized style of the 19th century, with an imposing columned portico, as well as mosaics and frescoes in the style of Late Antiquity. It is well worth making a visit to the medieval cloister, which was protected from the fire and which, with its elegant double marble columns decorated in Cosmati style, is considered to be the city's finest. The church's high degree of religious importance has always been based on the pious tradition that St Paul is supposedly buried here. Recent archaeological findings almost completely confirm this. The martyrdom of the apostle, missionary and first Christian theologian in Rome can also be assumed as historic fact: St Paul died during the persecution of Christians under Nero in 67 AD, and, after his beheading, was buried "outside the city walls", as was the custom in ancient Rome. Emperor Constantine the Great (r. 306–337) had a chapel built over his tomb on the road to Ostia. This was the first predecessor building to San Paolo fuori le Mura on the present-day Via Ostiense. St Paul's tomb has been one of Rome's most important pilgrimage destinations since ancient times. It is situated beneath the neo-Gothic high altar of the Basilica of St Paul, where only the pope can celebrate mass.

After being destroyed by a fire, the five-naved papal church of St Paul "Outside the Wall" was rebuilt in antique style in the 19th century. Beneath its main altar, which is spanned by a ciborium, is the sarcophagus of Paul the Apostle (left).

SAN MARINO

Città di San Marino is the official name of the capital of the mini-state of San Marino. The picturesque old mountain town has some 4,000 inhabitants – and around two million visitors each year.

This small city with a long history is perched atop the Monte Titano, not far from Rimini and the neighboring seaside resorts on Italy's Adriatic coast. Many legends surround its origins, but one thing which is certain is that San Marino was an independent city republic in the 13th century, and, over the years, was consistently able to defend its

The forts

The three towers on the coat of arms display three medieval forts which the city republic of San Marino used to defend its autonomy. The so-called "first tower", the Guaita Fortress, dates back to the 11th century: a veritable "picture-book" fort with two surrounding walls! Visitors can enjoy the magical view, and admire the old cannonry which fires the salutes on the national day. The "Witches' Pass" leads to the Cesta Fortress (13th century), which sits atop the highest peak of the Monte Titano (750 m/2,641 ft) as the "second tower". The fortress museum displays weapons from the 13th to the 19th century. The "third tower" (Montale) can only be visited from the outside. But to make up for this, its former long-distance observation decks provide what is probably

the most impressive view of San Marino, sweeping over the Adriatic Sea, which is only 10 km (6 miles) away. To the north-east, one can see Emilia Romagna, to the south-west the Marche region. And of course, one can also look out over the entire national territory of San Marino, spanning an area of just 61 sq km (24 sq miles). According to old tradition, it is divided into nine castelli, or townships, clustered around a fortress. Borgo Maggiore, which is connected to the capital via a funicular railway, is particularly worth seeing.

A walk on the fortress wall provides sensational panoramic views (above). The picturesque Guaita on Monte Titano looks like a picture postcard at dusk (large picture).

freedom against its mighty neighbors' cravings for conquest; forts, towers, walls and city gates today still attest to the city's defense-based character. Even when the new Kingdom of Italy was proclaimed in 1861, San Marino retained its sovereignty within the Italian national territory. This unique continuity of the republicanist tradition, as well as the historic townscape which has developed over the centuries, prompted UNESCO to include the Old Town of San Marino, with Monte Titano, on its list of World Heritage Sites in 2008. Strolling through the town, you will notice a fine mix of "genuine" medieval architecture and 19th-century reconstructions.

Souvenir shops, bars and restaurants line the medieval lane of the Città di San Marino (far left). The Piazza della Libertà, with the neo-Gothic Palazzo Pubblico (left), is the finest square in the town.

Resplendent uniforms

The guards of the mini-state look very smart in their gala uniforms. No tourist should miss the changing of the guard in front of the Government Palace. In the summer months, they take place every half hour.

Basilica di San Marino

The relics of the patron saint, Marinus, are the most precious treasures in the neo-classicist basilica (1836). According to legend, he fled to Monte Titano during the persecution of the Christians, and founded the first settlement there.

Old Town

Much like a staircase, the historic buildings of the Città di San Marino, not defaced by any modern eyesores, climb all the way up the hill, culminating in the Palazzo Pubblico, the town hall and the Government Palace of San Marino.

LJUBLJANA

A heritage-listed Old Town, magnificent baroque buildings, bridges with a special character, and the newer architecture characterized by a top Slovenian architect – Ljubljana is full of surprises.

The capital of Slovenia lies on the banks of the Ljubljanica, a small river that clearly divides the city into two halves. On one side is the Old Town, with its narrow alleys, the cathedral and the bishop's palace. These are closely packed around the three central squares (Town Square, Old Square and Upper Square), and form the oldest part of the city. On the other side of the river is the livelier district of Ljubljana, with Prešeren Square and numerous cafés and restaurants, as well as pedestrian zones with their department stores and boutiques. Architecturally, Ljubljana is largely baroque, but parts of the city are also the work of architect Jože Plečnik (1872–1957), a native to Ljubljana who designed countless different types of buildings in and around his hometown. This connection between the Old and the New gives the city unique character. Ljubljana is the seat of government and economic center of Slovenia. With a population of around 280,000, it is also the country's largest city.

Franciscan church and Tromostovje

Prešeren Square in the center of Ljubljana is dominated by the Franciscan Church of the Annunciation. The baroque basilica was erected between 1646 and 1660, but the façade was not given its present-day appearance until around 1700, and the altar was created in the mid-18th century. An earthquake in 1895 damaged the ceiling in the interior, thereby also destroying most of the original frescoes. These were recreated by Slovenian impressionist Matej

Ljubljana's heraldic animal

The dragon is the symbol of the city. According to legend it was founded by the Greek hero and dragon conqueror, Jason.

Sternen in the mid-1930s. Prešeren Square is also home to one of the symbols of Ljubljana, the "Tromostovje", literally "Triple Bridge" or "Three Bridges". And three bridges do, in fact, span the river directly alongside one another. After the original medieval wooden bridge burned down in 1657, it was replaced by a new one, which eventually also had to make way for a new river crossing in 1842, this time built of stone. Based on Jože Plečnik's plans, two pedestrian bridges were added on either side between 1929 and 1932. The Tromostovje have spanned the Ljubljanica as an ensemble ever since.

The ensemble of the Tromostovje – a tight group of three, virtually parallel bridges – has spanned the Ljubljanica River (left) in the shadow of the Franciscan Church (large picture) since 1932.

LJUBLJANA

Colonnades and Križanke Summer Theater – Jože Plečnik

A long row of colonnades runs directly along the banks of the Ljubljanica from the Triple Bridge to the Dragon Bridge. Built by Jože Plečnik between 1939 and 1940, it gives the inner city a charming Mediterranean ambiance. Hidden behind the colonnades are the market halls which also bear the unmistakable signature of the great architect but which can be easily overlooked. The elegant shapes of the white arcades are reminiscent of Greek temples, while inside, fresh produce from the surrounding area is on offer. The former monastery of the Teutonic Order at

Shoemaker's Bridge and Old Town

The Shoemaker's Bridge (Čevljarski most) is also the work of Jože Plečnik. Before the architect began his work here, it was the site of a 19th-century cast-iron bridge which Plečnik quickly had moved further downriver. But even this bridge had been preceded by one built of wood in the Middle Ages, on which huts with shoemakers' workshops had stood. This gave the first bridge its name, which was retained for the later structures. On the site of these previous bridges, Plečnik's new Shoemaker's Bridge was a type of wide square over the water. The construction, made of artificial stone and concrete, was given simple railings and a row of six tall columns topped with orbs on either side. These were originally meant to support a roof construction that was never completed. In the middle of the bridge, candlesticks soar up outside the concrete area on either side of the girders. These are effectively positioned a little lower than the columns on the balustrades. The bridge was built between 1931 and 1932, and connects the districts on both sides of the river more like a piazza than a classic bridge.

The best street cafés are also situated on the Old Town side, where the Shoemaker's Bridge opens out into the Town Square (Mestni trg). This is the heart of the oldest, and today largely traffic-calmed, part of the city. Almost all of the surrounding houses are baroque structures, although some of their gables suggest they were originally Gothic.

The main attractions are not far from here, such as the town hall dating from the year 1718, the Fountain of the Three Carniolan Rivers, also known as the Robba Fountain, at the Town Square, and St Florian's Church at the Upper Square (Gornji trg), which was completed in 1672.

With its balustrades and columns, the Shoemaker's Bridge (Čevljarski most) looks like a piazza floating above the water (large picture).

French Revolution Square (Trg francoske revolucije) was also redesigned by Plečnik, who gave the complex, which had already been remodeled in baroque style, a new look between 1952 and 1956. Today, the site is home to a school of design and photography, as well as the popular Križanke Summer Theater.

Beneath the colonnades along the Ljubljanica is an open market, with the market halls (far left) behind. A former monastery of the Teutonic Order houses the renowned Križanke Summer Theater (left). When the complex was redesigned in the 1950s, the architect Jože Plečnik used stylistic elements of the Renaissance period.

Central market

The lively central market by St Nicholas' Cathedral is worth a visit. Most of the stallholders come from the surrounding area, and their products, which range from honey to schnapps, are very popular among Ljubljana's locals.

National Gallery

The National Gallery building was constructed in 1896 by Czech architect František Skabrout as a venue for Slovenian associations, and was known as the "National House". The National Gallery has been housed here since 1918.

Fountain of the Three Carniolan Rivers

The fountain on the Town Square was built by the Venetian Francesco Robba from 1743 to 1751. The three statues depict the river gods, and represent the three rivers of the Carniola region: the Krka, Ljubljanica and Sava.

ZAGREB

In the times when the Orient Express used to stop in Zagreb, the city would provide the distinguished passengers with plenty of appropriate entertainment. A lot has changed since, but traces of that grandeur still remain.

With a population of just under 800,000, Zagreb is the largest city in Croatia, as well as the country's most important industrial city and economic and cultural center. It is the seat of government, and also a Catholic and Orthodox archbishopric. Magnificent palaces, baroque churches and colorful roofs, along with parks and grassed areas, char-

Gornji Grad and Kaptol

The districts of Gornji Grad (Upper Town) and Kaptol reveal the most scenic side of Zagreb – for instance, the remains of the triangular fortress wall erected as a precautionary measure after the Tartar attacks of the 13th century, or St Mark's parish church at St Mark's Square in the center of Gornji Grad. The originally Romanesque church was rebuilt in Gothic style in the 14th century. Its impressive tiled roof, with the large emblems of the city and the former kingdom, dates back to the year

Dolac

The Dolac Market at Ban Jelačić Square is spread over two levels: Market stalls offer fruit and vegetables on the upper level, while the market halls down below sell meat, cheese and bread. A number of old houses and even streets had to be sacrificed when the market was established in 1926.

1880. Zagreb's main landmark, the cathedral, with its twin spires visible from almost all areas of the city, stands in Kaptol, the ancient heart of the Old Town. Nearby is the Prislin Tower, which was once part of the old fortress complex.

The Ban Jelaăiç Square constitutes the historic center of Zagreb. It was named after the Croatian national hero to whom the equestrian statue at its center is also dedicated (large picture).

acterize the townscape. A large part of the city spreads over the two hills of Gradec and Kaptol. The two independent settlements which once existed here have long been merged, and today form the Upper Town (Gornji Grad) with the Kaptol district. It is home to Zagreb's tallest building, the cathedral, as well as a museum of naïve art and the roman-

tic Mirogoj Cemetery. Beneath the Gornji Grad lies the newer, modern Lower Town (Donji Grad), the center of Zagreb, with major hotels and impressive townhouses. The picturesque old funicular railway, which is popular among visitors and locals alike, acts as a quick link between the Upper and Lower Town.

Evening ambiance in the streets of the picturesque Old Town quarter, Kaptol (far left). At sunset, the 105-m- (345-ft-) high twin spires of the cathedral shine over the city's rooftops (left).

Crkva Svetog Marka

St Mark's Church not only captivates visitors with its colorful roof, but also with the numerous statues in its interior. The southern porch was created by artists from Prague in the 14th century.

Katedrala Svetog Stjepana

The former St Stephen's Cathedral (Katedrala Svetog Stjepana) is today called the Cathedral of the Assumption of the Blessed Virgin Mary. The square outside the church has a large fountain, its column topped with a statue of the Virgin Mary and four golden angels.

Sabor

The Sabor is the Croatian Parliament, and also the Houses of Parliament. The building erected at St Mark's Square in 1908 was once the residence of the bans, the viceroys appointed for a fixed term.

ZAGREB

Strossmayer Promenade

At the edge of one of the city's hills, Gradec, the Strossmayer Promenade follows the course of the former southern ring of fortifications, which was demolished in the early 18th century. The walkway offers a stunning view of the rooftops and labyrinthine alleyways of the Lower City, and heads past quaint, colorful houses. Soaring up at the end of the Promenade is the Lotršćak Tower, which was erected in the 13th century as part of the former fortress complex. A cannon is traditionally fired here at midday to, as the saying goes, inform the citizens of Zagreb of the correct time. The Promenade was laid out

Donji Grad

The Lower Town or center, as the locals call it, is the modern business district of Zagreb. Not only is it home to office blocks and banks, but also museums, cafés and restaurants, as well as the shopping streets found in every major city. In addition to this there are many classicist palaces and other prominent buildings. Marshal Tito Square is the site of the Croatian National Theater, built in 1895, in front of which stands the bronze "Well of Life" by a student of

Rodin, Ivan Meštrović (1883 to 1962). The Palace Hotel, erected in Secession style in 1891, is located on ornate Strossmayer Square, while the park-like King Tomislav Square is home to the Art Pavilion, opened in 1898. This building was one of the world's first pre-fabricated constructions. Lying on the border with the Upper Town is Ban Jelačić Square, Zagreb's large central square surrounded by stately buildings in neo-classicist and Viennese Secessionist style. The present-day Lower Town dates back to an urban redevelopment which took place at the end of the 19th century. Under the direction of Milan Lenucci, the Donji Grad was given a new, semicircular layout which connects the large squares and parks, and is known as the city's "Green Horseshoe". Many buildings and planning details can be traced back to Viennese architect, Hermann Bollé. During this time, numerous ornate buildings were also erected in the spirit of the Belle Époque.

Tomislav was crowned the first King of Croatia in the year 925. An equestrian statue in his honor stands in a small park at Tomislav Square (above). The Croatian National Theater was inaugurated in 1895, in the presence of Emperor Franz Joseph I (right).

in 1812, and later named after the bishop, politician and art patron, Josip Juraj Strossmayer (1815–1905). A statue of the Croatian writer Antun Gustav Matoš (1873–1914) sits on one of the park benches beneath the chestnut trees of the picturesque boulevard. The statue was created in 1978 by the famous Croatian artist, Ivan Kožarić. Several staircases connect the Lower and Upper Towns, but for many people, the funicular railway, which was built in 1888 and has been in operation since 1889, is a much more convenient alternative. The summit station is located right by the Lotrščak Tower. The bright blue carriage makes its short journey every ten minutes.

Antun Gustav Matoš – whose monument on Strossmayer Promenade is pictured on the far left – is considered one of the most prominent writers of the Croatian Modernity. The Uspinjača, a funicular railway (left), operates regularly between the Lower and Upper Town.

Regent Esplanade

The lavish emerald ballroom in the Regent Esplanade Hotel, opened in 1925. The historic luxury hotel continues to be one of Zagreb's most exclusive properties even today.

Muzej Miramara

The museum, opened in 1987 and housed in a 19th-century building on Roosevelt Square, is home to art treasures from many different epochs, as well as ancient archaeological exhibits.

Mirogoj Cemetery

The crypts at picturesque Mirogoj Cemetery, established in a park in 1876 and based on the plans of Austrian architect Hermann Bollé.

SARAJEVO

Nestled in the beautiful Miljacka Valley in the Dinaric Alps, the capital of Bosnia-Herzegovina, Sarajevo, is an old, atmospheric city looking enthusiastically toward the future.

Many people only associate Sarajevo with the horrors of the Bosnian War, when the city was besieged and shelled by the Serbs for 43 months (1992–1996). Ten thousand people died, and 50,000 were wounded. The war damage to the buildings has now largely been repaired, and the tourists are now also returning. Not only does it have a spectacular loca-

The new Sarajevo

Although Sarajevo only has a population of 300,000, its energy pulsates like that of a large metropolis. The war is over; the wounds are now just scars. People no longer talk a lot about it, and instead prefer to invest their energies and ideas in the future. A special city tour of the wartime "hotspots" is offered to interested visitors; however, of all the tourists who journey out to Princeva Park to enjoy the spectacular view over Sarajevo, very few of them probably realize that the observation terrace was also a good vantage point for the Serbian snipers during the siege.

The new, Europe-oriented Sarajevo can be found in the new business district established near the train station, and in the trendy clubs and cinemas by the Miljacka, in the city center. Young people dance to electro-pop, discuss film projects, review the latest art exhibitions, and plan the next theater performance. Foreign visitors are most welcome, because hospitality is a tradition in Sarajevo, where people are also trying to connect to the outside world. International celebrities are now often seen at the Sarajevo Film Festival, which was founded during the war (1995) and has since progressed to become the city's most important cultural event. Film is indeed a source of immense excitement and enthusiasm, but even the die-hard cineastes will agree it's not all about the art. People in Sarajevo also like to party.

The minaret of the Emperor's Mosque and the 17th-century Turkish bell tower (above) typify the old Sarajevo, which, with its many mosques, adjoins modern Sarajevo (right).

tion, but also a historic legacy in which Eastern and Western influences have merged to form their own cultural identity. The Ottomans dominated the city for four centuries, and mosques and bazaars in the Old Town's narrow alleyways attest to this. Impressive monuments from the time of the Austro-Hungarian Monarchy (1878–1918) have al-

so been preserved, while high-rise façades gleam in the new commercial district of Marijin Dvor. Enthusiasm for new beginnings has been in full swing since the end of the brutal war for independence, but the city's old roots have not been forgotten either. People still eat burek and baklava in preference to hamburgers and soft ice cream.

The Baščaršija quarter, with its narrow alleyways, handicraft shops and cafés, exudes a Turkish bazaar atmosphere (far left). Sarajevo has recorded the highest economic growth of all the capitals in south-eastern Europe since 2004. The new 40-story Avaz Twist Tower (left) symbolizes the boom the city has experienced since the end of the war.

SARAJEVO

Oriental Old Town and Turkish quarter

Baščaršija is the pulse of old Sarajevo. Even the name of the district, which stretches northward from the banks of the Miljacka, alludes to its Turkish origins. And anyone who strolls through the maze of narrow alleys will actually feel as if they are in an Oriental bazaar. All kinds of traditional handicrafts are on offer in the small shops – delicately engraved copperware, pottery and silver jewelry, as well as a plethora of tourist trinkets. In Baščaršija or on Kazandžiluk Street, one of Sarajevo's oldest, everyone is sure to find a souvenir to their liking. The numerous food stands and snack bars are also very traditional – they typically sell mouth-watering pitas with various fillings. Although Sarajevo is anything but a fundamentalist stronghold, many pubs and eateries in the Old Town uphold the Islamic alcohol ban. Apart from the Albanian capital, Tirana, Sarajevo is the only European city where the majority of the population is Muslim. This legacy of the four centuries in which it was part of the Ottoman Empire (1463–1878) is also reflected in the many mosques. As the seat of the Grand Mufti of Bosnia-Herzegovina, the Emperor's Mosque (the name refers to Sultan Süleyman I) plays a key role in religious life. It was built right on the banks of the Miljacka in 1566, and constitutes the

Symbol of the city – the National Library

Sarajevo's largest and most imposing building from the Austro-Hungarian period (1878 to 1918) is the old town hall, today the National Library and one of the city's landmarks. It was designed by Czech architect Alexander Witteck, who worked extensively in the Balkans on instructions from Vienna, and was considered a specialist in Oriental architecture since he had studied in

Arts Academy

The striking monument on the banks of the Miljacka, built in the late 19th century in an ornate neo-Romanesque/Byzantine style, originally served as a church for Evangelical Christians. Today, it is the prestigious home of Sarajevo's Academy of Fine Arts.

Cairo. Sarajevo's town hall, built during the 1890s, was his most famous and also his last work. Even today, it is said he went insane in the face of this enormous challenge. In fact, Witteck committed suicide while construction was still under way. The medieval inspirations for Sarajevo's grandiose town hall were the Mozarabic/Moorish architecture of the Maghreb and Spain. The highlight of the interior is the hexagonal hall topped with a glass dome. The magnificent building was severely damaged during the Bosnian War, but has since been rebuilt.

oldest center within the city. This is where the first Ottoman governor erected his castle in 1463, and it was this saray ("serail") which gave Sarajevo its name. The largest mosque, which is also one of the country's oldest, is the Gazi Husrev Mosque, a classic domed mosque with an almost 50-m- (164-ft-) high minaret and a fountain in an interior courtyard. Also worth seeing is the building opposite the mosque, which was erected as an Islamic college (Medresa) in 1547 and which, with its numerous lead-plated domes, is particularly picturesque.

The Roman Catholic cathedral was built in the late 19th century, after the end of Ottoman rule, when Austria-Hungary rose to supremacy in the Balkans (left). The National Library is Sarajevo's most magnificent building from the Austro-Hungarian era (large picture).

Bazaar and Turkish Fountain

Lying at the heart of the Oriental Old Town is the original Baščaršija Square with its small shops and stalls. There is always something happening here. If you are thirsty from all the browsing, dealing and shopping, you can drink at the Sebilj public fountain, built in a pseudo-Moorish style in 1891. Don't worry; the water is clean, fresh and delicious.

Latin Bridge

Sarajevo's townscape includes the bridges over the Miljacka. One of them, the Latin Bridge constructed in 1798, gained notoriety in the early 20th century: It was here that the Serbian nationalist, Gavrilo Princip, assassinated the Austrian heir apparent, Franz Ferdinand, and his wife on 28 June 1914. In doing so, he triggered a fatal chain of events which eventually led to the outbreak of World War I.

PODGORICA

When Montenegro was still part of the multiethnic state that was Yugoslavia, Podgorica was the subordinate capital of a constituent republic. Today, the country is independent, and Podgorica has set off towards a new future.

The ambitious capital of Montenegro is a city on the move. Along with the historic structures such as the 10th-century St George's Church and the mosques from Ottoman times, there are an increasing number of modern buildings and attractions such as the National Theater building, newly erected in 1997, and the Millennium Bridge, opened in

Old and new capital

Montenegro was controlled by the Ottoman Empire until 1878, and the mosques in the Drač and Stara Varoš (Old Town) districts attest to this; the latter has a famous clock tower worth seeing. The city's traditional symbol and landmark is, however, the 10th-century Serbian Orthodox Cathedral of the Resurrection of Christ.

Cetinje – The President's Residence

The residence of Montenegro's president is situated not in the capital, Podgorica, but in Cetinje, some 20 km (12 miles) away. The small town of 15,000 inhabitants was the nation's capital for three centuries until 1918. The picture shows the former ducal and royal palace, which today houses a museum.

A phase of active construction, which has changed the face of Podgorica and seen the emergence of structures such as the famous Millennium Bridge and numerous office and administrative buildings, began even before the country attained full sovereignty in 2006 and continues to the present day. Republic Square on the Hercegovačka pedestrian street was completely redesigned in 2006 and is today the center of an entertainment district with restaurants, cafés and pubs.

Podgorica's Serbian Orthodox cathedral, topped with gold crosses, was built in the 10th century.

2005. The industry, trade and economy of the young state are concentrated in Podgorica. With its museums and numerous theaters, the city is also Montenegro's cultural hub, as well as an administrative center and seat of government. The president's official residence is the only important state institution to be located outside the capital.

The Millennium Bridge, a cable-stayed bridge built over the Morača in 2005, is the new symbol of Podgorica (far left; left, with a modern sculpture in the foreground). The Parliament (center) represents Montenegro's independence, which it gained after breaking away from Serbia in 2006.

BELGRADE

Belgrade boasts an old fortress in a picturesque location between two rivers and the anachronism of 20th-century royal palaces, as well as boat-restaurants and Turkish coffee.

Belgrade has some 1.5 million inhabitants and is the largest town in Serbia as well as the seat of the government. As early as the 19th century, Belgrade developed as an economic and cultural center and today it is also a major location for heavy and light industries. The city is located at the confluence of the Sava River with the Danube, with the Old Town (Stari

Kalemegdan Fortress, Center

The mighty Belgrade Fortress rises on a hill above the confluence of the Sava and Danube. Over the course of the centuries, the castles that were built here were conquered, destroyed and rebuilt. The present fortress mostly dates from the 18th century, although many structures from that time repeatedly became the casualties of bloody disputes. The fortress complex is divided into the Upper Town and the Lower Town. In the Upper Town, some ancient gates are particularly interesting and well preserved, for example, the Zindan Gate

(1460), which was previously used as a dungeon, and the Despot's Gate (1470). Also part of the castle complex is Kalemegdan Park. This expansive green space encircles the entire core of the fortress. Within the park are Belgrade Zoo as well as several museums. Behind the fortress, the modern inner city of Belgrade begins, with a pedestrian mall (Knez Mihailova) lined with cafés and souvenir shops. Many houses in this district are protected buildings, for example the Belgrade Library, the Serbian Academy of Sciences and Arts and the Cultural Center, but also some elegant town houses from the 1880s. Knez Mihailova street links Kalemegdan Park below the fortress with Terazije, the official center of Belgrade.

Since 1928, the 14-m- (46-ft-) tall war memorial "The Victor" by Ivan Meštrović (above) has stood in Kalemegdan Fortress, majestically located where the Sava flows into the Danube (large picture).

Grad) positioned between the Sava right bank and the Danube. On the left bank of the Sava are the districts of New Belgrade (Novi Beograd), which were not developed until the 20th century. Established in medieval times and standing on a rock above the Danube and the Sava, Kalemegdan Fortress dominates the cityscape. Behind the castle extends the modern city center. Here lies boulevardlike Terazije Square, which represents the official center of Belgrade; thus, the house numbers in Belgrade streets ascend depending on their distance from the square. Particularly fascinating are the houseboats on the banks of both rivers. Some of these are restaurant ships, which also offer fine views over the city.

One of the most elegant establishments in town is the luxury Hotel Moskva on the Terazije, built in 1908 (left). The main shopping street is the Knez Mihailova in the center of the city. Cafés and souvenir shops define the scene here, but equally represented are the elegant boutiques of leading fashion brands (far left).

Skadarlija

In past times, many of Serbia's famous poets and artists lived in the old town district of Skadarlija. Visitors can find charming bars, art galleries, antiques shops and trendy hangouts on its cobbled streets.

Slavija Square

In the 1890s, there was still a lake here where wild ducks were hunted. Today, Trg Slavija square is a central traffic hub, with a monument to the Socialist leader Dimitrije Tucović (1881–1914) standing in the center.

Cathedral of Saint Sava

The largest church of all the Balkan countries is dedicated to Serbia's national saint. Building was begun in 1935 but interrupted several times and only completed in 2009.

BELGRADE

Novi Beograd and Zemun

Novi Beograd (New Belgrade) was systematically developed on the Sava left bank, opposite the old town, from 1948. Aside from residential tower blocks, industrial complexes and office buildings were built, such as the angular glass Block 25 structure and the "West Gate" skyscraper, two towers that are linked at the top. The adjacent, once independent Zemun, however, was only incorporated in 1945. Here stand a number of historic buildings, including some baroque churches, an local museum and the Millennium Tower of 1896. The romantic Danube promenade (Zemunski kej), fringed by inns, is a popular destination for excursions.

Beli dvor and Dedinje

The Beli dvor, or White Palace (literally: White Court), completed in 1936, is one of two royal palaces in the Belgrade district of Dedinje. The palace stands in a large park, where the Kraljevski dvor (Royal Palace), the Chapel dedicated to St Andrew

Museum of Yugoslav History

This museum was formerly called Museum May 25 because May 25, 1892, was the official birth date of Josip Broz Tito (the actual date was May 7), the President of the Republic Yugoslavia, who died in 1980 The museum dedicated to him displays Tito memorabilia.

the Apostle and a luxurious guesthouse can also be found.
The Beli dvor palace was built on the orders of King Alexander I, who himself lived at the Kraljevski dvor and wanted this new structure as a residential palace for his sons. After World War II, the Beli dvor became the presidential residence of Yugoslavia, and later Slobodan Milošević lived there. At the time of the monarchy, the villa district of Dedinje was still outside Belgrade; it only became an exclusive residential area in the first half of the 20th century. Today, many diplomats' villas and embassies are based here, and so the area enjoys a reputation as the most expensive district in the city.

The Beli dvor palace, built in 1936, features luxuriously furnished rooms as well as a valuable collection of paintings (right).

The Zemun district with its baroque church (far left: view across the Sava) and Novi Beograd, which was not developed until after World War II, lie on a spit of land between the two rivers Sava and Danube. One of the largest sports halls in Europe was opened here in 2004, the Belgrade Arena (left).

PRIŠTINA

When, in February 2008, the parliament in Priština declared the sovereignty of the Serbian province of Kosovo, the town rose from a regional center to becoming the capital of the youngest state in Europe.

Awakening City

Since the formation of the state of Kosovo, there has been a mood of optimism in this, Europe's youngest capital of some 500,000 inhabitants, apparent not only in the new cafés, restaurants and hotels. Despite modernization, some of which was fairly

Mosques

Since the 15th century, the main religion in Kosovo has been Islam, since then, numerous mosques have also been built here. Among the oldest buildings in the old town is the Fatih or Imperial Mosque, built in 1460. Just outside the city stands the Lap Mosque, which is only ten years younger.

radical, during the time it belonged to Yugoslavia, a number of interesting historic buildings from the Ottoman and more recent periods have survived. The National Library, opened in 1982, is impressive, a futurist composition of glass and concrete cubes with domes and enveloped in a net of steel.

On Independence Day in 2008, this installation was set up in the middle of the city, and people could inscribe their names on it with a felt-tip pen.

Gračanica Monastery

This major Serbian Orthodox monastery is located in the small village of the same name, only a few miles south of Priština, and inhabited mainly by Serbs. An exceptionally beautiful example of Serbian Byzantine architecture, the monastery church is among the most famous sacred buildings in the entire region and the most important in the Balkans. It was built as a "cross-in-square" church, as is typical in Byzantine church architecture. This means that its plan is the shape of a Greek cross, above which rise five domes, one above the central bay, or naos, and the others above the four arms of the cross. The church was built during the reign of the Serbian King Stefan Uroš II Milutin, who commissioned several sacred structures from the end of the 13th century. It was completed in 1311, but some of the frescoes were added later. Today, the church is the residence of the Orthodox bishop and the building itself has been a UNESCO World Cultural Heritage Site since 2006.

Gračanica Monastery (far left) is adorned by magnificent frescoes, such as this one depicting the Blessed Virgin Mary (left). The portrait of the royal founder, complete with halo, and the image of Queen Simonida are also famous.

TIRANA

Under the leadership of Enver Hoxha and his successors, Albania eked out a dire, isolated existence for many years. But the country has now opened up to the outside world, and the capital's appearance is noticeably transforming.

The city's history began in the year 1614, when the nobleman Sulejman Pasha built a mosque at the junction of two trade routes. Tirana became the capital of Albania in 1920, prompting rapid growth and development of the once rather small town. In particular, after Enver Hoxha founded the People's Republic of Albania in 1946, Tirana experienced an intensive phase of modernization which radically changed the face of the city. However, this also led to the loss of many historic buildings, as well as cultural monuments which had survived over the centuries. Today, Tirana has a population of some 600,000. With a university founded in 1957, numerous museums and diverse industry, it is the focal point of the country both economically and culturally. The main buildings worth seeing are located in the center, around Skanderbeg Square, which was created in the 1960s. It is named after the Albanian national hero, who, over a long period of time, prevented the country from being conquered by the Turks, and is considered to be its founding father.

Skanderbeg Square

Tirana's main square was created in the 1960s. Today, it is partly bordered by large, block-shaped buildings such as the Tirana International Hotel, and also partly by Oriental-looking buildings, including the famous Et'hem Bey Mosque. This structure, with its richly decorated interior, took well over thirty years to build – from 1789 to 1823. The two master-builders who succeeded one another were father and son, and also, it is said, the grandson and great-grandson of the city's founder, Sulejman Pasha. The Palace of Culture

Standing before the mosque at Skanderbeg Square since 1968 is the equestrian statue of the national hero and founding father, Gjergj Kastrioti, known as Skanderbeg (1405–1468), after whom the square is named.

directly opposite houses the National Library and Albanian State Opera. The foundation stone of this mighty building, with its columned porch open on three sides, was laid by the Soviet party leader and head of government, Nikita Khrushchev. Skanderbeg Square also marks the start of the wide streets leading into the outer districts. One of these is the grand Bulevardi Deshmoret e Kombit, which is home to the "Pyramid", the former modern Enver Hoxha Museum.

Skanderbeg Square is located in the center of Tirana. To the left is the elongated building Palace of Culture, and opposite it, the Et'hem Bey Mosque. Demonstrators toppled the monumental statue of Enver Hoxha here in 1991.

In recent times, the grey concrete façades of many houses and streets in Tirana have been painted with brightly colored patterns (left). The Mayor of the city, Edi Rama, initiated these cosmetic changes and also planted trees and greenery as well as personally participating in the waste disposal measures taken.

Blloku quarter

Tirana has a vibrant nightlife – which comes as a surprise to many visitors. Restaurants and cafés are concentrated in the Blloku entertainment quarter, a district of villas which was previously almost entirely inhabited by party members.

National Museum

The National Museum, opened in 1981, with its striking façade mosaics, is located at Skanderbeg Square. Its exhibits relate to the country's history, from earliest times to the change of the regime in 1992.

Et'hem-Bey Mosque

The frescoes inside the mosque are considered to be the country's most beautiful. As the Hoxha regime banned all religious practice in 1967, the building remained closed until 1991, and visitors were unable to view the frescoes.

SKOPJE

Skopje is a modern European city with an Oriental appearance. It is characterized by churches, some of whose exteriors are reminiscent of mosques, as well as what is allegedly the largest bazaar west of Istanbul.

Skopje is located in a fertile plain on the Vardar River. This river forms the border between the industrial center on the southern bank and the historic Old Town (Stara Čaršija) with its Oriental air. Perched on a mountain above the Old Town, the ruins of the Byzantine Kale fortress look down on the maze of houses and alleyways. Skopje is the capital of the

A city with a turbulent history

Skopje's development has been shaped by various political and cultural factors over the centuries. From the Middle Ages onwards, the city belonged successively to Bulgaria, Byzantium and Serbia; this was followed by 500 years under the rule of the Ottoman Empire. Skopje formed part of the later Kingdom of Yugoslavia from 1918, and became

Church of St Panteleimon

With its frescoes, the church and monastery complex built in 1164 in Gorno Nerzi, not far from Skopje, is one of the country's most famous. It was founded by Alexius Angelus Comnenus of the noble Byzantine Komnenos dynasty, and dedicated to the patron saint of physicians.

the capital of the Yugoslavian constituent republic of Macedonia from 1945. The city has a population comprising several ethnic groups, and is indeed home to churches and mosques alike. It is both a metropolitan's and a bishop's see. The new experiences gained since the revolutions of the late 20th century now merge with the old influences which have developed over time, and all of this is reflected in the city's variety of cultural monuments, as well as the people's attitude to life.

Occident and Orient meet in Skopje. While the Old Town still displays the city's Ottoman heritage, high-rises soar in the background (right).

Republic of Macedonia, which emerged from the Yugoslavian constituent republic in 1991. The city has a population of around 580,000, five times greater than the country's second most populated city. Skopje is the seat of government, a university city with research institutes and museums, as well as an important industrial center. Various international trade fairs also make it Macedonia's economic hub. In 1963, the city suffered a severe earthquake which caused serious damage. Only the bazaar quarter remained relatively intact. Large parts of the rest of Skopje had to be rebuilt, resulting in the emergence of a modern city in some areas.

The stone bridge over the Vardar River, which connects Skopje's Old Town with the newer districts, dates back to the 15th century (far left). This sculpture (left) adorns the Kale Fortress, which was built high above Skopje during Byzantine times. The old fortress was restored after being destroyed in the earthquake of 1963.

Mustafa Pasha Mosque

The mosque, constructed in 1492, is situated on a hill above the bazaar. It was built by, and named after, Mustafa Pasha, the vizier of Sultan Selim I.

Mother Teresa House

The memorial to the Skopje-born Nobel Peace Prize winner, situated on Boulevard Makedonija, was given an unusual design, and incorporates elements of her adopted country of India.

Čaršija Bazaar

The Čaršija Bazaar north of the Old Town once stretched as far as the river. The Turkish influence can still be felt here among the teahouses, barber shops and mosques.

ATHENS

The cradle of democracy, the birth-place of European philosophy, theater and art – all this is ancient Athens. And the historic heritage of antiquity lives on in the hectic, modern metropolis.

The Greek capital is located in the heart of Attica, not far from the Mediterranean Sea and surrounded by mountain ranges. Counting 2.8 million inhabitants in the municipal area alone and more than three million in the commuter belt, Athens is the cultural and economic center of Greece. The city and the wider area around Athens suffer from huge traffic and environmental problems. Illustrious ancient names are linked with the city, philosophers, poets and statesmen, to whom we owe the ideals of democracy, as well as many world-famous buildings. Yet, aside from the beholders of this great past in the age-old settlement area around the Acropolis, there is also modern Athens, featuring structures from the 18th, 19th and 20th centuries. Even so, it is most of all Classicism, developed elsewhere and modeled on Greek antiquity, then "re-imported" to Greece, that is represented in different forms in the numerous public buildings. Even the old town district of Plaka boasts neoclassical villas dating from the 19th century, although otherwise a

very different atmosphere predominates here. In the narrow lanes, often connected by staircases, pubs, bars and restaurants stand shoulder to shoulder next to countless souvenir shops. This largely pedestrian area is often the first port of call for visitors, but it is also a desirable residential area for Athenians.

In Psirri, the former merchants' and artisans' quarter right next to the old town district of Plaka, the many bars and street cafés make for a very lively scene in the evenings (left). Large picture: Spectacular views across Athens and the Saronic Gulf unfold from Lykavittos Hill.

ATHENS

New Acropolis Museum

The museum, housed in a monumental new glass and steel structure at the foot of the Acropolis, was inaugurated in June 2009. On an exhibition area of 25,000 sq m (269,000 sq ft), spread across three floors, the ancient finds from the Athens temple mountain are displayed here. The new museum replaces an older one that was built in the 19th century and enlarged in the 20th century. The old Acropolis museum was located in a hollow below the Acropolis rock and could not be enlarged any further. This, however, had become necessary because archeological excavations had unearthed such a wealth of new objects in the meantime that many exhibits had to be put into storage instead of being displayed. The construction of a new museum had been debated since the 1970s. Finally, the decision was made to replace the museum, and construction commenced in 2002 following several architectural competitions. The old museum closed its doors two years before the inauguration of the new one so that the exhibits could be prepared for the move. The new building consciously sets modern standards in its museum presentation. Large columned halls reminiscent of the ancient temples admit plenty of light, bringing the exhibits to life. During construction, the rich remains of hitherto unknown ancient

Acropolis

The Acropolis perches on a 156-m-(512-ft-) high rock, in the middle of the city, enjoying views of the sea. In ancient Greece, an acropolis was a castle mountain overlooking a city. The one in Athens is the best known; since 1987 it has been a UNESCO World Cultural Heritage Site. The earliest structures served as a royal fortress and were erected in the Mycenaean period. When these had been destroyed during the Persian Wars, the statesman Pericles ordered

Theater of Dionysus

The Theater of Dionysus below the Acropolis was originally built as part of a sanctuary for Dionysus, the god of fertility. It is considered the cradle of theater in antiquity. Its sheer size, accommodating about 17,000 spectators, makes apparent how important the theater was for life in the city.

the mountain to be newly built up in 447 BC. In Athens, by then a democracy, the Acropolis was dedicated to the gods. The Parthenon was the first to be built, the temple of the patron goddess of Athens, together with the Propylaea, which formed the entrance gates to the sanctuary. Next, the Erechtheion and the Nike Temple were added. The structures of the Acropolis, especially the Parthenon and the Propylaea, became architectural models for the neoclassical style.

The Acropolis temple mountain and the Parthenon Temple dominate the cityscape in the heart of Athens (right).

structures were unearthed where the new building was to be sited. These were eventually integrated so that the load-bearing columns of the museum now stand on the foundations of ancient and medieval town houses. A glass floor permits visitors to glimpse the ancient walls, situated 8 m (26 ft) below their feet.

With the New Acropolis Museum, Athens at last boasts a generously sized forum where the many ancient objects found in the Acropolis area can be displayed in a dignified manner (left). Connected with this is also the expectation that the Parthenon Frieze, which had been removed by Lord Elgin and taken to the British Museum in London, will one day be returned to its ancient home.

Caryatids of Erechtheion

Stone statues of women with flowing robes serving as the load-bearing columns of important buildings are known as caryatids. This example is from the Ionic Erechtheion temple on the Acropolis, completed in 406 BC.

Nike Temple

The smallest temple of the Acropolis, dedicated to Nike, the goddess of victory, was probably the last built. Parts of the altar can still be seen today.

Parthenon

The largest temple of the Acropolis was the Parthenon, built between 447 and 432 BC. It was the sanctuary of Athena, the daughter of Zeus, eternal virgin and patron goddess of the city. Parthenon means "maiden's chamber".

ATHENS

Presidential Palace and Syntagma Square

On Syntagma Square, in the heart of the city, stand the Houses of Parliament, built from 1836 to 1840. The neoclassical structure was erected as a royal palace for Otto I of the Wittelsbach dynasty, who, after a series of diplomatic entanglements, was elected the king of Greece by the National Assembly in 1832. The building was financed by his father, the Bavarian King Ludwig I, and the master-builder was Friedrich von Gärtner, court architect to Ludwig I. It has been the seat of the Greek parliament since the 1930s. By the retaining wall of the ramp to the main entrance is the Tomb of the

Lykavittos Hill

Lykavittos, or Lycabettus Hill rises to 277 m (909 ft); it is Athens' highest elevation and backyard mountain. From its rocky summit, breathtaking views across the city and often far beyond can be enjoyed. A funicular railway proceeds through a tunnel in the rock to the top of the hill. In addition, there is a footpath in the upper parts guiding visitors via steep zigzag staircases.

At the summit of the cone-shaped mountain stands a picturesque, whitewashed chapel (Chapel of St George) featuring many turrets and crosses on its roof. An observation deck and a restaurant also

National Archeological Museum

The museum holds the most important collection of prehistoric and ancient artifacts relating to the art and everyday culture of the Hellenic world, including many sculptures. It is housed in a neoclassical building completed in 1874.

attract visitors. Below the peak is a large open-air stage where concerts and plays are performed during the summer months. According to Greek mythology, the goddess Athena created the Lykavittos when she accidentally dropped a large rock that was intended for the construction of the Acropolis.

View from the Acropolis of the pulsating old town and entertainment district of Plaka toward the Lykavittos Hill, the local mountain of the Greek metropolis.

Unknown Soldier. Here, the Evzones keep vigil, the president's guard wearing distinctive uniforms (picture right). At every full hour, visitors may witness the ceremonious changing of the guard.

The construction of the presidential palace heralded the start of a major phase in the urban development of Athens. National administrative and other public buildings appeared in various places, all in the classicist style, which generally predominates in the city's newer buildings. Also on Syntagma stands the elegant Hotel Grande Bretagne, one of three luxury hotels. It was built in 1862 and then as now served as a guesthouse for important state visitors.

The Houses of Parliament stand on Syntagma, or "Constitution Square" (Platia Sintagmátos) (far left). In front of the neoclassical building erected by the Wittelsbach King Otto, soldiers in historic costume ("Evzones") perform the changing of the guard every hour at the Tomb of the Unknown Soldier (left).

BUDAPEST

Magnificent buildings and wide boulevards, elegant coffee-houses and opulent Art Nouveau baths, just like in Arabian Nights – the Hungarian capital is often called the "Paris of the East", and not just because of its glamorous musical, theatrical and cultural scene.

Budapest was created in 1873, when the towns of Buda and Óbuda on the Danube right bank were combined with Pest on the left bank to form the new capital of Hungary. Today, Buda, located at the foot of the Castle Hill and the steeply rising Gellért Hill, is the calmer, more sedate part of the city. Shopping streets, business and banking quarters, the representative buildings of the state administration as well as the nightlife are all concentrated in Pest. The history of this area, which for a long time was the link and at the same time the point of conflict between East and West, has bequeathed an extraordinarily rich variety of historic monuments to the city. Baroque and Classicism alternate with Art Nouveau, Bauhaus and Postmodernism. The 150-year Turkish rule contributed much to the present look of the city, and evidence of the 19th-century Danube Monarchy is hard to overlook. At about two million inhabitants, Budapest is the largest and most important town in Hungary. It is also the seat of government as well as the cultural and economic center of the country.

The Danube divides Hungary's capital into the hilly district of Buda with its Castle complex on one side and the flat district of Pest with the domed Parliament Building on the opposite bank (large picture). Budapest is also famous for its thermal spas, such as the Széchenyi Bath, located in the middle of the municipal forest and the world-famous Gellért Spa and Bath (above, from the left).

BUDAPEST

Spas

Budapest is the only city in the world to be both, a capital and a health resort at the same time. Within the municipal area, 32 baths are fed with mineral water by 123 developed thermal spas today, and nine of these are officially approved health spas. Many other springs pour themselves into the Danube below ground. This means that the city possesses the largest linked mineral water deposits in Europe. The Celts already appreciated the hot springs, and the Romans called the city they built here in the first century BC, the capital of their Pannonia province, "Aquincum", roughly meaning "lots of water". Among the ruins of the ancient settlement in northern Buda, plenty of mosaics can be seen, featuring scenes from the Roman therapeutic and leisure baths. So far, 21 Roman baths have been accounted for. During the Ottoman rule, the bathing culture experienced a new boom. At least five of the present large spas were originally set up by the Turks. The most beautiful baths are elegant Art Nouveau structures from the time of the Austro-Hungarian Empire. In the Rudas Baths, on the Buda side of the Erzsébet or Elizabeth Bridge, the dome and the octagonal main room of the former Turkish building, dating from the 16th century, were kept. The Széchenyi Bath, situated in a small city forest, boasts the hottest thermal springs in Budapest.

World Cultural Heritage: the Buda Castle District

Buda Castle was built in the 13th century as a fortress on the southern tip of the Castle Hill and soon became the royal castle. Around the same time, a medieval town developed on the remaining part of the peak. Today the Castle District extends across roughly two-thirds of the plateau, from Bécsi kapu (Vienna Gate) in the north to Szent György tér (St George's Square) in front of the castle gates. For centuries, the focal point and the

center of power in the country were based here. After the devastations during the Turkish wars, the entire quarter had to be rebuilt. The narrow cobbled streets are lined by low baroque town houses with façades in different colors. Also standing in the castle district are the old Matthias Church, one of the main attractions, which was converted to the neo-Gothic style in the 19th century, as well as the former town hall, built around 1710, and the popular Fisherman's Bastion. The new Hilton Hotel, beside the Matthias Church, successfully integrated the ruins of the old Dominican Monastery in 1976. The Castle District with Castle Hill and Castle as well as the Danube banks and Andrássy út boulevard have all been listed as a UNESCO World Cultural Heritage Site since 1987.

View from Gellért Hill toward Castle Hill with Buda Castle in the foreground (above). The triple-aisled Gothic Matthias Church, the coronation church of the Hungarian monarchs, dates back to the 13th century (right).

This water basin in the men's steam room in the Gellért Bath is embellished with lavish Art Nouveau decorations. Probably the most famous of the baths in Budapest, it and the luxury hotel of the same name are located at the southern tip of Gellért Hill.

Fisherman's Bastion

The playful, fortress-like ensemble of the Fisherman's Bastion stands on the edge of the forecourt of the Matthias Church, on a steep slope down to the Danube. It was built in 1902 to plans by the Budapest architect Frigyes Schulek, combining Romanesque shapes with those from other periods. From the Víziváros or "Watertown" district below, monumental stairs lead up the Hill. The "Fisherman's Bastion" recalls the fact that once the guild of fishermen had a defensive installation there.

National Gallery

The museum, presenting Hungarian painting, sculpture and graphic arts from the Middle Ages to the present day, is housed on four floors of the Royal Palace. The gallery was founded in 1957 from the holdings of private and municipal collections. It also puts on changing special exhibitions on a variety of topics.

BUDAPEST

Parliament Building

Until 1847, the Hungarian diet or estate assembly had its seat in present-day Bratislava, which in the 19th century was part of Hungary. After the settlement with Austria and the establishment of the Austro-Hungarian double monarchy in 1867, a new building for the state parliament in Budapest was also soon planned. It was to take another 15 years however, until 1884, before the first spade of earth was turned, and another 20 years, until 1904, before the monumental structure was finally ready to be handed over for its intended use. The complex is situated in a commanding spot right on the Danube bank in Pest, forming a counterweight to the Buda Castle on the opposite riverbank – as was certainly intended by the builders. The building is adorned with 365 turrets and 88 statues and figures. It consists of a central tract and two symmetrical side-wings with a mostly neo-gothic façade that also features elements of the Baroque and the Renaissance. The top of the dome is 96 m (315 ft) above floor level, and the ceiling of the domed hall, which rests on pillars, attains a height of 27 m (89 ft). Altogether, the structure is 268 m (879 ft) long and comprises 691 rooms and ten courtyards, making it one of the largest parliamentary buildings in the world – some even call it the largest of all.

Inner City and Europe's Largest Synagogue

The inner-city districts of Budapest are situated within the 4-km- (2.5-mile-) long Grand Boulevard or Big Ring Road (Nagykörút), which traverses the city on the Pest side in a sweeping semicircle from the Petőfi Bridge in the south to the Margaret Bridge in the north. This boulevard was set out in the 19th century as part of a reorganization of the entire cityscape. Its route is lined by re-

markable fin-de-siècle buildings as well as major central squares. At the octagon, the Andrássy út boulevard crosses the ring road, and a short way farther along stands the West Station, built by Gustave Eiffel who also built the Eiffel Tower in Paris. The heart of old Pest is encircled by the inner Small Ring Road (Kiskörút), which also connects two Danube bridges in a semicircle. Near the Freedom Bridge stands the Great Market Hall. Built in 1894 to 1896, the structure has a steel frame and its façade is clad with colorful glazed tiles. Also in the center of the city, on the edge of the former ghetto, stands the Great Synagogue, dedicated in 1859, a three-aisled building with a flat roof. It accommodates 3,000 faithful and is the second-largest Jewish place of worship in the world after the synagogue in New York. Its courtyard features a Holocaust memorial as well as the mass graves where several thousand Jewish victims of National Socialism were buried. The birthplace of Theodor Herzl, the father of Zionism, once stood next to the Synagogue, until 1930; today the Jewish Museum is based here.

The main shopping street in the center of the city is the pedestrian mall Váci utca (above), which is dotted with expensive boutiques. The Oriental-looking Great Synagogue (right) presents itself in an historicizing Byzantine style.

Probably the most famous landmark in Budapest is the Parliament building on the left bank of the Danube (left). The design of the colossal complex paid homage to British democracy and London's Westminster Palace.

Great Market Hall

With its tall central section and side aisles, the iron and glass structure of the largest market hall of the city, dating back to the end of the 19th century, recalls a medieval church.

St Stephen's Basilica

The basilica, built between 1845 and 1906 in the style of the Neo-Renaissance, is the largest and most important church in the city. It is dedicated to the first king of Hungary, Stephen I (969–1038), who was canonized in 1083.

Heroes' Square

Commissioned for the millennium celebrations in 1896 and finally inaugurated in 1927, the square and its monuments to the heroes of Hungarian history form the worthy end of the Andrássy Avenue.

BUCHAREST

Despite its political, economic and social problems, Romania's capital, Bucharest, a metropolis of two million people in the historic Wallachia region, also has some very beautiful aspects.

The crucial turning point in the city's recent history came with the 1989 revolution, which ended with the execution of communist dictator, Nicolae Ceauşescu. Since then, Bucharest, once known as the "Paris of the East", has again been seeking connections with Europe, and entry into the European Union in 2007 was an important step towards this.

Bucharest acts as the focal point of Romania in every aspect – politically, economically and culturally. Those who live here not only have the best income possibilities in the country, but can also enjoy all the benefits of the metropolis: museums, theaters, universities, entertainment, shopping, recreational facilities, as well as Romania's largest sports stadium, and,

with Steaua Bucharest, also one of the most successful football clubs in Eastern Europe. Bucharest has been the capital for 350 years, but the proud princes of Wallachia, who were considered the founding fathers of present-day Romania, resided here as early as the 15th century. Bucharest became the royal residence of the newly established monarchy in 1877.

The elegant Macca Villacrosse Passage (left), built in Art Nouveau style in 1890/91, connects the commercial quarter with the Calea Victoriei, and is today home to shops and cafés. In the 1980s, Nicolae Ceauşescu ordered the construction of Boulevard Unirii, with its many fountains, which leads up to the gigantic Palace of Parliament (large picture).

Palace of Parliament

By building the "People's House" (today "Palace of Parliament"), the communist dictator Ceauşescu erected a memorial in his honor which really is impossible to miss. The monstrosity of a building (above) stands for the totalitarian state from which the Romanians freed themselves in the revolution of December 1989. Ceauşescu mercilessly had an entire historic quarter demolished to erect his neo-classicist "Cathedral of Power". The construction costs were astronomical, which was no surprise given the dimensions (65,000 sq m/ 699,400 sq ft base area, 450,000 sq m/ 4,842,000 sq ft useable floor area) of the elaborate interior, with ceremonial rooms and galleries (below), the underground bunker system and the

ritzy palace surrounds. Between 1984 and 1989, tens of thousands of people were employed to erect the second largest building in the world. However, Ceauşescu and his equally detested wife, Elena, were shot before its completion. The new government finished the construction and made it the headquarters of the parliament and various authorities. The dictator's eternalized megalomania has now also become a tourist attraction.

BUCHAREST

Hanul lui Manuc and the Lipscani Quarter

Those wanting to experience the charm of the old Bucharest should make their way to the Old Town quarter surrounding Lipscani Street, which was once the most important economic center in all of Wallachia. Every type of craftsman, from cob-

blers to goldsmiths, had their work-shop in the cramped alleyways, but it was the merchants who profited the most here, at the junction be-tween the East and West. And the traders with goods from Leipzig, i.e. the West, finally also gave their name to the largest street; it was called Lipscani, or "persons from Leipzig", from the 17th century on-

wards. South of Lipscani Street, however, things go even further back in time: Bucharest's oldest church, Curtea Veche (16th century) serves as a reminder of the Wal-lachian court, established in the 15th century, and which is now nothing but ruins. Next door, also on the site of the former court, is a particularly picturesque structure:

City center, Calea Victoriei

The best way to get around the vast city center is to follow the Calea Victoriei, Bucharest's grand boule-vard, which, lined with (sometimes grandiose) buildings from the 19th and early 20th centuries, cuts diago-nally through the entire inner city in a north-south direction. Here, it be-comes clear why Bucharest was nicknamed "the Paris of the East" before World War II. The Calea Victo-riei runs along the medieval trade route to Transylvania; since the 18th century, it has been Bucharest's most exclusive street, the "premier address", so to speak. The name "Victory Avenue" dates back to 1877-78, when Romania had fought for national independence, and be-came an autonomous kingdom after centuries of Turkish and Austro-Hun-garian rule. Of course, the neo-clas-sicist royal palace (Palatul Regal;

1937) was also built here, and today it houses the National Museum of Art. Also located on the Calea Vic-toriei, in the classicist building of the former main post office, is the inter-esting National History Museum, with the treasury of the Wallachian princes. The high-class hotels along the Calea Victoriei are similarly steeped in tradition, particularly the Athénée Palace Hilton in magnifi-cent Art Nouveau style – the most expensive hotel not only on that street, but probably in the whole country.

In the center of the city lies the magical Parcul Cişmigiu park complex built in 1810 (above). The oldest buildings along the grand boulevard, Calea Victoriei, include the ornately painted Kretzulescu Church from 1722 (right).

Hanul lui Manuc, which could be translated as "Manuc's Inn and Hospice". It was built in the early 19th century in the style of a caravanserai, with a large interior courtyard, wooden access balconies and extensive cellar vaults. Today, it once again serves its traditional purpose as a hotel and restaurant.

Built in the early 19th century as a hospice and inn for traveling merchants, Hanul lui Manuc is today one of Bucharest's finest historic monuments (far left). An unusual mix of Oriental bazaar and hip Western quarter can be experienced around Lipscani Street (left).

Romanian Athenaeum

The classicist domed building (around 1885) with its superb columned portico today serves as a concert hall. The statue of national dictator, Mihai Eminescu (1850–1889), stands guard in front of the Athenaeum.

National Museum of Art

Take a tour through 1,000 years of Romanian painting in the National Museum of Art, housed in the former royal palace. The icons in late-Byzantine style are particularly worth seeing.

Revolution Square

On December 21, 1989, 100,000 people gathered at the square before the then Central Committee of the Communist Party, and demanded Ceaușescu's resignation. Today, the square is called Piata Revolutiei, and the modern monument serves as a reminder of the people's bloody victory over the dictatorship.

BUCHAREST

The Village Museum (Muzeul satului)

The little Colentina River forms a series of natural lakes in Bucharest's north, and this charming landscape is home to one of Europe's oldest and largest open-air museums. The Muzeul Satului Village Museum on Kisileff Avenue was founded in 1936; today, it houses some 300 monuments from all over the country. These were taken down at their original locations and rebuilt here, at the capital's gates, true to original plans. Wooden churches, stately homesteads and thatched mud huts, watermills and windmills, as well as rural craft workshops, were thus saved from dilapidation, and now provide an overview of Romania's old village culture. Thanks to the authentic construction of monuments and historic buildings, visitors can also gain insights into pre-industrial everyday life – it is like traveling back in time. The aesthetic beauty of the folk art is particularly admired: furniture, pottery, wall hangings, carpets and icons are displayed in their original form, not yet diluted by tourist folklore. Its exhibitions and events also make the Village Museum a popular day trip for locals and foreigners alike. At least two hours should be allowed to tour the museum.

Palaces

Despite the many socialist high-rise blocks and gigantic buildings in the neo-classicist "wedding cake" style, Bucharest's old splendor can still be seen today in its numerous palaces. On the grand Calea Victoriei boulevard stands the luxurious Cantacuzino Palace, erected in the French Eclectic style in the early 20th century. It was built by Gheorghe G. Cantacuzino, who was the prime minister and one of Romania's richest citizens at the time. Lavishly decorated both inside and out, the ceiling paintings in the central hall, created by reputable painters of the time, are also impressive. The magnificent building was later briefly the home of the famous Romanian composer, George Enescu. It now serves as a museum,

which was established in Enescu's honor and memory in 1956.

Mogosoaia Palace is situated in an idyllic location by a lake approximately 14 km (9 miles) north of Bucharest. It is among Romania's best-known cultural monuments. Built from 1698 to 1702 by order of Prince Brâncoveanu, it had a turbulent history, but has largely preserved its very decorative architecture. This style, characterized by many stone sculptures and stuccowork, combines Italian Venetian with Oriental elements and coined the "typical" Romanian Brâncoveanu style. The nationalized palace has been a museum of feudal art since 1957.

The neo-baroque Cantacuzino Palace (right) was built on Calea Victoriei boulevard in the early 20th century. Mogosoaia Palace (above), built in 1698 and located somewhat out of the city, is typical of the Brâncoveanu style.

The Village Museum invites visitors to take a journey back through time into Romania's rural past. The churches, mills and farmhouses from the Wallachian and Transylvanian villages which can be viewed in this idyllic location just outside the metropolis of Bucharest are up to 300 years old.

CHIŞINĂU

With a population of 600,000, the capital of the former Soviet Republic of Moldova, which has been independent since 1991, is the country's largest city, and lies at its center, by the Bîc River.

Chişinău is certainly not a dazzling hub of activity. Just by looking at the capital, it is clear that Moldova is one of Europe's poorest countries. The average monthly income is 30 Euros, so it is no wonder that so many Moldovans work abroad. Democracy is also on shaky ground, and the ethnic minorities in a country predominantly inhabited by Ro-manians mean there is potential for further political conflicts. Moldova's problems are also those of its capital city, and travelers should be prepared for this. One tourist attraction is located outside the city: In the wine-growing village of Cricova, it is possible to visit a giant underground tunnel system storing over a million wine bottles.

Green capital

Chişinău is known for its many beautiful parks. And as its climate is very pleasant due to its proximity to the Black Sea, the green oases can be enjoyed to the fullest extent. Located centrally on the Bulevardul Ştefan cel Mare şi Sfînt is the park of the same name, with the "Alley of Classics" lined with bronze busts of famous Moldovans. The statue of the national hero, whom the Moldovans incidentally share with the Romanians, greets visitors at the entrance. Ştefan cel Mare, or Stephen the Great (1433–1504), is considered to be Moldova's most prominent voivode. His principality stretched over present-day Moldova, as well as the Romanian province of the same name. In forty-seven legendary battles, he defended it against the Ottomans and Tartars.

The Parcul Catedralei is also centrally located. It was opened like the Nativity Cathedral in 1836, and is closely associated with the extensive urban redevelopment under Russian rule, which also produced the representational Bulevardul Ştefan cel Mare şi Sfînt. As the capital of the tsarist Governorate of Bessarabia (1818–1918), during which time it was called Kishinev, Chişinău went from being a rural settlement to a proper metropolis.

The parks at the edge of the city, created during the 1950s, are significantly larger. South of the center is the Valley of Mills (Parcul Vale Morilor; 114 ha/282 acres), with its vast artificial lake, and the Rose Valley (Parcul Valea Trandafirilor; 145 ha (358 acres). This amusement park with its big wheel is particularly popular among locals from the Botanica district, a gigantic settlement of pre-fabricated high-rise blocks. Its name dates back to the Botanical Garden near the 19th-century College of Viticulture. The largest park sprawls north of the city center: with its two lakes, the "Park at the Spring" (Parcul La Izvor; 150 ha/371 acres) is a true haven of local recreation.

The square in front of the Nativity Cathedral, with the Parcul Catedralei (right), is a popular meeting place.

The Catedrala Sfîntul Mare Mucenic Teodor Torin, inaugurated in 1858, attracts attention with its pale-blue paintwork and lovely onion domes (far left). This monument (left) serves as a reminder of the liberation from fascism.

Triumphal Arch

Chişinău gained importance as the capital of the Russian Governorate of Bessarabia in the 19th century. The Porţile Sfînte triumphal arch, erected in 1841, which stands in the Parcul Catedralei opposite the present-day seat of government, expresses the imperialistic aims of the tsars.

Nativity Cathedral

Chişinău's most important church is the Catedrala Naşterea Domnului – the Cathedral of the Nativity of the Lord – with its freestanding bell tower and high dome. The domicile of the metropolitan of the Moldovan Orthodox Church, built in classicist style from 1830 to 1836, forms a line of sight with the Triumphal Arch and the parliament building (in the background).

SOFIA

Bulgaria's vivacious capital, which has been the country's political and cultural center since the nation was founded in 1879, after 500 years of Ottoman rule, lies in a spectacular mountain landscape.

Bulgaria's capital, Sofia, rises up in front of the Vitosha Mountains, which start to emerge in the city's south, like a cleverly designed stage setting. Archaeologists found millennia-old traces of settlements here, while other structures today stand on the ruins of Roman buildings. Although twenty years have passed since the fall of communism, Bulgaria and its capital are still wrestling for economic ties with Europe. But this does not mean the metropolis is sinking into a state of lethargy; on the contrary, it is teeming with life. The love of folk music, whether traditional or pop ("Chalga"), runs deep: Sofia is famous for its many clubs and restaurants offering live music. However, art lovers will also find what they are looking for. Although Sofia presents itself as a city of the 19th to 20th centuries in which examples of historic architecture are few and far between – hardly anything has been preserved from Ottoman times –, the medieval church in the Boyana district and the art treasures in the National History Museum alone are worth the trip.

Alexander Nevsky Cathedral

Sofia is symbolized by the neo-Byzantine Alexander Nevsky Cathedral, which is probably the most impressive 20th-century religious building in the entire Balkan region. It was completed in 1912 and inaugurated in 1924. The exterior of the giant building, made up of several different domes, is overwhelming, not least because of its exposed location at a vast square in the heart of the city. Inside, the opulent furnishings with mosaics, wall paintings and icons captivate visitors. Bulgarian artists and well-known Russian masters were involved in its construction. The architect was also a Russian – Alexander Pomerantsev, who built Moscow's GUM department store. And the church's patron, the Russian national hero Alexander Nevsky, is yet another link to Russia. The close relationship between little

Bulgaria and its big Slavic brother can be explained in terms of history: To liberate the Orthodox Balkan people from the rule of the Muslim Turks and provide them with access to the Mediterranean, Russia waged war on the Ottoman Empire in 1877–78 and enabled the founding of the independent Principality of Bulgaria (1879).

Alexander Nevsky Cathedral (above) impresses visitors with its magnificent furnishings. Standing in front of the monumental domed construction is the parliament building, with the equestrian statue of Russian Tsar Alexander I (right).

A monument, standing in front of the National Library, is commemorated to the two patrons SS. Cyril and Methodius – the famous apostles to the Slavs and founders of the Old Bulgarian literature (left). The Ivan Vazov National Theater is a neo-classicist gem by Viennese theater architects Hermann Hellmer and Ferdinand Fellner (far left).

SOFIA

Boyana Church

Boyana was once the preferred residential area of high-ranking communist officers due to its beautiful location in the Vitosha Mountains and its proximity to the city center (approx. 8 km/5 miles). But for art connoisseurs, the main attraction is the unique church (UNESCO World Heritage Site), whose oldest sections date back to the 10th century. In the 13th century, it was given a two-story annex building which was painted with stunning frescoes by an unknown artist. They are among the most important medieval artworks of the Eastern Church, and portray the biblical history in vivid images.

City center

In the planned inner city, the best way to get one's bearings is to follow the wide boulevards which terminate at the central Ploštad Nezavisimost Square – a good starting point for city tours. (Those with language problems should ask for the Sheraton; it is very close by and everyone knows it). To the north are the market halls, the Banya Bashi Mosque (1576) – one of the few monuments preserved from Otto-

Sofia, the city's patron saint

Perched atop a column above bustling Batemberg Square is the modern statue of Sofia, with her golden face. The old Byzantine church of Sveta Sofia (6th century), after whom the city is named, lies in the nearby university quarter.

man times –, as well as the largest synagogue in the Balkans. Running westwards is the Bulevar Zar Osvoboditel, whose side streets lead to representational public buildings and the Alexander Nevsky Cathedral. For strolling and shopping, head south along the Bulevar Vitoša: the whole city seems to gather here in fine weather.

Only small churches were allowed to be built under Ottoman rule – for example the late-medieval Sveta Petka Samardjiiska (right), which is dwarfed by the ZUM department store, the former Bulgarian Communist Party headquarters and the Presidential Palace (from left).

National History Museum

Boyana is also home to Bulgaria's largest and richest museum, housed in the former residence of the national leader, Todor Zhivkov, who was toppled in 1989. Nine thousand years of history comes alive in the National History Museum.

The frescoes in the Boyana Church are considered the highlight of Bulgaria's medieval religious paintings, and are a UNESCO World Heritage Site (far left). The treasures of the National History Museum (left) also include the world-famous "Thracian gold".

The Rotunda of St George

Sofia's oldest monument, the Rotonda Sveti Georgi, can be visited in the court-yard of the Sheraton Hotel. The small rotunda from Late Antiquity (fourth to fifth centuries), with its medieval wall paintings, marks out the area where the thermae were once situated during Roman times. It served as a mosque under Ottoman rule (1396–1878).

Central market hall

An appetizing variety of Bulgaria's special treats is on offer in the restored market hall (Centralni Hali). Look, smell and taste is the motto at the approximately 100 stalls, which are open from seven o'clock in the morning until midnight. The Bulgarian wines are also worth tasting. They are better than their reputation suggests!

VALLETTA

Once built by knights, the smallest capital in the European Union is perched picturesquely on a peninsula between two natural bays. With its bastions and old limestone houses, Valletta is a veritable treasure trove.

After the knights of the Order of St John were given the islands of Malta as a fief in 1530, they were forced to defend their new home against Turkish attacks on several occasions, prompting them to build the Saint Elmo Fort at the tip of a headland on the peninsula. In 1566, the Grand Master of the knights' order, Jean de la Valletta, decided to create a city beneath the fort: this was to be their new capital, named after its founder. Today, the city has a population of just under 10,000, making it the largest in the country. As an archbishopric, a university town and major port regularly visited by cruise ships, Valletta is the economic and cultural center of Malta. The most famous buildings are St John's Cathedral, erected from 1573 to 1577, and the Grand Master's Palace (1574), where the Maltese Parliament today convenes. There are so many buildings and monuments of historic importance in Valletta that UNESCO declared the entire Old Town a World Heritage Site in 1980.

Old Town and bastions

The warlike circumstances existing at the time of Valletta's founding are unmistakably reflected in the city's overall appearance: It is surrounded on all sides by a ring of defense walls and bastions, which soar to heights of up to 100 m (328 ft). From the chessboard layout of the streets, it is clear that the city was planned to a specific design. These plans were devised by Francesco Laparelli, the leading military architect of his time, whom Pope Pius V had initially sent to Malta as an advisor in 1565. Contained within the ring of forts is a delightful Old Town with numerous churches and grand palaces dating back to the time of the city's founding. The church of Ta' Vittoria (Our Lady of Victories) was the first building to be completed by the knights of the order in 1578. Many of the palaces originally served as the seat of the nationality-

based sections of the knightly order, the so-called "langues" (tongues). Some of these are today the headquarters of state authorities. The Old Town is characterized by countless oriels of all shapes and sizes, which adorn almost every façade. Even in early times, the knights created magnificent gardens on the bastions, and, with their lush vegetation, these form the green oases in a townscape otherwise characterized by rock and stone. The view from the Upper Barracca Gardens over the Grand Harbour is famous.

Oriels and balconies adorn the houses in the narrow alleyways of the Old Town (above). Valletta lies on a rocky peninsula, protected by mighty walls and bastions covered in vegetation (large picture).

The opulent baroque interior of
St John's Cathedral is considered one
of the finest in all the Mediterranean.
The church's art treasures include the
Grand Masters' sarcophagi, as well
as Caravaggio's famous painting
"The Beheading of John the Baptist".

Carmelite Church

Over twenty-five churches crowd
Valletta's small area of just 900 m
by 630 m (2,953 ft by 2,067 ft). The
Carmelite Church, built in 1573, whose
imposing white dome appears to
float above the rooftops, is one of
the largest on the island.

Grand Master's Palace

The simple Renaissance palace is
lavishly decorated inside, including the
Armory Corridor with its paintings, colorful marble floors, and suits of armor.

Auberge de Castille
et Léon

In the 16th century, an auberge was
established in Valletta for every language community within the Order
of Malta. The most impressive is the
baroque-style building by Andrea Belli.

NICOSIA

Nicosia has been a divided city for decades. Under international law, the entire city belongs to the Republic of Cyprus; but in actual fact, the northern part of Nicosia falls under the administration of the non-internationally-recognized Turkish Republic of Northern Cyprus.

Northern part of the city

The northern part of Nicosia is the capital of the Turkish Republic of Northern Cyprus, which was proclaimed in 1983, but which is only acknowledged as a sovereign state by Turkey. North Nicosia, with some 75,000 inhabitants is the largest city in northern Cyprus. It is the seat of government and administrative center of the country, which is nevertheless heavily economically dependent on Turkey. Atatürk Square, surrounded by taverns and cafés, is the main square in the Old Town. Here, monumental depictions of the father of modern Turkey peer down on street café patrons from roofs and façades. The historic monuments include the

Capital of (southern) Cyprus

After the north broke away, the southern part of Nicosia remained the capital of the now smaller Republic of Cyprus. With a population of some 350,000, this section, primarily inhabited by Greek-speaking Cypriots, is the larger of the city's two halves. Like North Nicosia for the north, so south Nicosia is the most important city in the southern region. When the country was divided in 1974, the border was drawn down the middle of the historic Old Town, which has nonetheless preserved its lively character. The traditional restaurants and cafés are joined by the Laikí Jitoniá entertainment district, which was created in 1984 through systematic restorations and re-openings. The southern

Old Town is also home to Odos Lidras (Ledra Street), a pedestrian zone and shopping street with stores, boutiques and outlets of famous international stores. The focal point of South Nicosia is lively Platía Eleftherías (Freedom Square), situated in front of the d'Avila Bastion at the southern edge of the Old Town. The attractions here include the Ágios Giannis Cathedral (St John's Cathedral), built on the foundations of a Crusaders' church in 1662, and housing an impressive fresco depicting the crucifixion. Adjacent to this is the Archbishop's Palace, constructed from 1956 to 1961 to mark the independence of what was then a still-united Cyprus. It was the residence of Makarios III, who was both the archbishop and country's president.

The statue of Archbishop Makarios III, who led Cyprus to independence from British colonial rule, watches over the Archbishop's Palace (above). The commemorative freedom monument in the Old Town is also a reminder of this event (right).

"Great Inn" (Büyük Han), a giant complex from the 16th century, as well as the 17th-century Arabahmet Mosque, with an interesting Muslim cemetery. The city's main mosque, the Selimiye Mosque, was built as a Christian coronation cathedral under the name of St Sophia Cathedral in the 13th century.

The "Great Inn" Büyük Han, built in 1572, is today home to art and craft stores, galleries and a restaurant (far left). The Selimiye Mosque in the Turkish part of Nicosia has Gothic origins. It was erected as the St Sophia Cathedral, and re-dedicated by the Ottomans in 1571 (left).

St John's Cathedral

The interior of the Orthodox Cathedral was painted from 1736 to 1756. The frescoes depict themes such as a crucifixion and the legend of the church's foundation, which is based on an apparition of Barnabas the Apostle.

Laikí Jitoniá

The Laikí Jitoniá entertainment district in South Nicosia was created as part of extensive restorations in the area. It is home to many fine taverns with alfresco dining areas conducive to enjoying the balmy summer nights.

Archeological Museum

Bronze nude statue of Roman Emperor Septimius Severus in the Archeological Museum (Cyprus Museum), which houses the world's largest collection of archeological finds originating from Cyprus.

ANKARA

The insignificant Anatolian provincial city became the capital when the Turkish Republic was founded in 1923. It then rapidly developed into a large metropolis, which is today home to some five million people.

Ankara is the country's seat of government and second largest city after Istanbul, and is also one of Turkey's most important economic centers. Two international airports, three opera houses, theaters and universities, the imposing skyline, the subway system and the eight-lane ring road are proof that Ankara has long shed its small-town image: The Central Anatolian metropolis is booming! Whether it becomes part of Europe in future depends on the decisions made by the EU and the government in Ankara. Orient or Occident, the Western or Islamic world – Turkey's affiliation is not so clearly defined. Even Ankara's cityscape has two faces, with winding alleyways on the one hand, and main urban arteries on the other; traditional Turkish architecture is juxtaposed with post-modern highrises. The ideas of the city's founder, Mustafa Kemal, who proclaimed the republic in 1923 and bore the honorary name of Atatürk (the Father of the Turks), were oriented towards the West. He abolished the sultanate and caliphate, introduced the Latin

Modern Ankara

With Turkey's largest opera house, numerous theaters, five symphony and chamber orchestras and a classical ballet company, Western high culture is certainly very much at home in Ankara. The Turkish metropolis has a typically European look and feel in its inner districts of Kizilay and Kavaklidere. The fact that Atatürk was advised by German architects and town planners when creating his new capital is today still evident in the wide boulevards, parks and representational administrative and government buildings.

The chic promenades and new Atakule Tower are great for shopping. However, at every turn, one is reminded that this is not just any old European metropolis: The background noises and smells are distinctly oriental. It is said that the people of Ankara have their head in Europe and their heart in Asia. And visitors will enjoy the exciting mix. This city is full of surprises. And energy – which is no wonder, given that two-thirds of the population are under the age of 30. The city's incessant growth does, however, pose a problem. The urban sprawl extends to the outskirts, where more and more haphazard settlements are springing up. These are home to all the new arrivals who come here from rural Anatolia seeking a better future.

The Turkish capital appears here as an endless sea of houses with striking high-rise buildings (above). The giant Kocatepe Mosque (right) was modeled on the classic Ottoman mosques (right).

script and the concept of Sunday as a day of rest, made religion a private matter in his secular state, and moved the capital to the geographic center of the country, far from Istanbul, the old capital of the Ottoman Empire, which was now history and had been replaced by a modern, national state.

The mausoleum of Turkey's founding father, Mustafa Kemal Atatürk (1881–1938), rises up on a hill above Ankara. The visitor numbers prove how popular the "Father of the Turks" still is: Every year, over ten million Turks come here to pay homage to Atatürk.

ANKARA

Citadel (Kalesi)

Old Ankara is symbolized by the so-called Citadel (Kalesi), which perches atop an exposed, 978-m- (2,329-ft-) high rocky hill and constitutes the city's oldest urban center. It is more than just a fortress: it is a historic residential area with an inner and outer city, established during Byzantine times, probably the 7th century. The inner city is of great historic interest, and its walls and gates serve as a reminder of its original function as a fortress. According to legend, it was founded by the fabulously rich King Midas of Greek legend, but archaeological finds suggest it emerged during the heyday of the Hittite culture

Eski Ankara – the Old Town

Sprawling beneath the citadel is the Old Town (Eski Ankara), the former Anatolian provincial town which, in 1923, had just 30,000 inhabitants. It has an extremely loud, lively atmosphere, the streets are congested with traffic, and the narrow alleyways do not always live up to the romantic expectations of what the Orient should be. The bazaar quarter, however, is a dream come true: Narrow streets and spacious courtyards with countless little shops, including the grocery and flea market, are all conducive to a spot of shopping and strolling – and not just for tourists either. Because, as picturesque as the bazaar quarter is, it is part of everyday life for the locals here. The Old Town has been settled since ancient times. The Romans have left their mark on the architecture, and relics from the time of the Seljuks have also been preserved, such

as a rare 12th-century mosque with wooden columns. There are also many fine examples of Ottoman architecture, namely the Haci Bayram Mosque (15th and 18th centuries). Anyone who visits the outstanding Museum of Anatolian Cultures will kill two birds with one stone, so to speak. Not only is it home to unique treasures from Antiquity, but it also displays them in interesting historic buildings: the bazaar and caravanserai, which are today part of the museum complex, were established at the base of the citadel as early as the 15th century.

Residential homes built using the ancient wooden construction method can be found not far from the citadel in Ankara (above). Several hills in the metropolis serve as lookout points, offering sweeping views over the Old and New Town (right).

(c. 1450–1200 BC). Today, tourists amble through the citadel's picturesque winding alleys. Since the renovation, restaurants, cafés, carpet merchants and antique dealers have all moved into the old houses, some of which are still built of clay and wood. Hawkers offer souvenirs, while spices and the popular snack Kuruyemifl can be bought at roadside stalls. The Alaadin Mosque, in traditional Ottoman style, is also worth seeing. And, of course, no visitor should miss out on the magnificent view from the White Castle (Akkale), erected at the highest point of the citadel.

Traditional Turkish architecture with protruding upper floors can still be seen in Ankara's citadel (far left). Visitors can buy refreshments from the small grocery stores in the narrow alleyways (left)

Temple of Augustus

The Temple of Augustus, whose ruins can be visited in the Old Town at the base of the citadel, was built on the remains of an old Phrygian temple in 10 AD. The Kingdom of Galatia in Anatolia was influenced by the Romans even then, but did not become a Roman province, with its capital of Ancyra, for another fifteen years. Other ancient relics include the Roman bath, amphitheater and the Column of Julian.

Hittite Museum

Ankara's biggest attraction is the Museum of Anatolian Cultures (Anadolu Medeniyetleri Müzesi), which is usually epitomized in the Hittite Museum. The unique archaeological collection is world famous, and displays millennia-old treasures of advanced Anatolian civilizations, from the Paleolithic to Roman Antiquity. The picture above shows a Hittite stone relief depicting a hunting scene.

Notre-Dame Cathedral in the heart
of the French capital, Paris, is one of
the iconic images of Europe. From
here, the gothic style advanced across
large parts of Europe.

EUROPE AT A GLANCE

SVERIGE
SUOMI FINLAND
ROSSIJA
Respublika Komi
Zapadno- Sibirskaja ravnina

Nordkapp · Hammerfest · Vadsø · Nordkyn · Kirkenes · Severomorsk · Murmansk · Surgut
Tromsø · Alta · Inari · Muonio · Moncegorsk · Apatity · Kandalakša · o.Kolguev · Nar'jan-Mar · Njagan' · Hanty-Mansijsk · 125
Narvik · Kiruna · Rovaniemi · Kuusamo · m.Kanin Nos · p-ov Kanin · Pečora · gora Telpoziz 1617 · Ob' · Kujbyšev
2111 Kebnekaise · 539 · Sodankylä · Ust'-Cil'ma · Njagan' · Tara · Tatarsk
Gällivare · Kemi · Luleå · Kuhmo · Čésskaja guba · Uhta · Mezen' · Tobol'sk
Storuman · Hailuoto Karlö · Oulu · Respublika Karelija · Arhangel'sk · Pinega · Konda · OMSK
Östersund · Umeå · Kokkola · Kajaani · Segozero · Severodvinsk · Onega · Tavda · Isil'kul' · k-l.Siletiteniz
Härnösand · Vaasa · Jyväskylä · Savonlinna · Petrozavodsk · Onežskoe ozero · Kem' · Beloe more · Kotlas · Serov · Tjumen' · Irbit · Išim · Petropavl
Sundsvall · Pori · Tampere · Mikkeli · Lappeenranta · Vel'sk · Muraši · gora Konžakovskij Kamen' 1569 · Kamensk-Ural'skij · Kurgan · Köksetau
Hudiksvall · Hämeenlinna · Lahti · Lodejnoe Pole · Konoša · Syktyvkar · Solikamsk · Berezniki · Nižnij Tagil · EKATERINBURG · Zapadnoe · Ščučinsk
Gävle · Helsinki Helsingfors · Kolpino · oz.Beloe · Vologda · Kirov · Krasnokamsk · PERM' · Glazov · Votkinsk · Zlatoust · Miass · ČELJABINSK · Esim · Kostanaj
Åbo Turku · Puškin · SANKT-PETERBURG · Čerepovec · Galič · Kotel'nič · Igra Udmurtskaja Resp. · Sarapul · Neftekamsk · g.Jamántau · Troick · k-l.Kušmuryn · Rudnyj
Uppsala · Tallinn · Narva · Rybinskoe vdhr. · Kostroma · Joškar-Ola Resp.Marij-El · KAZAN' · UFA 1640 · Magnitogorsk · Arkalyk
Västerås · EESTI · Luga · Novgorod · Rybinsk · Jaroslavl' · Ivanovo · Čeboksary Čavš Resp. · Naberežnye Čelny · Respublika Baškortostan · Torgai ústírti
Stockholm · Hiiumaa s. · Pärnu · Tartu · Pskov · Borovici · Kinešma · NIŽNIJ NOVGOROD · Vladimir · Murom · Simbirsk · Oktjabr'skij · Salavat · Kumertau · Orsk · Torgaj
Norrköping · Saaremaa s. · Kuressaare · Čudskoe ozero · Tver' · Toržok · Sergiev-Posad · Orehovo-Zuevo · Saransk · SAMARA · Dimitrovgrad · Buguruslan · Novotroick
Linköping · Visby · Gotland · LATVIJA · oz.Il'men · Ržev · Odincovo · Kolomna · Mordovskaja Resp. · Tol'jatti · Buzuluk · Orenburg · Aktöbe · Oktjabr'
Kalmar Öland · Jūrmala · Rīga · Velikie Luki · Vjaz'ma · MOSKVA · Rjazan' · Šack · Syzran' · Novokujbyševsk · Oral · Šalkar · Aralsk
Karlskrona · Liepāja · Daugavpils · Vitebsk · Smolensk · Obinsk · Tula · Kuznck · Penza · Vol'sk · Balakovo · Žambejtü · Ateke Bi
Bornholm · Ventspils · LIETUVA · Polack · Orša · Kaluga · Micurinsk · Tambov · Saratov · Eršov · Čapaev · Embi · Aral tengizi
Gdynia · Klaipėda · Šiauliai · Panevėžys · 293 · Orel · Elec · Balašov · Engel's · KAZAHSTAN · 53 · Orol dengizi
Gdańsk · Kaliningrad · Kaunas · Vilnius · ROSSIJA · Mahilëv · Brjansk · Voronež · Borisoglebsk · Kamyšin · Inderborskij · Makat · 250 · Moynak
Elbląg · MINSK · BELARUS' · Klincy · Železnogorsk · Kursk · Volgogradskoe vodohranilišče · Aterau · UZBEKISTAN · Nukus
Koszalin · Olsztyn · Hrodna · Sluck · Homel' · Černihiv · Belgorod · Possoš · VOLGOGRAD · Volžskij · Antubinsk · Ústírt
Bydgoszcz · Białystok · Baranaviči · Mazyr · Sumy · Surovikino · Millerovo · Svetlyj Jar · Ganjuškino · Zhanaozen
Poznań · WARSZAWA · Brėst · Pinsk · Korosten' · KYJIV · Brovary · CHARKIV · Šahty · Volgodonsk · Astrahan' · a-l Kulandy · Tubek Tub-Karagan · Aktau
POLSKA · Siedlce · Radom · Lublin · Rivne · Žytomyr · Lubny · Poltava · Slovjans'k · Luhans'k · ROSTOV-NA-DONU · Jaškul' · Kalmykija · Elista
Łódź · Wrocław · Kielce · Łuc'k · Bila Cerkva · Kremenčuk · DONEC'K · Taganrog · Ipatovo · Lagan · Kočubej · m.Pesčany
Legnica · Opole · Częstochowa · Rzeszów · UKRAJINA · Vinnycja · DNIPROPETROVS'K · Mariupol' · Kropotkin · Stavropol' · Čečenskaja Respublika · Mahačkala
Liberec · Ostrava · Kraków · Katowice · Beskidy 2655 · L'viv · Ternopil' · Kirovohrad · Nikopol' · Zaporižž'ja · Novo-rossijsk · Majkop · Čerkessk · Nazran · Groznyj · Dagestan · Derbent · TURKMENISTAN
Brno · ČESKÁ REP. · Olomouc · Ivano-Frankivs'k · Kam'janec-Podil'skyj · Mykolajiv · Melitopol' · Berdjans'k · Adygeja · Kar.-Cerk. · g.El'brus 5642 · Kab.-Balk. · Vladikavkaz · Guba · BAKI · m.Tjulenij
Wien · SLOVENSKÁ REP. · Černivci · MOLDOVA · Bălţi · Cherson · Kerč · Krasnodar · Kutaisi · TBILISI · AZERBAIJAN · Gyzylarbat · Balkanabat
Bratislava · Debrecen · Užhorod · Satu Mare · Suceava · Chişinău · Azovskoe More · Džankoj · GEORGIA · Gjumri · ARMENIA · Kirovakan · Gänžä · Türkmenbaši · Čeleken · Gonbad-e
Graz · Győr · BUDAPEST · Oradea · Iaşi · Bender · ODESA · Jevpatorija · Tuapse · Soči · Suhumi · Batumi · ERWAN · Agdam · Bilasuvar · Gorgan
Maribor · MAGYARORSZÁG · Miskolc · Baia Mare · Carpaţii Orientali 2100 · Bacău · Simferopol' · Sevastopol' · Kryms'kyj p-iv · Jalta · Artvin · Kars · Maku · Sari
Zagreb · Pécs · Szeged · Arad · ROMÂNIA · Sibiu 2544 · Târgu Mureş · Braşov · Galaţi · Ba · Trabzon · Horasan · Ağrı · TABRÎZ · Kuhha-ye Alborz 5601
HRVATSKA · Subotica · Timişoara · Deva · Buzău · Brăila · Delta Dunării · Sinop · Ordu · Bayburt · Erzurum · Van · Miyaneh · Qazvin · Semnan
Novi Sad · Osijek · Carpaţii Meridionali · Ploieşti · BUCUREŞTI · Constanţa · Samsun · Erzincan · Van Gölü · Orūmīyeh · Zanjan · Saveh · TEHRĀN
Banja Luka · BEOGRAD · Drobeta-Turnu Severin · Pitești · Ruse · N.Kaliakra · Varna · Küre Dağları · Çorum · Bingöl · Güney Doğu Toroslar · Bukan · Qom · Qazvin
BOSNA I HERCEGOVINA · SRBIJA · Craiova · Vidin · Dunărea · Pleven · Šumen · Burgas · Gerede · Yozgat · Sivas · Elâzığ · Diyarbakır · Nusaybin · Arbil · Sanandaj · Hamadan
Split · Sarajevo · Foča · Niš · BĂLGARIJA · Stara Zagora · Zonguldak · Kocaeli · Düzce · Kırıkkale · Kayseri · Malatya · Gaziantep · Hasakeh · As Sulaymaniyah · Kermanshah · ESFAHAN
Mostar · Dubrovnik · CRNA GORA · Priština · Plovdiv · İSTANBUL · Sakarya · Yalova · ANKARA · Kahraman-Maraş · Şanlıurfa · AL MAWSIL (MOSUL) · Kirkuk · Qars-e-Shirin · 4294
Podgorica · KOSOVO · Skopje · SOFIJA · Blagoevgrad · Edirne · Eskişehir · Bursa · TÜRKİYE · Adıyaman · HALAB · Raqqa · Dei Al Zôr · Khorramabad · 2900 · Dezful
Foggia · Bari · Durrës · Tiranë · MACEDONIA · Bitola · Seres · Kavala · Alexandroúpoli · Bandırma · Balıkesir · Kütahya · Afyon · Niğde · ADANA · Gaziantep · İskenderun · Hama · HALAB · Mari · Euphrates · Ba'qubah · BAGHDAD · Ahvaz
Táranto · Brindisi · ALBANIA · Vlorë · Thessaloníki · Çanakkale · Limnos · Manisa · Uşak · Tarsus · İçel · Hatay · Al-Ladiqiya · SYRIA · Ar Ramadi · Al Kut · Al 'Amarah
Lecce · S.Maria di Léuca · Kérkyra (Korfu) · Ioánnina · Lárissa · Vólos · Mitilíni · Lésvos · İZMİR · Denizli · Isparta · Konya · Karaman · Silifke · Antalya · Hatay · Al Kuwayt
2917 · ELLÁDA · Évia · Hios · Çeşme · Aydın · Toros Dağları · Alanya · KIBRIS · Hama · 1390 · Ar Ramadi · Karbala · IRAQ · Al Basra · Abadan
Reggio di Calabria · Ólimpos · Pátra · Pireás · ATHÍNA · Kikládes · Bodrum · Marmaris · Kale · Yardımcı Burnu · Lefkosia · Ammochostos · Tartus · Homs · Tadmur · An Najaf · An Nasiriyah · Khorram Shar
Catánia · Agrínio · Pirgos · Pelopónnisos · Spárti · Sparti · Kos · Ródos · Pafos · Lemesos · DIMASHQ (DAMASCUS) · As Salmy · Jahrah
Siracusa · Kalamáta · Kíthira · Kárpathos · LEBANON BEIRUT · 1803 · 402 · KUWAIT Al Kuwayt (Kuwait)
Capo delle Correnti · Hania · Irákliio · Kríti · Sitía · KÝPROS · Hefa (Haifa) · Nezerat · As Sweidaa · Turayf · Ar'ar · As Salmy · Hafar al Batin
Akra Kriós 2456 · Tel Aviv · AMMAN · Al Haditha · Al Harrah · JORDAN · SAUDI ARABIA
MEDITERRANEAN SEA · ISRAEL · Jerusalem · Yeriho · Al Wádyan · Rafha

Black Sea
Caspian Sea
Aegean Sea
Ionian Sea
Baltic Sea
Adriatic Sea
Gulf of Bothnia
Azovskoe More
Mesopotamia

The Parthenon Temple on the Acropolis in Athens. In ancient Greece, the intellectual foundations were laid for our present-day democracies.

The Ancient Roots of Democracy in Europe

Solon, Cleisthenes, Pericles, Plato and Aristotle, Cicero and Marcus Aurelius – did those ancient philosophers and statesmen guess that their ideas and work might one day become the foundations of European culture? Hardly, nor was it their objective. Nevertheless, their intellectual heritage has in many ways become the basis for our Western philosophy of state.

In ancient Athens, after the triumph over the monarchy, the first tender seedlings of democracy (Greek: demos "people" and kratein "rule") germinated. There was no longer a single all-powerful ruler. Rather, opinions were formed and decisions made by a variety of bodies. The people's assembly, which however only comprised free and enfranchised men, passed laws, appointed officials and also decided on war and peace. From today's point of view, that was not yet a complete democracy, yet when compared with the other forms of government found elsewhere in Antiquity, that is, monarchy or tyranny, it was downright revolutionary. After all, government and legislation were scrutinized, and major decisions needed to be approved by the people's assembly. Reformers like Solon and Cleisthenes repeatedly brought about practical improvements, while philosophers like Plato and Aristotle concerned themselves with the theoretical basis for various forms of government.

In ancient Rome, ferocious struggles raged for centuries between different population groups, who either claimed their rights or defended their privileges. Against this background, meanwhile, various precisely defined government offices or institutions developed, such as the Senate or the jurisdiction, that were subject to a degree of control by other authorities. The corpus iuris civilis, an important statute book, came into being during the reign of the East Roman Emperor Justinian at the beginning of the sixth century and was to influence modern European jurisdiction into the 21st century. Democracy of our time – the form of government valid in all of Europe and the Western world – was theoretically justified by the philosophers of the Enlightenment and won in bitter struggles by the people. The memory of the beginnings of democracy in ancient Athens and Rome, however, is still present and still informs our thinking today.

Europe – a far-reaching concept. The borders of the continent are not clear, and it is even debatable whether Europe is a continent at all. Geographically speaking, Europe is a subcontinent, which together with Asia forms the continent of Eurasia; its autonomy as a continent is founded in history and culture. Beginning with the cradle of Western culture in ancient Greece, something like a unified European area perhaps first existed during the Imperium Romanum – which fell with the turbulences of the Migration Period and rose again centuries later in the France of Charlemagne, the "first European". During the course of the Middle Ages and the Modern Era, the peoples of Europe mercilessly fought each other in vicious religious wars and dynastic power struggles. This sad tradition continued with the two world wars, and still found its late echoes in the Balkan conflicts after the dissolution of the Soviet Union and the countries of the Communist bloc in the late 20th century. Today, Europe is one of the most peaceful regions on Earth; 27 countries together form the European Union, and further countries are hoping to join it. The following excursion through the periods of European history shows how Europe became what it is today.

Antiquity

Although hunter-gatherers populated Europe some 1.5 million years ago, the advanced civilizations that were so meaningful for Europe only developed during the third and second millennia BC. Greek mythology knows Europa as the daughter of a Phoenician king; she was abducted by Zeus in the shape of a bull and later bore him the future king of Crete. In actual fact, Crete was the cultural bridge between the Middle East and Mediterranean Europe. Around 1100 BC, the Greek cultural sphere transferred to Asia Minor, and the first city-states emerged. There followed the Archaic Period, lasting from 800 till 500 BC, during which the monarchs were replaced by aristocrats as rulers and the entire Mediterranean region was colonized. The political centers were Sparta, Athens, Thessaly, Thebes, Corinth, Argos and Miletus. This extreme political fragmentation was offset by a unified culture, which found its expression in great Pan-Hellenic festivals, such as the Olympic Games, and by the collective religious centers (Oracle of Delphi). The Classical Period from 500 to 336 BC was characterized by the struggle for hegemony between Athens and Sparta as well as attacks from outside. After repelling the Persian invasion under Xerxes and the Carthaginian attack on Sicily, and with the formation of the Delian League in 478 BC, Athens became the dominant power. Sparta then took over the leading position when Athens was defeated in the Peloponnesian War, until it was ousted again, after the formation of the Second Athenian Empire. A series of internal disputes in Greece allowed Philip II of Macedonia to assume the reign over Greece. With the Battle of Issus in 333 BC, the Macedonian King Alexander III the Great started his "revenge campaign" and the period of Hellenism. Greece, Asia Minor and Egypt became united as a great empire. The attempts to restore Greek sovereignty after the death of Alexander failed. Eventually, in 146 BC, Greece was occupied by a young, emerging power from the West: Rome.

According to legend, the city of Rome was founded in 753 BC and ruled by seven kings until a republican constitution came into force in subsequent years. In 509 BC, the last Etruscan king was defeated, and by 272 BC, after a series of wars, Rome controlled the entire Apennine Peninsula south of the Po Valley. Carthage, the most important power in the western Mediterranean at that time, was defeated by the Romans in the three Punic Wars until 146 BC. Irrespective of the continual expansion of its territory, several civil wars took place in Rome that shook the republican system. When Caesar was murdered in 44 BC, the Senate had already lost its powers. Formally, Rome was still a republic during the imperial period, yet there was a strong trend toward establishing a hereditary monarchy. A first crisis occurred with the Germanic invasions during the reign of Marcus Aurelius.

A Greek vase depicting The Abduction of Europa, from the 4th century BC; fragments of a statue of the Roman Emperor Constantine; the Battle of Hastings (1066) in the Bayeux Tapestry; the Declaration of Human Rights of August 28, 1789, following the French Revolution; Jacques Louis David's Coronation of Empress Josephine by Napoleon (from left to right).

Within the Roman Empire, the spread of Christianity became a serious threat to the system, which it countered with the bloody persecution of all Christians. Constantine put an end to this and founded Constantinople as a second capital in 330. In 379, Christianity became the state religion, and in 395 the division into a Western Roman and an Eastern Roman empire became final. The West lost vast territories and in 476, the last Western Roman Emperor, Romulus Augustulus, was deposed. The Eastern Roman Byzantium continued to exist until it was conquered by the Turks in 1453 and renamed Constantinople.

The Middle Ages

After the formal end of the Western Roman Empire, and following the Migration of Peoples, numerous Germanic empires were founded in the former Roman territories. Vandals, Visigoths; Ostrogoths and Lombards formed their own state entities, but eventually the Franks prevailed as the dominant power. The Frankish dynasty of the Merovingians, whose outstanding ruler was Clovis, was followed in 751 by Carolingian rule under Pepin the Short, a son of Charles Martel, who had managed to halt the Arab advance in France in 732. Under Charlemagne, who was crowned emperor in 800, a politically and culturally unified empire emerged, which however disintegrated again after his death.

England was ruled by the Danes, whose reign was brought to a violent end by William the Conqueror in the Battle of Hastings in 1066. The originally predatory Vikings arranged themselves over time with the papacy and established Norman empires in Lower Italy and Russia, among others.

In the West Frankish Kingdom, the Capetians endured internal strife for a long time. In 962, the imperial crown of Charlemagne went to the East Frankish King Otto I, who halted the onslaught of the Magyars and went on to establish a great empire. During his reign, the Czechs, Danes and Poles were bound to Rome.

The Middle Ages were largely characterized by the power struggle between the pope and the emperor, with Henry IV's Walk to Canossa, to Pope Gregory VII, a first climax. The Investiture Controversy was settled by a compromise agreed at the Concordat of Worms in 1122, yet it could not contain in the long term the conflict between spiritual and secular powers, which continued to define European politics. Another characteristic feature of the Middle Ages in Europe was the often-violent conflict with Islam. After Charles Martel's first successful defense, the Moors were finally expelled from the Iberian peninsula in 1492. The occupation of the "Holy Land" and the "liberation" of Jerusalem were the objectives of eight Crusades between 1095 and 1275. The alienation between Latin Western Europe and the Byzantine East expressed itself particularly clearly in the division of the church, the so-called Schism of 1054. The North Italian city-states, which had now become very powerful, also stood in open conflict with the Byzantine Empire.

The papacy had to fight powerful attacks from heretic movements. With the help of the Inquisition, these were more or less violently suppressed. Conflicts and wars between the individual princes also caused the secular rule in the empire to rock.

The medieval feudal structures evolved noticeably as early as the 14th century, although this process did not happen at the same time everywhere. In England and France, modern nation-states gradually formed after the Hundred Years' War, Spain and Portugal followed some time later. The establishments of banking houses and the extension of trade as an economic basis, as witnessed also in the German Hanseatic League, indicated the arrival of new times. The enormous demographic changes brought about by the plague, the great journeys of exploration made by the Spanish and the Portuguese, the emergence of humanism in the Renaissance and the activities of reformers, such as Luther, Zwingli and Calvin, all marked the end of the Middle Ages at the turn of the 15th to the 16th centuries.

Early Modern Period

The discovery of America and the studies of scientists such as Copernicus and Galileo finally put an end to the medieval worldview. The nation-states of Portugal, Spain, and later also England, France and the Netherlands, now sailed across all the oceans and established the first colonial empires.

The power of the Pope was deeply shaken by the religious wars. Reformation and Counter-Reformation finally culminated in the Thirty Years' War in 1618, which was brought to an end by the Peace of Westphalia in 1648. Europe was now also politically divided into a Protestant and a Catholic camp. During the reign of Henry VIII, England established a separate state church as early as 1534. While Germany consisted of a patchwork of small and very small sovereign states, England was able to establish itself after the defeat of the Spanish Armada in 1588 as a maritime nation alongside the Spanish and the Portuguese, and the Netherlands, liberated from Spain, became one of the wealthiest nations in Europe. The wars of the 17th century paved the way for the formation of the great European powers.

When the Turkish advance in Eastern Europe had been warded off, France's claim to hegemony in Europe was also rejected. The quest for a single power to dominate no longer had any chance of success, at the very latest after the end of the Spanish War of Succession in 1714. Politically, the European monarchies were absolutist into the late 18th century, and some even longer. With Peter I, Russia too raised its voice in the European concert of superpowers. In Germany, two large states fought for predominance: strict, military, organized Prussia and the Habsburg monarchy in Austria. The clear loser of this dispute was Poland, which was divided up between its neighbors three times between 1772 and 1795.

The baroque display of splendor at the royal courts and the unfettered reign "by the grace of God" were soon called into question by the Enlightenment. In England and Prussia especially, but also in the other European states, reforms were attempted. However, these largely remained piecemeal, and feudal society was unable to offer much to the middle classes striving for emancipation.

The French Revolution

Human rights, a government elected by all citizens and control over the rulers were the demands that swept away the Ancien Régime in France in 1789. With the storming of the Bastille, the call for "liberty, equality and fraternity" was forcefully made. The newly created National Assembly declared human and citizens' rights, worked out the shape of a constitutional monarchy, redivided the country and curtailed the power of the Church.

With the proclamation of the republic in 1792, the revolutionary wars with the other European powers began, initially clocking up successes for France. The external threat led to a radicalization of the revolutionaries. Louis XVI was executed, and the Jacobins around Robespierre started a reign of terror. In 1794, the terror regime ended with a new constitution. The army relied on a young Corsican general, who also gained an ever-greater political influence: Napoleon Bonaparte. In 1804, after a dubious popular poll, Napoleon crowned himself the emperor. His code civil and numerous legal and administrative reforms indicate that he was not only an ingenious military strategist but also an extremely capable politician. In 1810 he attained the height of his powers. However, resistance grew with the emergence of national movements. England's navy seemed unbeatable, and the French troops had to accept a decisive defeat in their Russian campaign. In 1813 finally, Paris was occupied by coalition troops, Napoleon was sent into exile and the reign of the Bourbon dynasty was restored by Louis XVIII.

EUROPE – YESTERDAY AND TOMORROW

The Reorganization of Europe

Under the direction of Metternich, the European powers in Vienna negotiated the territorial reorganization. The conference was interrupted by the brief return of Napoleon. When his Hundred Days was finally put to an end in the Battle of Waterloo in 1815, the countries in Vienna agreed to restore the principle of legitimacy. However, the old sovereigns were not reappointed, and the reforms, such as the Stein-Hardenberg Reforms in Prussia, were not revoked. The Austrian Netherlands and the United Provinces were combined in the Kingdom of the Netherlands, and the formerly several hundred sovereign German territories now became but 39 independent states, loosely organized in the German Confederation. Despite the growing conflict between the two German power centers of Vienna and Berlin, the desire for a unified German nation-state became stronger.

The Nineteenth Century

The Industrial Revolution, which started in England, and the mindset of liberalism and nationalism, defined the further course of European history in the 19th century.
Initially, the reactionary regimes successfully defended themselves against the demands for reform from the liberal bourgeoisie. Yet social tensions erupted everywhere in Europe, and the call for national integrity became louder. Greece managed to free itself from Turkish rule in 1829. The Irish demanded independence from the British monarchy, and the Poles temporarily expelled the Russian military from Warsaw. In 1830, the Bourbons in France were finally toppled and under Louis-Philippe, King of the French, a constitutional monarchy was agreed. In Italy, Giuseppe Mazzini formed the "Giovane Italia" group, which promoted a united free Republic of Italy. Among the people of Austria and Hungary, too, resistance against the Habsburg rulers began to arise.
In Germany, the national mood erupted during the pre-March era in 1848 in a revolution that was to grip all of Europe with the exception of England and Russia. At first, Louis-Philippe was toppled, Metternich fled from Vienna, the Prussian king had to bow to the victims of the Revolution, and in Frankfurt, a constituent assembly discussed the democratic unity of a future Germany.
Nevertheless, the revolutionary enthusiasm waned, and by the end of 1849, the status quo had been restored almost everywhere by armed force. Only Sardinia and Switzerland were able to preserve their liberal constitutions.

Clash of the Great Powers

After a long period of peace, the subsequent era was defined by huge conflicts between the great powers. Russia used the obvious weakness of the Ottoman Empire as an opportunity to extend its sphere of influence in Eastern Europe. Together with the Turks and the Piedmontese, the English and the French resoundingly defeated the Tsarist Empire in the Crimean War (1853–1856). Austria had to cede its Northern Italian possessions, and Garibaldi and Cavour pressed ahead with the unification of Italy.
Germany, too, was en route to national unity. The Prussian Prime Minister Bismarck pursued a "Lesser German Solution": a unified state without Austria. In 1871, the German Empire was proclaimed in Versailles.

The Industrialization of Europe

The inexorable march of technological progress was matched by the emergence of a new industrial proletariat. Under the aegis of Karl Marx, workers' parties organized as international associations that sought the revolutionary overthrow of bourgeois society.

At the same time, the tensions between the European powers intensified through the imperialist ambitions of the industrial nations. France, England, Russia, and later also Italy and Germany, resorted to a race for the partition of the world.

World War I

When Bismarck had been "dropped" in 1890, Emperor Wilhelm II took over the reins. His policy of sabre-rattling and a maritime arms race with Great Britain prepared the mood for World War I, which began in August 1914. In South-Eastern Europe, the Balkan states had fought several wars after being freed from Ottoman rule. When the Austrian successor to the throne and his wife were shot by a Serb assassin on June 28, 1914, in Sarajevo, the atmosphere was explosive, and one month later, Austria declared war on Serbia.
Subsequently, the complicated network of alliances led to a rapid succession of mobilizations and war declarations. Germany, Austria-Hungary, Bulgaria and the Ottoman Empire faced the entente of England, France and Russia. Mobile warfare quickly turned into trench warfare. In Russia, war weariness led to the overthrow of the tsar. A civilian government under Kerensky initially continued with the war, until Lenin took power after the October Revolution of 1917. The United States' entry into the war on the side of the entente led to the final defeat of the Central Powers in November 1918. The German military dictatorship under Hindenburg and Ludendorff washed their hands of all responsibility; the emperor and all other German monarchs abdicated. "Workers' and soldiers' councils" filled the power vacuum until the Weimar Constitution finally restored political order in Germany – although this was later to prove not very stable.
Lenin's war against Poland ended in a fiasco. In 1919 and 1920, peace treaties were signed in villages outside Paris, in the absence of the defeated powers. Not much remained of a just post-war order, like the one U.S. President Wilson had envisaged. Germany had to cede large territories and make enormous reparation payments.
The Danube Monarchy and the Ottoman Empire were dissolved; Poland, Yugoslavia, Czechoslovakia, Finland and the Baltic countries became independent states. The League of Nations was formed to safeguard the peace, but it was without power.

On the Eve of World War II

Initially, parliamentary democracy seemed to prevail in the newly ordered Europe, but gradually the authoritarian regimes gained in strength. In 1922, the Fascists under Mussolini came to power in Italy. At the climax of the world economic crisis, in 1933, Hitler became the Chancellor of the German Reich, and in Spain General Francisco Franco asserted himself in 1939 after a bloody civil war – and remained the head of state until his death in 1975. In the Soviet Union, Stalin advanced as seemingly all-powerful dictator, had his political opponents executed after show trials and was responsible for the deaths of millions and millions of citizens.
The aggressive policies of the National Socialists initially promised to be successful. Despite the brutal suppression of any opposition and the ruthless persecution of the German Jews, Hitler was at first able to push through his foreign-policy objectives without any appreciable resistance from the other European powers. The German invasion of Poland on September 1, 1939, finally, led to England and France declaring war against the German Reich. Within only a few weeks, the German Poland campaign was finished, and after the "Blitzkrieg" in the west and Rommel's Africa campaign, the German army and its allies were in control of large parts of Europe. After initial successes, however, the German offensive ran aground and the Battle of Stalingrad in the winter of 1942/43 marked the turning of the tide. When the United States entered the war in 1941, the German defeat was

Scene from the Congress of Vienna on the reorganization of Europe (woodcut from 1880); French soldiers in a trench during World War I; deportation of Jews from the Warsaw Ghetto in 1942; Soviet soldiers unfurl the red flag on the Reichstag in Berlin in May 1945; the Fall of the Berlin Wall in the autumn of 1989 (from left to right).

only a question of time. The racial hatred of the Nazis led to the death of about six million Jews in extermination camps.

The Postwar Period

In May 1945, the German troops capitulated. Germany was divided into four occupation zones, and subsequently two German states came into being.
The Europe of 1945 was razed to the ground, and the global balance of power had shifted significantly. Western Europe looked closely to the United States, whereas in the East, Stalin established a system of satellite states. The military alliances of NATO and the Warsaw Pact faced each other with the gigantic potential for annihilation.
The Vietnam War gave rise to the student rebellions at the end of the 1960s. In Prague, reform socialism was put down by Soviet tanks, just as previously the uprisings in Hungary and the GDR.
The 1970s were characterized by Willy Brandt's Ostpolitik or politics of détente toward the East, and the politics of "revolutionary conformism" by Olof Palme in Sweden and Bruno Kreisky in Austria. The European Community, which had been called into being with the Treaties of Rome, was continually enlarged.
The last remaining military dictatorships in Spain, Greece and Portugal were toppled and colonialism came to an end. At the same time, the Western democracies had to contend with organized terrorism. In Northern Ireland, in the Basque Country and on Corsica self-proclaimed liberation movements planted bombs. The Red Brigades carried out assassinations in Italy, the RAF in Germany.

The "End of Socialism"

In the 1980s, "real socialism" began to crumble. In Poland, the "Solidarity" trade union went on strike for the right to freedom, and in the Soviet Union, Gorbachev's politics of glasnost and perestroika triggered the end of the people's democracies. In 1989, the inner-German border was opened, and in 1990 Germany was reunited. Parliamentary democracies established themselves in the Eastern European countries, the USSR and the Warsaw Pact fell apart. The hopes for a lasting peace in Europe were overshadowed, however, by the wars in disintegrating Yugoslavia.

Europe in the 21st century

On September 11, 2001, hijacked passenger planes destroyed the World Trade Center in New York and damaged the Pentagon in Washington. The countries of the European Union increased their cooperation in the fight against terror. With the accession of ten new countries to the EU in 2004, the political division between Eastern and Western Europe was declared a thing of the past. Many Europeans believe that the time is ripe for a European constitution, but they cannot agree on what form this should take. The discussion on the future of Europe in a globalized world continues.

Parliamentary building in Strasbourg: gradually, more and more powers within the EU have been signed over to the European Parliament.

The European Union

The European Union is a highly complex, politically difficult, but historically extremely significant entity. After centuries of wars, especially after the immense human and material destruction of World War II, the European Union was created as a platform and framework for the non-violent cooperation between the European peoples on a political, economic and cultural level.
At the beginning stood the European Coal and Steel Community, founded in 1952, which made possible a common market for coal, steel, iron ore and scrap iron for the signatory countries: Belgium, Germany, France, Italy, Luxembourg and the Netherlands. The next step came on March 25, 1957, when the Treaties of Rome brought into effect the European Economic Community (EEC), creating the basis for a common agricultural and industrial market, with the aim of the long-term integration of the national political economies. Within the framework of the Treaties of Rome, the European Atomic Community (Euratom) was also established, which was to ensure the peaceful application of nuclear energy. From these three bodies, the European Community (EC) was created in 1967, and by 1986 Denmark, Great Britain, Ireland, Greece, Portugal and Spain had joined. In 1992 the union was given a superordinate political framework in the Maastricht Treaty, which combined the various EC institutions under the banner of the European Union (EU). A European Economic Area has existed since 1993, without internal borders, in which the free exchange of people, goods, services and capital is guaranteed. Since then, every EU citizen has had the right to live, work and (within limits) also to vote in every country of the EU.
In further rounds, Austria, Finland und Sweden, Latvia, Estonia as well as Lithuania, Poland, Hungary, the Czech Republic, Slovakia, Slovenia, Malta and Cyprus were accepted as members.
Among the achievements of the EU, the one most readily felt by the people of Europe is the introduction of the common currency of the euro, which is today the currency in 16 of the 27 member states. Many European states have not yet joined the European Union – the future is open.

EUROPE AT A GLANCE | 229

REYKJAVÍK

Country: Iceland
Capital since: 1918, 1944 (Republic)
Time zone: GMT
Geographical location: 64° 09′ N, 21° 57′ W
Altitude above sea level: 54 m (177 ft)
Area: 274.5 sq km (106 sq miles)
Inhabitants: 119,848
Inhabitants of the urban agglomeration: over 200,000
Population density: 429 inhabitants/sq km (1,111/sq mile)
Internet: www.rvk.is
Currency: Icelandic krona (ISK)
Dialing code with country code: (+354) 5
Most important sights: National Museum of Iceland, Árbæjarsafn
Open-Air Museum, Dómkirkjan Church, Church of Hallgrímur, Perlan
Hot Water Storage

OSLO

Country: Norway
Capital since: 1299
Time zone: GMT +1 (+ summer time)
Geographical location: 59° 55′ N, 10° 45′ E
Altitude above sea level: 1 m (3 ft)
Area: 454 sq km (175 sq miles)
Inhabitants: 575,475
Inhabitants of the urban agglomeration: 1.4 million
Population density: 268 inhabitants/sq km (694/sq mile)
Internet: www.oslo.kommune.no
Currency: Norwegian crown (NOK)
Dialing code with country code: (+47) 02
Most important sights: Akershus Fortress, Viking Ship Museum
(Vikingskipshuset), Edvard Munch Museum, Karl Johans gate boulevard,
Vigeland Park, Holmenkollen Ski Complex

COPENHAGEN

Country: Denmark
Capital since: 1443
Time zone: GMT +1 (+ summer time)
Geographical location: 55° 41′ N, 12° 35′ E
Altitude above sea level: 0–24 m (0–79 ft)
Area: 88.25 sq km (34 sq miles)
Inhabitants: 509,861
Inhabitants of the urban agglomeration: 1.8 million
Population density: 5,777 inhabitants/sq km (14,962/sq mile)
Internet: www.kk.dk
Currency: Danish krona (DKR)
Dialing code with country code: (+45) 077
Most important sights: Christiansborg Palace, Amalienborg Palace (and
Changing of the Guard), Frederikskirche, Nyhavn (New Port), Little Mermaid,
Tivoli Theme Park

STOCKHOLM

Country: Sweden
Capital since: 1634
Time zone: GMT +1 (+ summer time)
Geographical location: 59° 20′ N, 18° 3′ E
Altitude above sea level: 15 m (49 ft)
Area: 209 sq km (80.7 sq miles) (21% of which is water)
Inhabitants: 810,120
Inhabitants of the urban agglomeration: 1,981,263
Population density: 4,252 inhabitants/sq km (11,013/sq mile)
Internet: www.stockholm.se
Currency: Swedish krona (SEK)
Dialing code with country code: (+46) 8
Most important sights: Gamla Stan (old town on Stadsholmen island),
German Church (Tyska kyrkan), Storkyrkan Cathedral, Royal Palace, Sergels
torg (Sergels Square), Vasa Museum (Djurgården)

HELSINKI

Country: Finland
Capital since: 1918
Time zone: GMT +2 (+ summer time)
Geographical location: 60° 10′ N, 24° 56′ E
Altitude above sea level: 25 m (82 ft)
Area: 686 sq km (264.9 sq miles)
Inhabitants: 576,623
Inhabitants of the urban agglomeration: 1,303,579
Population density: 3,044 inhabitants/sq km (7,883/sq mile)
Internet: www.hel2.fi
Currency: Euro (EUR)
Dialing code with country code: (+358) 09
Most important sights: Senate Square (Senaatintori) and Cathedral,
Aleksanterinkatu and Esplanadi promenades, National Museum of Finladn
(Suomen kansallismuseo), modern Temppeliaukio Church in the Töölö
district, Finlandia Hall, Suomenlinna Fortress

TALLINN

Country: Estonia
Capital since: 1918
Time zone: GMT +2 (+ summer time)
Geographical location: 59° 25′ N, 24° 46′ E
Altitude above sea level: 44 m (144 ft)
Area: 159.2 sq km (61.5 sq miles)
Inhabitants: 402,798
Inhabitants of the urban agglomeration: not known
Population density: 2,534 inhabitants/sq km (6,563/sq mile)
Internet: www.tallinn.ee
Currency: Estonian krona (EEK)
Dialing code with country code: (+372) 6
Most important sights: Old Town, Town Hall Square (Raekoja plats),
gothic Town Hall, Ramparts, Dome Church, Alexander Nevsky Cathedral
(Aleksander Nevski katedraal), KUMU Art Museum, House of the Blackheads,
Kadriorg Palace

The Little Mermaid watches over Copenhagen. Riddarholmen Island in Stockholm is home to the Swedish Chancellor of Justice. Dublin's Temple Bar entertainment district attracts visitors with its numerous pubs and restaurants. The neo-gothic Tower Bridge (1894) spans the Thames, leading into the modern financial district of the City of London (from left to right).

RIGA

Country: Latvia
Capital since: 1918
Time zone: GMT + 2 (+ summer time)
Geographical location: 56° 57' N, 24° 6' E
Altitude above sea level: 7 m (23 ft)
Area: 307.17 sq km (118.6 sq miles)
Inhabitants: 719,613
Inhabitants of the urban agglomeration: 882,270
Population density: 2,343 inhabitants/sq km (6,068/sq mile)
Internet: www.riga.lv
Currency: Latvian lats (LVL)
Dialing code with country code: +371 (no city dialing code)
Most important sights: Old Town, Riga Dome Cathedral, Statue of Roland, St Peter's Church, House of the Blackheads, Powder Tower, Riga Castle, New Town and Art Nouveau façades, Central Market

VILNIUS

Country: Lithuania
Capital since: 1323
Time zone: GMT +2 (+ summer time)
Geographical location: 59° 55' N, 10° 45' E
Altitude above sea level: 112 m (367 ft)
Area: 402 sq km (155.2 sq miles)
Inhabitants: c. 553,000
Inhabitants of the urban agglomeration: not known
Population density: 1,379 inhabitants/sq km (3,572/sq mile)
Internet: www.vilnius.lt
Currency: Lithuanian litas (LTL)
Dialing code with country code: (+ 370) 05
Most important sights: Gediminas Castle, St Stanislaus Cathedral and bell tower, Gate of Dawn (Aušros Vartai), baroque University complex, KGB Museum and Museum of Genocide, Užupis Artists' Quarter, Europa Tower, Trakai Castle

DUBLIN

Country: Ireland
Capital since: 1922, 1949 (Republic)
Time zone: GMT
Geographical location: 53° 21' N, 6° 16' W
Altitude above sea level: 20 m (66 ft)
Area: 17.8 sq km (6.9 sq miles)
Inhabitants: 506,211
Inhabitants of the urban agglomeration: 1.2 million
Population density: 4,293 inhabitants/sq km (11,119/sq mile)
Internet: www.dublin.ie
Currency: Euro (EUR)
Dialing code with country code: (+353) 01
Most important sights: Trinity College, O'Connell-Bridge/O'Connell Street, Temple Bar, Custom House, Ha'Penny Bridge, Christ Church Cathedral, St. Patrick's Cathedral

LONDON

Country: United Kingdom
Capital since: 1066
Time zone: GMT
Geographical location: 51° 31' N, 0° 7' W
Altitude above sea level: 15 m (49 ft)
Area: 1,600 sq km (617.8 sq miles)
Inhabitants: 7,512,400
Inhabitants of the urban agglomeration: c. 14 million
Population density: 4,758 inhabitants/sq km (12,323/sq mile)
Internet: www.london.gov.uk
Currency: British pound (GBP)
Dialing code with country code: (+44) 020
Most important sights: Tower, Tower Bridge, St. Paul's Cathedral, Buckingham Palace, Trafalgar Square, Westminster Palace, Big Ben, Westminster Abbey, Guild Hall, British Museum, Tate Modern, Victoria and Albert Museum, National Gallery, Harrod's, Camden, Notting Hill

AMSTERDAM/THE HAGUE

Country: Netherlands
Capital since: 1813 (Amsterdam); seat of government The Hague since: 1588
Time zone: GMT +1 (+ summer time)
Geographical location: 52° 22' N, 4° 53' E
Altitude above sea level: –2 m (–6 ft)
Area: 219 sq km (84.6 sq miles)
Inhabitants: 747,290
Inhabitants of the urban agglomeration: 2,158,592
Population density: 4,457 inhabitants/sq km (11,544/sq mile)
Internet: www.amsterdam.nl
Currency: Euro (EUR)
Dialing code with country code: (+31) 020
Most important sights: Canals, Keizersgracht, Paleis Noordeinde, Westerkerk, Montelbaanstoren, De Waag, Paleis op de Dam, Rijksmuseum, Scheveningen, Binnnehof, Peace Palace, Amsterdam South, Mauritshuis, Anne Frank House, Van Gogh Museum

BRUSSELS

Country: Belgium
Capital since: 1830
Time zone: GMT +1 (+ summer time)
Geographical location: 50° 51' N, 4° 21' E
Altitude above sea level: 70 m (230 ft)
Area: 32.61 sq km (12.6 sq miles)
Inhabitants: 148,900
Inhabitants of the urban agglomeration: 1,067,557
Population density: 4,566 inhabitants/sq km (11,826/sq mile)
Internet: www.brucity.be
Currency: Euro (EUR)
Dialing code with country code: (+32) 02
Most important sights: Grand-Place, Atomium, Stock Exchange, Rue des Bouchers, Manneken Pis, Cathedral, Quartier Européen, Triumphal Arch in the Jubelpark/Parc du Cinquantenaire, Palace of Justice, Royal Palace, La Monnaie Opera House

LUXEMBOURG

Country: Luxembourg
Capital since: 1815
Time zone: GMT +1 (+ summer time)
Geographical location: 49° 37′ N, 6° 8′ E
Altitude above sea level: 307 m (1007 ft)
Area: 51.73 sq km (20 sq miles)
Inhabitants: 90,000
Inhabitants of the urban agglomeration: 142,033
Population density: 1,515 inhabitants/sq km (3,924/sq mile)
Internet: www.luxembourg-ville.lu
Currency: Euro (EUR)
Dialing code with country code: +352 (no city dialing code)
Most important sights: Lower Town, Upper Town, Grand Ducal Palace, Notre-Dame Cathedral, Pétrusse Valley (Péitrusdall), Musée d'Art Moderne Grand-Duc Jean (MUDAM), Luxembourg Castle, Citadel of the Holy Spirit, Church of St John

PARIS

Country: France
Capital since: c. 990 A.D.
Time zone: GMT +1 (+ summer time)
Geographical location: 48° 52′ N, 2° 21′ E
Altitude above sea level: 65 m (213 ft)
Area: 105.40 sq km (40.7 sq miles)
Inhabitants: 2,181,371
Inhabitants of the urban agglomeration: 11.6 million
Population density: 1,925 inhabitants/sq km (4,986/sq mile)
Internet: www.paris.fr
Currency: Euro (EUR)
Dialing code with country code: (+33) 01
Most important sights: Eiffel Tower, Louvre, Notre-Dame, Place de la Concorde, Champs Élysées, Arc de Triomphe, Pompidou Center, Opéra Garnier, Jardin du Luxembourg, Saint-Germain-des-Prés, Panthéon, Les Invalides, Pont Neuf, Montmartre, Sacré-Cœur, Père-Lachaise Cemetery

MONACO

Country: Monaco
Capital since: 1440 (independence)
Time zone: GMT +1 (+ summer time)
Geographical location: 43° 44′ N, 7° 25′ E
Altitude above sea level: 55 m (180 ft)
Area: 1.97 sq km (0.76 sq miles)
Inhabitants: 32,796
Inhabitants of the urban agglomeration: not known
Population density: 16,600 inhabitants/sq km (42,944/sq mile)
Internet: www.visitmonaco.com
Currency: Euro (EUR)
Dialing code with country code: +377 (no city dialing code)
Most important sights: Old Town on the Rock of Monaco, Prince's Palace, Notre-Dame Immaculée Cathedral, Casino, Exotic Garden (Jardin Exotique), Oceanographic Museum, Yachting Harbor

BERLIN

Country: Germany
Capital since: 1991 [before 1999: Berlin (capital), Bonn (seat of government)]
Time zone: GMT +1 (+ summer time)
Geographical location: 52° 31′ N, 13° 24′ E
Altitude above sea level: 34–115 m (111–377 ft)
Area: 897.85 sq km (346.7 sq miles)
Inhabitants: 3,431,473
Inhabitants of the urban agglomeration: 4,500,000
Population density: 3,848 inhabitants/sq km (9,966/sq mile)
Internet: www.berlin.de
Currency: Euro (EUR)
Dialing code with country code: (+49) 030
Most important sights: Brandenburg Gate, Reichstag, Museum Island, Unter den Linden, Kurfürstendamm, Kaiser Wilhelm Memorial Church, Holocaust Memorial, Government District, Potsdamer Platz, Zoo, German Historical Museum, East Side Gallery, Checkpoint Charlie

BERN

Country: Switzerland
Capital since: 1848
Time zone: GMT +1 (+ summer time)
Geographical location: 46° 57′ N, 7° 26′ E
Altitude above sea level: 542 m (1778 ft)
Area: 51.6 sq km (19.9 sq miles)
Inhabitants: 129,418
Inhabitants of the urban agglomeration: c. 300,000
Population density: 2,484 inhabitants/sq km (6,434/sq mile)
Internet: www.bern.ch
Currency: Swiss franc (CHF)
Dialing code with country code: (+41) 031
Most important sights: Clock Tower (Zytgloggeturm), Old Town, Bern Münster and Arcades, Nydegg Church, Untertorbrücke, Federation Square Fountain, Holländerturm (Dutch Tower), Bear Park, Nydegg Bridge, Museum of Fine Arts, Paul Klee Center, Einstein House

VADUZ

Country: Liechtenstein
Capital since: 1719 (main city), since 1939 residence of the prince
Time zone: GMT +1 (+ summer time)
Geographical location: 47° 08′ N, 09° 30′ E
Altitude above sea level: 455 m (1493 ft)
Area: 17.3 sq km (6.68 sq miles)
Inhabitants: 5,221
Inhabitants of the urban agglomeration: 35,350 (principality)
Population density: 288 inhabitants/sq km (746/sq mile)
Internet: www.vaduz.li
Currency: Swiss franc (CHF)
Dialing code with country code: +423 (no city dialing code)
Most important sights: Vaduz Castle, Städtle, Town Hall, Liechtenstein Parliament Building, St Florin's Cathedral, Ski Museum, Art Museum of Liechtenstein

National symbols: the building of the Swiss Federal Council and Federal Assembly (Federal Palace) in Bern and the Reichstag Building in Berlin. Bratislava Castle, in a commanding position above the Danube, is used as the Slovak National Museum and for state visits. The Red Square in Moscow with its historic buildings is one of the most important sites in Russia (from left to right).

VIENNA

Country: Austria
Capital since: 1804–1918; 1918–1938, 1945 (Republic)
Time zone: GMT +1 (+ summer time)
Geographical location: 48° 12′ N, 16° 22′ E
Altitude above sea level: 151–542 m (495–1778 ft)
Area: 414.89 sq km (160.2 sq miles)
Inhabitants: 1,691,468
Inhabitants of the urban agglomeration: c. 2,300,000
Population density: 4,550 inhabitants/sq km (11,784/sq mile)
Internet: www.wien.gv.at
Currency: Euro (EUR)
Dialing code with country code: (+43) 01
Most important sights: Hofburg Imperial Palace (Imperial Apartments, National Library of Austria, Spanish Riding School), St Stephen's Cathedral, Karlsplatz, St Charles's Church, Museums Quarter, Burgtheater, Museum of Art History, Jewish Vienna, Belvedere Palace, Schönbrunn Palace, Prater, Grinzing

PRAGUE

Country: Czech Republic
Capital since: second half of 14th c. (Holy Roman Empire), end of the 16th c. royal capital, 1918 (ČSSR), 1993 (Czech Republic)
Time zone: GMT +1 (+ summer time)
Geographical location: 50° 5′ N, 14° 25′ E
Altitude above sea level: 399 m (1309 ft)
Area: 496 sq km (191.5 sq miles)
Inhabitants: 1,223,368
Inhabitants of the urban agglomeration: c. 2,300,000
Population density: not known
Internet: www.praha-mesto.cz
Currency: Czech koruna (CZK)
Dialing code with country code: (+420) 02
Most important sights: Hradčany, St Vitus Cathedral, Strahov Monastery, Golden Lane, Malá Strana, Charles Bridge, Petřín, Old Town with Old Town Square, Wenceslas Square, National Museum, Jewish Quarter

BRATISLAVA

Country: Slovakia
Capital since: 1536–1783/1848 (Kingdom of Hungary), 1939–1945 (First Slovak Republic), 1968 (part of federalized Czechoslovakia), 1993 (Slovakia)
Time zone: GMT +1 (+ summer time)
Geographical location: 48° 9′ N, 17° 9′ E
Altitude above sea level: 140 m (459 ft)
Area: 367.58 sq km (141.9 sq miles)
Inhabitants: 426,927
Inhabitants of the urban agglomeration: 602,433
Population density: 1,161 inhabitants/sq km (3,006/sq mile)
Internet: www.bratislava.sk
Currency: Slovak koruna (SKK)
Dialing code with country code: (+421) 02
Most important sights: Bratislava Castle, Grassalkovich Palace, St Martin's Cathedral, Franciscan Church, New Danube Bridge, Town Hall on the Main Square, Primatial Palace, New Bridge (Novy Most), Slovak National Theater

WARSAW

Country: Poland
Capital since: 1815 (Congress Poland), 1918–1939, 1945 (Republic)
Time zone: GMT +1 (+ summer time)
Geographical location: 52° 13′ N, 21° 2′ E
Altitude above sea level: 103 m (338 ft)
Area: 517.9 sq km (200 sq miles)
Inhabitants: 1.69 million
Inhabitants of the urban agglomeration: 2.5 million
Population density: 3,300 inhabitants/sq km (8,547/sq mile)
Internet: www.um.warszawa.pl
Currency: Polish zloty (PLZ)
Dialing code with country code: (+48) 022
Most important sights: Palace of Culture and Science, Old Town, Market Square, Royal Castle with Zygmunt's Column, Royal Tract (Trakt Królewski), Presidential Palace, Grand Theater (Teatr Wielki), Krasiński Palace, Sapieha Place, Capuchin Church, Nowy Świat boulevard, Ujazdowski Avenue

MINSK

Country: Belarus
Capital since: 1919
Time zone: GMT +2 (+ summer time)
Geographical location: 53° 54′ N, 27° 33′ E
Altitude above sea level: 280 m (919 ft)
Area: 305.47 sq km (117.9 sq miles)
Inhabitants: 1,832,800
Inhabitants of the urban agglomeration: 2,650,000
Population density: 6,000 inhabitants/sq km (15,540/sq mile)
Internet: www.minsk.gov.by
Currency: Belarus ruble (BYR/BRB)
Dialing code with country code: (+375) 017
Most important sights: City Hall, Holy Spirit Cathedral, St Bernard's Nunnery, Cathedral of Saint Virgin Mary, National Library of Belarus, Independence Square, Independence Avenue, Victory Square, Freedom Square, Memorial Church (Chernobyl), Great Patriotic War Museum

MOSCOW

Country: Russia
Capital since: 1480
Time zone: GMT +2 (+ summer time)
Geographical location: 55° 45′ N, 37° 37′ E
Altitude above sea level: 156 m (512 ft)
Area: 1,081 sq km (417.4 sq miles)
Inhabitants: 10,508,971
Inhabitants of the urban agglomeration: 14,837,510
Population density: 9,722 inhabitants/sq km (25,180/sq mile)
Internet: http://mos.ru/
Currency: Russian ruble (RUB)
Dialing code with country code: (+7) 095
Most important sights: Kremlin: e.g., Church of the Deposition of the Robe, Hall of the Order of St Andrew, Palace of Facetts, Great Bell Tower; Red Square: e.g., St Basil's Cathedral, Lenin's Mausoleum, Resurrection Gate; Metro Stations, Arbat, Pushkin Museum of Fine Arts, Bolshoi Theater, "Seven Sisters" High Rises

FACT FILE

KIEV

Country: Ukraine
Capital since: 1934
Time zone: GMT +2 (+ summer time)
Geographical location: 50° 27' N, 30° 30' E
Altitude above sea level: 179 m (587 ft)
Area: 839 sq km (323.9 sq miles)
Inhabitants: 2.7 million
Inhabitants of the urban agglomeration: 3 million
Population density: 3,218 inhabitants/sq km (8,335/sq mile)
Internet: http://kmv.gov.ua/
Currency: Hryvnia (UAH)
Dialing code with country code: (+380) 044
Most important sights: St Sophia Cathedral, Cave Monastery (Kiev-Pechersk Lavra), Mariinsky Palace, Independence Square (Maidan) and Shevtshenko Boulevard, St Michael's Monastery, Golden Gate, National Museum of the History of the Great Patriotic War

LISBON

Country: Portugal
Capital since: 1256
Time zone: GMT (+ summer time)
Geographical location: 38° 43' N, 9° 10' W
Altitude above sea level: 0–200 m (0–656 ft)
Area: 84.7 sq km (32.7 sq miles)
Inhabitants: 499,700
Inhabitants of the urban agglomeration: 2.5 million
Population density: 5,900 inhabitants/sq km (15,281/sq mile)
Internet: www.cm-lisboa.pt
Currency: Euro (EUR)
Dialing code with country code: (+351) 021
Most important sights: Torre de Belém, Upper Town (Bairro Alto): Igreja de São Roque, Elevador de Santa Justa; Castelo de São Jorge, Old Town (Alfama), National Pantheon, Sé de Lisboa Cathedral, Praça Dom Pedro IV (Rossio), Praça do Comércio, São Vicente de For a Church

MADRID

Country: Spain
Capital since: 1606
Time zone: GMT +1 (+ summer time)
Geographical location: 40° 25' N, 3° 42' W
Altitude above sea level: 667 m (2188 ft)
Area: 605.77 sq km (233.9 sq miles)
Inhabitants: 3,332,463
Inhabitants of the urban agglomeration: c. 6 million
Population density: 5,501 inhabitants/sq km (14,248/sq mile)
Internet: www.munimadrid.es/
Currency: Euro (EUR)
Dialing code with country code: (+34) 091
Most important sights: Plaza de Cibeles, Gran Vía, Plaza de España, Royal palace (Palacio Real), Puerta del Sol, Plaza Mayor, Museum Triangle at the Paseo del Prado, Convent of the Royal Barefoot Nuns, Parque del Buen Retiro, trendy district Malasaña with the Plaza del Dos de Mayo

ANDORRA LA VELLA

Country: Andorra
Capital since: 1278 (officially 1993)
Time zone: GMT +1 (+ summer time)
Geographical location: 42° 30' N, 1° 31' E
Altitude above sea level: 1,011 m (3317 ft)
Area: 12 sq km (4.63 sq miles)
Inhabitants: 24,574
Inhabitants of the urban agglomeration: 83,888 (principality)
Population density: 2,048 inhabitants/sq km (5,304/sq mile)
Internet: www.comuandorra.ad
Currency: Euro (EUR)
Dialing code with country code: (+376) (no city dialing code)
Most important sights: Old Town, Sant Esteve and Santa Coloma churches, Margineda Bridge, Castle of Sant Vicenç d'Enclar, Casa de la Vall, Caldea Thermal Spa

ROME

Country: Italy
Capital since: 1871 (Antiquity: Roman Empire, Middle Ages–1871: Papal States)
Time zone: GMT +1 (+ summer time)
Geographical location: 41° 53' N, 12° 29' E
Altitude above sea level: 37 m (121 ft)
Area: 1,285.31 sq km (496.3 sq miles)
Inhabitants: 2,708,395
Inhabitants of the urban agglomeration: c. 4 million
Population density: 2,106 inhabitants/sq km (5,455/sq mile)
Internet: www.comune.roma.it
Currency: Euro (EUR)
Dialing code with country code: (+39) 06
Most important sights: Coliseum, Arch of Constantine, Largo Argentina, Forum Romanum, Imperial Forums, Theater of Marcellus, Pantheon, Capitoline Museums, House of Augustus, Castel Sant'Angelo, Piazza Navona, Piazza del Popolo, Campo de' Fiori, Fontana di Trevi, Spanish Steps, Villa Borghese

VATICAN CITY

Country: State of the Vatican City
Capital since: 1929
Time zone: GMT +1 (+ summer time)
Geographical location: 41° 54' N, 12° 27' E
Altitude above sea level: 51 m (167 ft)
Area: 0.44 sq km (0.17 sq miles)
Inhabitants: 932
Inhabitants of the urban agglomeration: not known
Population density: 2,100 inhabitants/sq km (5,439/sq mile)
Internet: www.vaticanstate.va/IT/homepage.htm
Currency: Euro (EUR)
Dialing code with country code: (+39) 06
Most important sights: St Peter's Basilica and St Peter's Square, Sistine Chapel, Santa Maria Maggiore, San Giovanni in Laterano, San Paolo fuori le Mura

The National Monument to Vittorio Emanuele II commemorates the first king of the newly unified Italy. The "white city" of Lisbon charms visitors with its picturesque location at the mouth of the Tagus River. View over the rooftops of Zagreb, toward the St Mark's Church and the twin towers of the cathedral. Preseren Square in Ljubljana, with the framed Franciscan Church (from left to right).

SAN MARINO

Country: San Marino
Capital since: 1549/1631 (independence) 1815 (after the Congress of Vienna)
Time zone: GMT +1 (+ summer time)
Geographical location: 43° 56′ N, 12° 27′ E
Altitude above sea level: 749 m (2457 ft)
Area: 7.09 sq km (2.74 sq miles)
Inhabitants: 4,376
Inhabitants of the urban agglomeration: 30,300 (country)
Population density: 617 inhabitants/sq km (1,598/sq mile)
Internet: www.sanmarinosite.com
Currency: Euro (EUR)
Dialing code with country code: (+378) 626
Most important sights: three forts on Monte Titano (including Guaita Fortress, Cesta Castle), Piazza della Libertà, Palazzo Pubblico, Palazzo del Governo, San Francesco della Vigna Church, Basilica di San Marino, Old Town

LJUBLJANA

Country: Slovenia
Capital since: 1945 (part republic of Yugoslavia), 1991 (Republic)
Time zone: GMT +1 (+ summer time)
Geographical location: 46° 3′ N, 14° 30′ E
Altitude above sea level: 298 m (978 ft)
Area: 275 sq km (106.2 sq miles)
Inhabitants: 278,638
Inhabitants of the urban agglomeration: not known
Population density: 1,013 inhabitants/sq km (2,624/sq mile)
Internet: www.ljubljana.si
Currency: Euro (EUR)
Dialing code with country code: (+386) 01
Most important sights: Tromostovje (Three Bridges), Church of the Annunciation, central squares (Prešeren Square, Town Square, Old Square and Upper Square), Ljubljana Castle, Old Town, Town Hall, Saint Nicholas's Cathedral, Shoemaker's Bridge, Dragon Bridge, National Gallery of Slovenia

ZAGREB

Country: Croatia
Capital since: 1945 (part republic of Yugoslavia), 1992 (Republic)
Time zone: GMT +1 (+ summer time)
Geographical location: 45° 48′ N, 15° 58′ E
Altitude above sea level: 120 m (394 ft)
Area: 641 sq km (247.5 sq miles)
Inhabitants: 779,145
Inhabitants of the urban agglomeration: 1,106,000
Population density: 1,215 inhabitants/sq km (3,147/sq mile)
Internet: www.zagreb.hr
Currency: Kuna (HRK)
Dialing code with country code: (+385) 01
Most important sights: Upper Town (Gornji Grad), Kaptol Quarter, Saint Mark's Church (Crkva svetog Marka), Funicular Railway, Cathedral of the Assumption of the Virgin Mary, Dolac Market on the Ban Jelačić Square, Lower Town (Donji Grad), Strossmayer Promenade, Mimara Museum (Muzej Mimara)

SARAJEVO

Country: Bosnia and Herzegovina
Capital since: 1945 (part republic of Yugoslavia), 1992 (Republic)
Time zone: GMT +1 (+ summer time)
Geographical location: 43° 51′ N, 18° 25′ E
Altitude above sea level: 511 m (1677 ft)
Area: 141 sq km (54.4 sq miles)
Inhabitants: 304,065
Inhabitants of the urban agglomeration: c. 500,000
Population density: 2,149 inhabitants/sq km (5,566/sq mile)
Internet: www.sarajevo.ba
Currency: Convertible mark (KM/BAM)
Dialing code with country code: (+387) 033
Most important sights: Gazi Husrev Mosque, Emperor's Mosque, Oriental Old Town with Turkish Quarter (Baščaršija), Turkish Fountain (Sebilj), Roman Catholic Cathedral, Town Hall, Latin Bridge, Academy of Fine Arts, National und University Library

PODGORICA

Country: Montenegro
Capital since: 1946 (part republic of Yugoslavia), 2006 (Republic); Cetinje: seat of the country's president (since 2006)
Time zone: GMT +1 (+ summer time)
Geographical location: 42° 26′ N, 19° 16′ E
Altitude above sea level: 45 m (148 ft)
Area: not known
Inhabitants: 143,718
Inhabitants of the urban agglomeration: not known
Population density: not known
Internet: www.podgorica.cg.yu
Currency: Euro (EUR)
Dialing code with country code: (+382) 020
Most important sights: Church of the Resurrection (Church of Saint George), Mosques in the Drač and Stara Varoš districts (Old Town), Republic Square, Montenegrin National Theater, Clock Tower, Millennium Bridge

BELGRADE

Country: Serbia
Capital since: 1945 (part republic of Yugoslavia), 1992 (Republic)
Time zone: GMT +1 (+ summer time)
Geographical location: 44° 49′ N, 20° 28′ E
Altitude above sea level: 131 m (430 ft)
Area: 359.96 sq km (139 sq miles)
Inhabitants: 1,546,812
Inhabitants of the urban agglomeration: 1.9 million
Population density: 4,297 inhabitants/sq km (11,129/sq mile)
Internet: www.beograd.rs
Currency: Serbian dinar (Din)
Dialing code with country code: (+381) 011
Most important sights: Kalemegdan Fortress and Park, Old Town (Stari Grad), Slavija Square (Trg Slavija), Cathedral of Saint Sava, Zemun, Danube Promenade (Zemunski kej), National Museum of Serbia, Museum of Yugoslav History, former Royal Palace Beli dvor, Residence of Princess Ljubica

PRIŠTINA

Country: Kosovo
Capital since: 2008
Time zone: GMT +1 (+ summer time)
Geographical location: 42° 40′ N, 21° 10′ E
Altitude above sea level: 652 m (2139 ft)
Area: 572 sq km (220.9 sq miles)
Inhabitants: 350,000
Inhabitants of the urban agglomeration: 550,000 (greater conurbation)
Population density: 962 inhabitants/sq km (2,492/sq mile) (greater conurbation)
Internet: www.prishtina-komuna.org
Currency: Euro (EUR) (not part of the European currency union)
Dialing code with country code: (+381) 038
Most important sights: Fatih or Imperial Mosque, Llap Mosque, Gračanica Monastery, National Library

TIRANA

Country: Albania
Capital since: 1920
Time zone: GMT +1 (+ summer time)
Geographical location: 41° 20′ N, 19° 49′ E
Altitude above sea level: 667 m (2188 ft)
Area: 41.8 sq km (16.14 sq miles)
Inhabitants: 616,396
Inhabitants of the urban agglomeration: 895,042
Population density: 14,746 inhabitants/sq km (38,192/sq mile)
Internet: www.tirana.gov.al
Currency: Albanian lek (ALL)
Dialing code with country code: (+355) 04
Most important sights: Skanderbeg Square, Et'hem Bey Mosque, Kulla e Sahatit Clock Tower, Palace of Culture, National History Museum, Blloku entertainment district

SKOPJE

Country: Macedonia
Capital since: 1918 (Kingdom of Yugoslavia), 1945 (part republic of Yugoslavia), 1991 (Republic)
Time zone: GMT +1 (+ summer time)
Geographical location: 41° 59′ N, 21° 25′ E
Altitude above sea level: 248 m (814 ft)
Area: 517.46 sq km (199.8 sq miles)
Inhabitants: 580,000
Inhabitants of the urban agglomeration: not known
Population density: 887 inhabitants/sq km (2,297/sq mile)
Internet: www.skopje.gov.mk
Currency: Macedonian denar (MKD)
Dialing code with country code: (+389) 020
Most important sights: Mustafa Pasha Mosque, Church of St Panteleimon, Mother Teresa House, Oriental feeling old town (Stara Čaršija), Kale Fortress, old stone bridge, Čaršija Bazaar

ATHENS

Country: Greece
Capital since: 1834
Time zone: GMT +2 (+ summer time)
Geographical location: 37° 59′ N, 23° 44′ E
Altitude above sea level: 70 m (230 ft) (average)
Area: 361.72 sq km (139.7 sq miles)
Inhabitants: 2,805,262
Inhabitants of the urban agglomeration: 3.23 million
Population density: 7,755 inhabitants/sq km (20,085/sq mile)
Internet: www.cityofathens.gr
Currency: Euro (EUR)
Dialing code with country code: (+30) 210
Most important sights: Acropolis: Parthenon, Propylaea, Erechtheion Temple, Nike Temple, New Acropolis Museum; Theater of Dionysus, Presidential Palace, Syntagma Square (Platia Sintagmátos), National Archeological Museum, Agora, Lykavittos Hill, old town district of Plaka, Daphni Monastery

BUDAPEST

Country: Hungary
Capital since: 1918
Time zone: GMT +1 (+ summer time)
Geographical location: 47° 30′ N, 19° 3′ E
Altitude above sea level: 102 m (335 ft)
Area: 525 sq km (202.7 sq miles)
Inhabitants: 1,702,297
Inhabitants of the urban agglomeration: 2,571,504
Population density: 3,242 inhabitants/sq km (8,397/sq mile)
Internet: www.budapest.hu
Currency: Hungarian forint (HUF)
Dialing code with country code: (+36) 01
Most important sights: Buda Castle District: Castle, Matthias Church, Fisherman's Bastion, Town Hall; Chain Bridge, National Galley, Spas, Nagykörút ring road, Andrássy út Boulevard, Heroes' Square, Hungarian Parliament Building, St Stephen's Basilica, Great Synagogue, Jewish Museum

BUCHAREST

Country: Romania
Capital since: 1862
Time zone: GMT +2 (+ summer time)
Geographical location: 44° 26′ N, 26° 6′ E
Altitude above sea level: 91 m (299 ft)
Area: 228 sq km (88 sq miles)
Inhabitants: 1,931,838
Inhabitants of the urban agglomeration: 2.6 million
Population density: 8,673 inhabitants/sq km (22,463/sq mile)
Internet: www.pmb.ro/
Currency: Romanian lei (RON)
Dialing code with country code: (+40) 021
Most important sights: Palace of the Parliament, Stavropoleos Monastery, Hanul lui Manuc, Lipscani Quarter, Calea Victoriei Boulevard, National Museum of Art of Romania, National History Museum, Kretzulescu Church, Revolution Square, Triumphal Arch, Cişmigiu Park, Village Museum (Muzeul satului)

Budapest on the Danube is also known as the "Paris of the East". From Lykavittos Hill, superb views over Athens unfold. Malta's small capital Valletta boasts more than 25 churches, among them the Carmelite Church with a dome that is visible from afar. The monumental Alexander Nevsky Cathedral is the emblem of Sofia (from left to right).

CHIŞINĂU?

Country: Moldova
Capital since: 1991
Time zone: GMT +2 (+ summer time)
Geographical location: 47° 1′ N, 28° 51′ E
Altitude above sea level: 85 m (279 ft)
Area: 120 sq km (46.3 sq miles)
Inhabitants: 593,800
Inhabitants of the urban agglomeration: 717,900
Population density: 4,938 inhabitants/sq km (12,789/sq mile)
Internet: www.chisinau.md
Currency: Moldovan leu (MDL)
Dialing code with country code: (+373) 22
Most important sights: Nasterea Domnului Cathedral, Portile Sfînte Triumphal Arch, Saint Teodor Tiron the Martyr Cathedral and Monastery, Pushkin Museum, Avenue of Moldavian rulers

SOFIA

Country: Bulgaria
Capital since: 1879
Time zone: GMT +2 (+ summer time)
Geographical location: 42° 41′ N, 23° 19′ E
Altitude above sea level: 550 m (1805 ft)
Area: 1,311 sq km (506.2 sq miles)
Inhabitants: 1,356,877
Inhabitants of the urban agglomeration: not known
Population density: 1,035 inhabitants/sq km (2,681/sq mile)
Internet: www.sofia.bg
Currency: Bulgarian lev (BGN)
Dialing code with country code: (+359) 02
Most important sights: Alexander Nevsky Cathedral, National Assembly Square, Bojana Church, National History Museum, Rotunda of St George (Rotonda Sveti Georgi), Batemberg Square, Sveta Sofija and Sveta Petka Samardjiiska churches, Vitoša promenade

VALLETTA

Country: Malta
Capital since: 1586
Time zone: GMT +1 (+ summer time)
Geographical location: 35° 54′ N, 14° 31′ E
Altitude above sea level: 70 m (230 ft)
Area: 0.55 sq km (0.21 sq miles)
Inhabitants: 6,300
Inhabitants of the urban agglomeration: not known
Population density: 12,815 inhabitants/sq km (33,191/sq mile)
Internet: www.cityofvalletta.org
Currency: Euro (EUR)
Dialing code with country code: (+356) 626
Most important sights: Old Town, St John's Cathedral, Grand Master's Palace, Carmelite Church, St Julian's Port, Victoria Gate, Church of Ta' Vittoria (Our Lady of Victories), Fort Saint Elmo, Auberge de Castile et Léon, National Archeological Museum

NICOSIA

Country: Republic of Cyprus (since 1983 also: Turkish Republic of Northern Cyprus, internationally recognized only by Turkey)
Capital since: 1960, 1974 division into N. (Turkish) and S. (Greek) Cyprus
Time zone: GMT +2 (+ summer time)
Geographical location: 35° 10′ N, 33° 22′ E
Altitude above sea level: 149 m (489 ft)
Area: 51 sq km (19.7 sq miles) (Greek part), 60 sq km (23.2 sq miles) (Turkish part), altogether 111 sq km (42.9 sq miles)
Inhabitants: c. 310,900 (Greek part), c. 75,000 (Turkish part)
Inhabitants of the urban agglomeration: c. 789,300 (Southern part)
Internet: www.nicosia.org.cy
Currency: southern part: Euro (EUR); northern part: Turkish lira (TL)
Dialing code with country code: (+357) 02
Most important sights: South: Old Town, Faneromeni Church, Cyprus Museum, Archbishop's Palace, St John's Cathedral, Venetian City Walls; North: "The Great Inn", Selimiye Mosque, Arabahmet Mosque

ANKARA

Country: Turkey
Capital since: 1923
Time zone: GMT +2 (+ summer time)
Geographical location: 39° 55′ N, 32° 51′ E
Altitude above sea level: 900 m (2953 ft)
Area: 2,498 sq km (964.5 sq miles)
Inhabitants: 4,395,888
Inhabitants of the urban agglomeration: not known
Population density: 1,760 inhabitants/sq km (4,558/sq mile)
Internet: www.ankara.bel.tr
Currency: Turkish Lira (TL)
Dialing code with country code: (+90) 312
Most important sights: Citadel (Kalesi), Old Town (Eski Ankara) with Bazaar Quarter, Haci Bayram Mosque and Museum of Anatolian Civilizations (Anadolu Medeniyetleri Müzesi), Mausoleum of Kemal Atatürk (Anitkabir), Kocatepe Mosque, Augustus Temple, Thermae, Column of Julian

LEGEND

GMT = Greenwich Mean Time

INDEX

PICTURE CREDITS/IMPRINT

Picture Credits

Abbreviations:
A = Alamy
C = Corbis
G = Getty
L = Laif
M = Mauritius

2/3: Zielske; 4/5: Huber; 6/7: C/Grand Tour; 8/9: Zielske; 10l + 10/11: L/Galli; 11t: C/Karnow; 11r 1: G/Messier; 11r 2: M/CuboImages; 11r 3: G/Allen; 12/13: BA-online; 13tl: Schapo/Sime; 13tr: M/CuboImages; 14t: Schapo/Irek; 14l: L/The New York Times; 14/15: vario; 15t: Huber; 15tr: Art Archive/Nasjonial Galleriet Oslo; 15br: C/Pearson; 16/17: L/Glaescher; 17t: L/Huber; 18l: G/Moos; 18/19: Huber/Damm; 19t: G/Barbour; 20t: L/Glaescher; 20c: Visum/Buellesbach; 20b: L/Kristensen; 21t: G/Pitamitz; 21c: L/Galli; 21b: L/Hemis; 22/23: Ifa; 23t: M/Cultura; 24l + 24/25: L/Kreuels; 25t: f1online/Tiophoto; 25tr: C/Ehlers; 25br: A/Anna Yu; 26t: TopicMedia/ib; 26l: A/Richardson; 26/27: Huber; 27t: Interfoto/Kreder; 28/29: C/Hicks; 29t: M/CuboImages; 29tr: L/Gonzalez; 29br: C/Borchi; 30t: f1online; 30l: DFA/Mayer; 30/31: C/Raymer; 31t: C/Lisle; 31.: artur/Hagen; 32/33: G/van der Elst 33tl: TopicMedia/ib; 33tr: L/Kirchner; 34l: TopicMedia/ib; 34/35: Vario; 35t: M/Buss; 36l: L/Kristensen; 36/37t: Huber/Simeone; 36/37b: G/Adams; 38l: Bilderberg/Wirtz; 38/39: Franz Marc Frei; 39t: M/Korall; 40t: Huber/Schmid; 40l: M/imagebroker; 40/41: Franz Marc Frei; 41t: M; 41tr: L/Eisermann; 41cr: Visum/Hackenberg; 41br: M/imagebroker; 42l: M/Harding; 42/43: Jochen Tack; 43t: L/Boening; 44l: G/Flaherty; 44/45: M/age; 45t: Premium; 46t: Interfoto; 46b: G/Flaherty; 47tl: Premium; 47tr: C/RH World Imagery; 47c: M/Dumrath; 47b: A/RH Picture Library; 48/49: Zielske; 49t: Bollen; 50t-51t: Zielske; 51t: Monheim; 51cr: Zielske; 51br: A1Pix; 52l: Schapo/Atlantide; 52tr: A/Ingram; 52br: G/Yeowell; 52/53t: A/Libera; 53tr: Bilderberg/Ellerbrock; 53c + 53b: Zielske; 54t: G/Krist; 54l: pictureNews/Vedder; 54/55: Zielske; 55t: L/Westrich; 55c: Zielske; 55bl: L/Heeb; 55br: G/Pistolesi; 56l: Premium; 56/57: Ifa/Jon Arnold; 57t: C/Amantini; 58t: Schapo/Harding; 58c: Look/Pompe; 58b: Avenue/Bibikow; 59t: Westend61/Mel Sturart; 59c: M/CuboImages; 59b: M; 60l: M/age; 60/61: M/O'Brien; 61t: TopicMedia/ib; 61tr: Huber; 61br: M/imagebroker; 62l: artur/Lautwein; 62/63t + b, 63t: Premium; 64l: TopicMedia/ib; 64/65: M; 65t: M/CuboImages; 65tr + 65br: M/image-broker; 66t: Huber; 66b: C/Busselle; 67t: M/imagebroker; 67c: Klammet; 67b: Visum/Wojciech; 68t: Huber: 68 : mediacolors/Wild; 68/69: L/Boehning; 69t: Vario; 69tr: M/Author's Image; 69br: Look/Herzig; 70/71 + 71t: L/Meyer; 72t: Premium; 72c: all-five; 72b: Huber; 73t: Premium; 73c: L/Hemis; 73b: L/Meyer; 74l: L/Hoa-Qui; 74/75t: A/Kehler; 74/75b: L/Meyer; 75t: A/mediacolors; 75 r: L/Zinn; 75cr: A/JTB; 75br: M/Superstock; 76l: L/Roemers; 76/77: BA-online; 77t: Helga Lade; 77tr: A/Matt Griggs; 77br + 78l: L/Hemis; 78/79: Visum/Buellesbach; 79t: f1online/Prisma; 79tr: M/Alamy; 79cr: F1online/Tips; 79br: bildstelle/Rex Features; 80/81: Zielske; 81t: Bredehorst; 82l: Zielske; 82/83 + 83t: L/Gaff; 83tr: Schapo/Menges; 83cr: L/Gaff; 83br: L/Galli; 84t: L/Boening; 84b: Zielske; 85t: L/Plombeck; 85c: Zielske; 85b: M/Leuzing; 86t: L/Galli; 86tl: C/Svenja-Foto; 86bl + 86/87: Böttcher; 87t: L/Hemis; 88l + 88/89: Visum/Buellesbach; 89t: f1online/Christensen Design; 90t: Visum/Buellesbach; 90l: M/Alamy; 90/91: Visum/Buellesbach; 91t: Look/Pompe; 91tr: Mehdi Chebil; 91c: Visum/Buellesbach; 91br: Look/Pompe; 92/93 + 93t: L/Boehning; 9 tr: alimdi/Lenz; 93cr: remotephoto/Hiltpold; 93br: Vario; 94/95: C/Damm; 95t: Anzenberger; 96t: Monheim; 96l: L/Huber; 96/97: Anzenberger; 97t: Bilderberg/Steinhilber; 97tr: A; 97cr: L/Hemis; 97br: Anzenberger; 98t + 98b: L/Heeb; 99t: Bilderberg/Steinhilber; 99c: L/Hoa-Qui; 99b: blickwinkel/Thomas; 99r: Bilderberg/Steinhilber; 100l: L/Henseler; 100/101t: Huber; 100b: M/Kaiser; 101t: L/Huber; 101b: L/Huber; 102/103: Bilderberg; 103t: Bilderberg/Peterschröder; 104t: Bilderberg/ Blickle; 104c: ifa; 104/105: Huber; 105t: Bilderberg/Modrak; 105c: A; 106t: DFA; 106/107: L/Knop; 107t: Vario; 107tr: DFA 107cr: Interfoto/Zill; 107br: Bilderberg/Blickle; 108l: TopicMedia/ib; 108/109: Huber; 109t: TopicMedia/Zill; 110t: alimdi/Lippert; 110/111: Vario; 111t + 111tr: Visum/Fragasso; 111cr + br: TopicMedia/Info; 112/113: M/Michalke; 113t: transit/Hirth; 11 t: Schapo/Huber; 114b: Avenue/Bibikow; 115t: C/Hicks; 115c + 115b: P. Widmann; 116l: Images; 116/117: f1online; 117t: L/ProPress; 118/119: M/Alamy; 119t: transit/Schütze; 120/121: L/Hannes; 121t: Caro/Bastian; 121tr: transit/Schulze; 121br: Ipon/Bonness; 122/123: Ifa/Arnold; 123t: Bilderberg/Drechsler; 124t: Bilderberg; 124l: C/Taylor; 124/125: Bilderberg/Ernsting; 125tr: L/Heuer; 125cr: Blume Bild; 125br: imagetrust/Kah; 126t: Look/van Velzen; 126c: M/age; 126b: Blume Bild; 127t: Premium/Hilger; 127c: M/Vidler; 127b: C/Itar-Tass; 128l: Caro/Muhs; 128/129t: Visum/PhotoXPress; 128/129b: A/Kovalev; 130t: argum/Thomas Einberger; 130/131: Huber; 131t: blickwinkel/Thomas; 132t + 132l: Holger Klaes; 132/133: phototek/Koehler; 133t: M/Alamy; 133tr: M; 133cr: Huber; 133br: Holger Klaes; 134/135: L/Hemis; 135t: G/Baxter; 135tr + br: G/vanderElst; 136t: M; 136b: TopicMedia; 137t: Premium; 137c: TopicMedia/Otto; 137b: M/age; 138l: M; 138/139: M/Alamy; 139t + 140/141: Premium; 141t: M/Alamy; 142t: Laif; 142c: Premium; 142b: M/Pixtal; 143t: Look; 143c: G/Christofori; 143b: blickwinkel/Teister; 144l 1 + 2: Interfoto; 144/145: Premium; 145t: Huber; 146l: M/age; 146/147: M/Leuzing; 147t: Interfoto/The Travel Library; 147tr: M; 147br: Huber; 148t: DFA/Calvo; 148l: blickwinkel/McPhoto; 148/149: Huber; 149t: A1PIX/PHB; 149r: Vario; 149cr: blickwinkel/Thomas; 149br: Huber; 150/151: L/Hemis; 151t: Cahjo Panorama Images; 152t: L/Galli; 152b: A/imagebroker; 153t: U. Bernhart; 153c: L/Hemis; 153b: Premium; 154t: G/Walker; 154l: G/Hemis; 154/155: L/Galli; 155t: L/Scorelletti; 155tr + cr: L/Galli; 155br: G; 156tl: Franz Marc Frei; 156bl: L/Gonzalez; 156/157: L/Galli; 157t: L/Bialobrzeski; 158/159: Huber; 159t: Ifa; 160l, 160/161 + 161t: L/Galli; 161tr: Udo Bernhart; 161cr: AKG; 161br: A/Robert Harding; 162l: Huber; 162r: Schapo/Sime; 163t: G/Image Bank; 163: C/Alinari Archives; 164t: Fotex/Cellai; 164l: alimdi/Siepmann; 164/165: C/Fuste Raga; 165t: Huber; 165tr: DFA/Xinhua; 165cr: Schapo/Sime; 165br: Caro/Riedmiller; 166l: Laif; 166/167: M/imagebroker; 167t: transit/Haertrich; 168t: M/Alamy; 168/169: Schapo/Sime; 169t + tr: M/Alamy; 169cr: Vario; 169br: blickwinkel/Gerth; 170t: G/Baxter; 170l: M/Alamy; 170/171: G/Bibikow; 171t: Jupiter; 171tr + cr: M/Alamy; 171br: Vario; 172t: DFA/Mayer; 172l: M/imagebroker; 172/173: G/Lawrence; 173t: Huber; 173tr: G/AFP; 173cr: G/Moos; 173br: G/Bibikow; 174t + 174l: M/Alamy; 174/175: G/Bibikow; 175t + 176l: Andreas Buck; 176/177 + 177: Jupiter; 177tr: M/Alamy; 177br: Jupiter; 178t: A/Jon Arnold; 178l: Schapo/Dormann; 178/179 + 179tl: M/Bibikow; 179tr: M/Alamy; 180t: A1PIX/KTP; 180l: M/O'Brien; 180/181: transit/Schulze; 181t: Lonely Planet/Horton; 181tr: Huber; 181cr: blickwinkel/Thomas; 181br: f1online/Austrophoto; 182t: M/Bibikow; 182l, 182/183 + 183t: M/Alamy; 184l: C/Bisson; 184/185: www.throughmyeyes.de; 185tl: bridgemanart; 185tr: A/Delimont; 186l: L/Reporters; 186/187: Andreas Buck; 187t: Marc Steffen Unger; 187 tr: Andreas Buck; 187cr: L/Redux; 187br: NN; 188t: M/Alamy; 188l: The Art Archive/Dagli Orti; 188/189: Look/age fotostock; 189t: G/The Image Bank; 189tr, c + b: M/Alamy; 190/191: Huber; 191t: L/Heuer; 192l: M/Photononstop; 192/193: Huber; 193t: L/Konots; 193r: L/Celentano; 193cr: AKG/Forman; 193br: Huber/Schmid; 194t: alimdi/Obermeyer; 194l: M; 194/195: M/Philochrome; 195t: M/imagebroker; 196/197: L/Barth; 197tl: L/Hahn; 197tr: Alamy; 198l: transit/Schulze; 198/199 + 199t: Visum; 199tr: L/Hahn; 199br: Visum/Ask; 200l: Huber; 200/201: Fnoxx/Hettrich; 201t: Ifa; 201tr: L/Hahn; 201cr: M; 201br: Visum/Keller; 202/203: L/Raach; 203tl: transit/Hirth; 203tr: L/Raach; 203 tr: L/Zuder; 203br: Bildstelle/Lethkuva OY; 204t: transit/Hirth; 204l: Schapo/Atlantide; 204/205: L/Raach; 205t: transit/Hirth; 205tr: M/imagebroker; 205cr + br: L/Hemis; 206l: L/Raach; 206/207: Huber; 207t: Schapo/Atlantide; 208t: A1Pix/KTP; 208/209: Andreas Buck; 209t: f1online; 209tr: M; 209 br: Andreas Buck; 210l: transit/Schulze; 210/211: Huber; 211tl: A/Jon Arnold; 211tr: G/Image Bank; 212t: G/Petrova; 212l: M/Alamy; 212/213: transit; 213t: L/Schwelle; 213tr: transit/Schulze; 213br: Huber; 214l: Bilderberg/Kunz; 214/215: Huber; 215t: L/Kirchner; 215tr: G/Renault; 215cr: M/Moxter; 215br: TopicMedia/ib; 216t: M/Alamy; 216l: L/Hemis; 216/217: M/Alamy; 217: DFA/Matrzel; 217tr, 217cr + br: Look/Richter; 218l + 218/219: G/Taner; 219t: Premium; 220t: Schapo/Atlantide; 220l: mediacolors/Peters; 220/221: Huber; 221t: Premium; 221tr: The Art Archive/Dagli Orti; 221br: AISIA; 222/223: G/Morandi; 224/225: M/Alamy; 226tl: AKG; 226tc: Visum/Wertrich; 226tr: A/Interfoto; 226l: A/Art Kowalsky; 227tl: AKG; 227tr: bridgeman; 22tl + c: AKG; 228tr + tl: Corbis; 229tr: AKG; 229r: C/Tanner; 230tl: L/Glaescher; 230tr: A/Bora; 231tl: C/World Imagery; 231tr: Zielske; 232tl: G/Woodhouse; 232tr: L/Plambeck; 233tl: Huber; 233tr: Interfoto/GPraf; 234tl: L/Hemis; 234tr: G/van der Elst; 235tl: Getty/Baxter; 235tr: M/Röder; 236tl: Ifa; 236tr: Huber; 237tl: Alamy/JA; 237tr: Huber.

Cover: N. N.

The publisher made every effort to find all of the copyright holders for the images herein. In some cases this was not possible. Any copyright holders are kindly asked to contact the publisher.

MONACO BOOKS is an imprint of Verlag Wolfgang Kunth
© Verlag Wolfgang Kunth GmbH & Co.KG, Munich, 2010

For distribution please contact:

Monaco Books
c/o Verlag Wolfgang Kunth, Königinstr. 11
80539 München, Germany
Tel: (+49) 89 45 80 20 23
Fax: (+49) 89 45 80 20 21
info@kunth-verlag.de
www.monacobooks.com
www.kunth-verlag.de

Translation: Mike Goulding, Sylvia Goulding, Emily Plank
Editor: Jane Michael for bookwise Medienproduktion GmbH, Munich
Coordination: bookwise Medienproduktion GmbH, Munich

Text: 16–27, 36–39, 44–55, 70–77, 94–117, 134–139, 16–201, 214–217: Andreas Stieber, Munich; 10–15, 28–35, 40–43, 56–69, 78–93, 118–133,140–165, 202–213, 218–221: Monika Baumüller, Munich. 2–5, 8, 222–237: Editorial offices interConcept/Verlag